The Burzynski Breakthrough

The Most Promising Cancer Treatment . . .

and the Government's Campaign to Squelch It

by
Thomas D. Elias

Lexikos
Nevada City, California

Publisher: Mike Witter
Design: Eva-Lena Rehnmark

For information:

Lexikos
PO Box 1289
Nevada City, California 95959

Library of Congress Cataloging-in-Publication Data

Elias, Thomas D.
    The Burzynski breakthrough: the most promising cancer
treatment and the government's campaign to squelch it / Thomas D. Elias
        p.   cm
    Includes bibliographical references and index.
    ISBN 0-938530-66-6
    1. Burzynski, S.R. 2. Oncologists–Texas–Houston–Biography
3. United States. Food and Drug Administration. I. Title.
RC279.6.B87A3   2000
362.1'96994082–dc21   97-17040
                                                        CIP

Printed in the USA by Sheridan Books
10 9 8 7 6 5 4 3 2 1

Lexikos
Nevada City, California

Dedication

This book is dedicated to Marilyn and Jordan, who always keep my life interesting and meaningful.

–Thomas D. Elias

Contents

Acknowledgments

When Mary Jo Siegel first approached me with the story of Dr. Stanislaw Burzynski, I didn't want anything to do with it. It was midsummer 1995, and as the West Coast correspondent for Scripps Howard News Service, I was deeply embroiled in covering the O.J. Simpson criminal trial. The last thing I needed was another controversial project.

I had known Mary Jo and her husband, Steve, briefly about 16 years earlier, while we were fellow students in an evening class. Even so, when they came to me with their deep concern that the government was trying to jail the doctor who had saved the lives of Mary Jo and many others, I was tempted to dismiss both them and their story. As a reporter, I had been confronted on a regular basis by cranks claiming to have unique or scandalous stories. They virtually never pan out. The Siegels' tale of vindictive government agencies and an anticancer establishment not really interested in finding a cure for this plague seemed like just another wild story. But because of our past relationship, I agreed at least to take a look at the material they'd brought to me.

The more I looked, the better Burzynski looked. Among the first telephone inquiries I made about Burzynski were to the American Cancer Society, the Food and Drug Administration and the National Cancer Institute. None would call him a quack. Neither would any such agency say his antineoplaston medication does not work. All said simply that it was an experimental, unproven treatment. Next, I tried to get a direct explanation from the FDA for its long campaign against Burzynski.

I expected the agency to tell me the man and his medicine were frauds and that he was bilking his patients out of millions of dollars. But that's not what the FDA said. The closest I could get to a direct answer was, "We can't discuss the Burzynski matter because it involves pending litigation." This statement was repeatedly made to me by FDA publicist Larry Bachorik and by Robert Spiller, the FDA's chief enforcement lawyer and one of the signers of the agency's 1983 "declaration of war" against Burzynski. Yet, in my experience, federal officials routinely and gladly comment on and explain pending litigation, especially when they believe they can make a strong case. When I covered the federal trial of Charles H. Keating Jr., prosecutors freely discussed why they were going after the accused savings and loan swindler. If federal officials can't reveal any information about pending trials, who was responsible for the reams of pretrial information linking Timothy McVeigh to the Oklahoma City bombing? And who was leaking armloads of information about the case against the purported Unabomber?

I began to sense that something was not quite kosher here. I decided to interview some of Burzynski's living patients and the survivors of some who had died. When I did, I heard not a single negative word about Burzynski, even from persons whose close relatives had come to him too late for antineoplastons to help them. I viewed CT and MRI scans of brain tumors that antineoplastons had apparently shrunk when nothing else would work. Skeptics may say that as a journalist, I'm not trained to read such scans. But anyone can see the white blob that a large brain tumor produces on film and anyone can compare its size on various dates.

Eventually, I produced a package of stories for Scripps Howard, carried by the wire service in August 1995. But even as I wrote those stories, I was aware that no newspaper could provide enough space to tell the entire fascinating story of Burzynski and his patients. Soon I resolved that I would make that story into a book.

Pursuing the new edition of this book would have been

impossible without the faith and trust of my new publisher Mike Witter of Lexikos Books, who stepped in when the publisher of the first edition, General Publishing Group, was unable to act. The book also would have lacked all authenticity and could not have contained such a large amount of previously unpublished material without the complete cooperation of Burzynski and his staff and patients. The charts that are such a vital addition to this printing were provided by The Burzynski Clinic. Burzynski originally told me his story in a series of late-night interviews conducted at the only time when he is not seeing patients, completing paperwork for the FDA, or being besieged by telephone calls. For the new printing, he indulged me with another series of sessions that went deep into the Houston nights. His former clinical trials director, Dean Mouscher, became a good friend and an invaluable source of many documents vital to this project. Later Burzynski's assistant Sherry Ysais proved extremely helpful in obtaining documents necessary to this edition. Whatever documents I requested, from Burzynski's tax returns to his correspondence with federal agencies and pharmaceutical companies, Mouscher and Ysais provided them quickly. I soon became convinced that Burzynski and his staff were not trying to conceal anything from me or the readers of this book.

When I sought information from those in Congress who have taken an interest in Burzynski's situation, I easily gained the cooperation of Alan Slobodin, counsel to the House Commerce Committee's Subcommittee on Oversight and Investigations. Documents in the subcommittee's files provided evidence of both the length and extent of the FDA's effort to "get" Burzynski. Transcripts of subcommittee hearings revealed that FDA officials had been as firm in stonewalling Congress as they were in refusing to cooperate both with Burzynski's patients and with me.

During Burzynski's criminal trials, I also received substantial cooperation from his capable corps of defense attorneys, including Michael Ramsey, Dan Cogdell, John Ackerman and Richard Jaffe. Chief prosecutor Michael Clark, while hostile to Burzynski, was never hostile to me even though he was fully aware of the direction this book would take. And while Judge Simeon T. Lake 3rd could not discuss details of the case or reveal in advance what his rulings during the trial might be, he did provide insights into his legal philosophy during two hour-long interviews in his chambers. I also had help from the late Dr. William Mask, who provided eyewitness information about the earliest use of antineoplastons in humans, and from Prof. Carlton Hazlewood, who confirmed most of what Burzynski remembered about his years at the Baylor College of Medicine.

This project would have been utterly impossible to complete without the help I received from Burzynski's dynamic and determined patients. Whether in person or via lengthy telephone interviews, every patient I contacted was eager to tell his or her story in great detail. For both editions of this book, each of their stories was verified either by conversations with their conventional doctors or by documents that detailed the nature and extent of their illness before and after seeking out Burzynski. I also owe a vote of thanks to my friend Charlie Peters.

Finally, this new edition could not have been completed without the presence of two utterly remarkable women: My wife Marilyn and my cousin Tammy Gilad. Even though she knew my kidneys were failing and that I might need to start dialysis very soon, Marilyn protested only mildly while I commuted weekly from my base in suburban Los Angeles to Houston during the two full months of Burzynski's first criminal trial. I will always be grateful to her for her support during that often-agonized time, during the months of dialysis that followed, and during my recovery from a kidney transplant. Just as the first edition of this book was published in 1997, Tammy donated one of her very healthy kidneys to me. Her act of almost the ultimate generosity provided me with the energy and physical ability to pursue this new edition—and many other activities. Without these two women, this book simply would not exist.

Thomas D. Elias
Santa Monica, California
May 2000

Prologue

Patients

S ydney Seaward's friendly freckled face was familiar to almost everyone in the sprawling, disorderly southeast Texas metropolis of Houston. At 40, she was an anchor-woman on the all-news television station KNWS—"sort of a local CNN," the California native and sometime Sorbonne student said, smiling, as she breezed into the waiting room of the Burzynski Clinic on the raw, partially developed western edge of her adopted Texas hometown.

A brief stir accompanied Seaward's entrance on that sunny day in May 1996. "Sydney's here!" a secretary shouted, bursting into the office of Dean Mouscher, clinical trials director and chief publicist for the maverick cancer-treatment center. "Sydney's here," Mouscher repeated moments later, catching the clinic's founder and chief scientist in a hallway between examining rooms.

This was the start of what could have been a classic opportunity for Dr. Stanislaw Burzynski, the man who 20 years earlier had discovered a family of naturally occurring peptides that demonstrated cancer-fighting properties. Seaward had arrived with a camera crew, itching for a dramatic, optimistic statement from Burzynski. She never got one. The doctor would make no far-reaching claims about the antineoplastons that were soon to land him in the defendant's chair in a federal courtroom. He also didn't come close to promising he could cure Seaward's cancer.

Instead, he tried to ignore her status as a local celebrity and treat her like any other patient. For Seaward, this would mean long and anxious hours in the waiting room. She may have arrived with a camera crew, but Burzynski never lost sight of the fact that she was there not as a reporter but as a cancer victim. So Sydney Seaward sank into one of the six long, high-backed green sofas, alone in the crowd, completely uncertain of her fate.

For Seaward, her entrance into Burzynski's spacious and airy waiting room was fraught with desperation. In this, she was no different from any of the other half-dozen cancer patients seated near her and her camera crew. Her trauma began in March 1994, when she was diagnosed with breast cancer. Taking advantage of a relatively new treatment tactic, she elected to undergo chemotherapy and radiation before surgery. That way, she figured, the size of the lump in her breast could be reduced before it was removed. "I'm not married and that seemed like a way I could save my breast," she said. "That was very important to me."

The plan appeared to work. The lump was eight centimeters in diameter when discovered; by the end of the preliminary chemo and radiation, it was half that size. The lump was removed in February 1995; her breast was saved and reconstructed. For the surgery, Seaward traveled to Los Angeles, where she was operated on by UCLA's renowned Dr. Susan Love. "Several doctors I saw didn't like this method of attack," Seaward recalled. "They wanted me to get a full mastectomy right away. But I know now that if I had had one, it wouldn't have made any difference."

In fact, nothing she did before entering Burzynski's waiting room made any real difference. In June 1995, a blood test revealed elevated tumor markers, and—under the care of Love and Houston oncologist Dr. Paul Holloye— she found she had ten small tumors growing throughout her lungs.

"They found that the cancer had spread through my vascular system," she said, grimacing. "I was eligible for more radiation and chemotherapy, but I'd had enough. I wasn't ready for more, because the treatments I'd undergone were supposed to prevent this, but they obviously didn't work. And in my gut I believe that the radiation helped cause the metastasis to my lungs."

As painful as this fruitless process would be to anyone, it was more so to Seaward. Reared as a Christian Scientist, she had never abandoned her faith. Her media career, in fact, began with stints on the radio and television services of the Christian Science Monitor.

"Medicine is foreign to me," she confessed. "I'm still a Christian Scientist. But I'm not willing to put my life on the line when treatments have been effective for some."

It was that thought which eventually brought Seaward to the Burzynski waiting room, ready for treatment. She first visited the clinic almost five months earlier, in January 1996. On that appointment, she didn't see Burzynski but consulted with his associate, Dr. Dorothy Sprecher. Sprecher had given Seaward more bad news. Perhaps because she knew Seaward's face so well from seeing it on television, Sprecher spotted a stiffness in one cheek and recommended a brain scan, guessing Seaward's cancer might have spread to her brain. It had. The new tumor was on the brain stem, perhaps the most delicate area of the brain and certainly one of the most difficult places for surgeons to operate.

Stunned, Seaward consulted more doctors. They recommended full-brain radiation. "But they told me that the procedure only improves the quality of life. It doesn't extend it. And they told me the possible side effects: loss of sight, loss of hearing, loss of motor skills, nausea. This is an improved quality of life? Doesn't sound that way to me. Plus, they said the chances of getting a response were just

10 to 15 percent. That's not enough for me. So I said 'Forget that!' and came here."

By the time she returned to Burzynski's clinic in May, she had concluded that she had no use for more radiation.

Burzynski already knew her medical history as he led Seaward and her camera crew into an examining room. Its light blue walls were adorned by two cheery Chinese prints of multicolored birds. "I've never seen so many elegant people!" he exclaimed, grinning at Seaward in her business suit, and at the crew, which had also recorded much of her earlier odyssey. Then he started talking.

"I have looked at your films," he began. "The lungs are the real concern. This can be a special problem if you get a lot of fluid. We have to watch carefully that your lungs don't become congested. But our best chance in your case is high dosage (of his medication). So we have to be careful with watching the infusion and the outflow of liquid." With her now impaired lungs, if Seaward were to take in more of the antineoplaston solution than her body could process, pneumonia could result.

This promised to make the course of her cancer cure more difficult, because most of Burzynski's patients take large quantities of his peptides, called antineoplastons because of their ability to fight neoplasms—the technical term for cancer tumors—via catheters inserted into the chest's blood vessels. The purified peptides, in solution, are packaged in plastic intravenous solvent bags and infused directly into the blood-stream by a small, lightweight pump. The more impaired a patient's lungs, the less fluid he or she can safely process. Seaward's case also confronted Burzynski with another potential problem: She had refused to allow insertion of a catheter into her chest, opting instead for one in her left arm. Because blood vessels in the arms are smaller than those in the chest, she could not receive as much antineoplaston as many of Burzynski's other patients generally did.

"Most likely," Burzynski explained to her, behaving as if her TV crew had disappeared, "you will take two quarts of fluid every day. We'll increase the dosage step by step, starting with 40 cubic centimeters the first day and working up to a 300-cc dose. The higher the dosage, the more effective it will be."

Then Burzynski took on a professorial tone, offering the details: "For breast cancer, we usually need a high dosage, especially if we are talking about the involvement of the lungs and the brain. We'll do blood tests after four days, after 15 days, and at other intervals. It may take five or six weeks of treatment for your CT (computed tomography) scan to show a reduction. We would like to see you here every day for the next 10 days. Once you feel comfortable with the pump and catheter, you can infuse the medicine on your own. But if your lungs become congested, your chances would be reduced. If these were brain nodules only, it would be better. Every day, you will be connected to the pump for at least 22 hours. If you slow down, the cancer will take advantage.

"This treatment can be effective for your cancer; it is just a matter of time and concentration. We were about to begin using a more concentrated version of the antineoplastons in February, but the Food and Drug Administration has refused to allow us to make any changes. This change would have been better for you—less fluid to deliver more medicine," he told her.

"What are your chances? A 30 percent chance of response seems reasonable. But this may be lower because of your lungs. The question here is not whether the medicine works, but whether you can tolerate the dosage."

Could Burzynski have offered a more optimistic prognosis? Yes, if his aim was merely to recruit more patients. No, if his aim was to play it safe for television audiences. But a more optimistic estimate would have made Sydney Seaward far more cheerful while she spent hour after hour on the green sofas of the Burzynski Clinic's waiting room seated beside a blue zippered canvas case containing her pump and an IV bag filled with enough medication to last about four hours. Like every antineoplaston patient taking the medication intravenously, she had to spend entire days in the waiting room as Burzynski's assistants monitored her for allergies, water retention, the state of her lungs and her general comfort.

"I don't give false hope," Burzynski said a little later, as he ate lunch at his desk. "I want no one to have any illusions. Everything we claim is right on the films."

Burzynski has never made those X-ray and CT scan films himself. His patients undergo scans and magnetic resonance imaging (MRI) at centers near their homes and then bring the results to Houston for sessions with Burzynski.

MRI films left no doubt about what had happened to William Boyd in April 1996. The virulent, fast-growing brain tumor that took up almost one-eighth of his cranium in late March was less than half as large five weeks later. Bill's MRI scans, like those from which he was originally diagnosed, were made at Moses Cones Hospital in Greensboro, North Carolina, not far from his home in Ashboro.

Bill's path to Burzynski was not as long, convoluted or tortured as Seaward's. Nor was it any less painful. It was only during the previous January that he learned he had a brain tumor.

"I had been passing out and the doctor thought I had low blood sugar," recalled the tall, muscular, gray-haired Boyd as he sat in Burzynski's waiting room. At 54, he had led a full life as a realtor, contractor, state legislator and runner-up in the 1988 Republican primary for lieutenant governor of North Carolina.

"I was never totally out when I'd keel over," he remembered. "They were more like brownouts than blackouts. And my mother and brother both had diabetes, so I don't blame the docs for thinking it was blood sugar. I passed out on New Year's Day in Myrtle Beach, South Carolina, and on January 10, in a sales meeting, I fell over just like a big log."

A smile lit up Bill Boyd's face as he told his story. His wife, Shirley, was seated on the same leather sofa, focusing on his every word. "So they did a CT scan, and I was referred right away to Dr. Ernesto Betero at Cones Hospital. He sent me for an MRI, which was conclusive for a brain tumor in my right temple. Dr. Betero said he could take out only part of the tumor. He likened it to cutting off an old oak tree: Unless you excavate deeply around the stump, you won't get all the roots, and pretty soon you'll have a lot of little oak trees growing up. He said he couldn't get all the roots of my tumor and recommended some kind of postoperative treatment. After my tumor was removed, it was rated as a Grade 4—that's pretty bad. They took out the tumor in late February, and then I had some radiation. When they did a CT scan in March, it had begun to grow back anyway. Just two weeks later. That's when we started doing a lot of research. We talked to all the oncologists and radiologists at Cones, and they never gave me a chance to keep going more than two years. Dr. Betero urged me to seek out every option. We found out about Dr. Burzynski very quickly through inquiries on the Internet, as well as a newsletter. I came to Houston in late March."

He'd seen the scans, one showing the inside of his skull on March 21, and another on April 29. They showed his recurring tumor, a mixed glioma, reduced to about 40 percent of its former size in that time through infusion of Burzynski's antineoplastons—without any use of radiation.

Bill's voice boomed around the large waiting room. "It's completely ridiculous, this thing with the FDA," he declared, indignant that government lawyers had indicted Burzynski for selling antineoplastons to people like him. And it became obvious that Bill would not be reluctant to use his political past to further a future he now feels is once more within his grasp. "I talked to Newt Gingrich's deputy just two weeks ago, and I told him it takes 10 years and $400 million to get a drug approved by the FDA. (Gingrich was the Republican Speaker of the House of Representatives at the time.) The deputy told me, 'You can't believe the political corruption that's involved in the FDA.'"

Now it was Shirley's turn. She'd listened quietly to her husband, but her own anger, frustration, faith and gratitude poured forth. "No one at the hospital gave us any hope. The nurses on the rehab floor told me, 'Please, please start him on radiation right away because it will at least give him some time.' But you can see now that he's hardly wasting away. In fact, he's gaining weight on the fluids. They have a lot of salt in them. So I am reminded constantly that doctors' reports are not the final report. God's is. You know, this makes me so mad, that people have to be terrified and suffer when there's something actually out there for them. It's just wrong."

Bill wasn't finished with his treatment yet, not by a long shot. He still faced more months of carrying around his blue canvas bag and pump, like a college-fraternity pledge with a paddle or a young home economics student learning how to care for a baby. And he still had to find energy for his ongoing battle with his insurance company, the Consolidated Administrator's Group of Raleigh, North Carolina, carrier for the state's Home Builder's Association. The firm had initially refused to pay for anything more than CT scans and MRIs when Bill began going to Houston.

"I told them I have a lawyer ready to sue and they said they might get back to me," he said, grinning, looking ready for combat. "I'm not asking for money for my flying to Houston or my hotels. Just the clinic. But if I sue, I promise all that will be in the suit—and a whole lot more."

Across the waiting room, Krystyna Pataluch listened quietly as Bill's voice caromed from wall to wall. Now 57, this small, olive-skinned woman had come to Chicago from Poland six years earlier with her bus driver husband and quickly found work in child care. "In January, I learned I have colon cancer," she said sadly, leaning forward and fingering the tube leading from her blue canvas bag to the shunt surgically placed into her chest. "It is colo-rectal cancer. I made a few tests in Chicago, and they pushed me for surgery. But the Polish people in Chicago know a lot about Dr. Burzynski. I decided I wouldn't do anything until after I see him."

But for more than two weeks in late April 1996, the Burzynski Clinic couldn't touch Krystyna on pain of prison for its founder. "I had to wait because he was on hold from the FDA," she said. "I don't understand. It sounds just like the Communists were in Poland. Who ever heard of stopping a dying person from getting whatever she wants? Not even the Communists did that. I couldn't start my treatment until two days ago. But I never knew when I would be able to start. So I had to stay here in Houston and wait and wait and wait."

All the while, of course, she knew her tumor was growing and that the chances of further metastasis (the spread of cancer from one site to others) were growing, too. Even before she reached Houston, the malignancy had spread far beyond her colon. Yet Burzynski couldn't treat her any sooner than he did. If he had, he might have gone to prison immediately. One condition of his bail as he awaited trial was that he take on no new patients except those expressly permitted by the FDA.

But Krystyna was determined that it would be Burzynski or no one. "If I could not start this treatment, I don't know what I would do. I don't believe surgery would work," she said, eyes large and bleak behind her oversize horn-rimmed glasses. "This has already spread to my liver. They can't take out my liver. But still, in Chicago, they tell me I have no choice but an operation."

As she fingered her catheter tube, wondering if the anti-neoplaston treatment was beginning to work, nurses called Mitzi Jo Goodfellow into an examining room from a near-by spot where she sat dozing. The petite, elfish-looking Goodfellow, 28, had flown in the day before from her home in the Detroit suburb of Royal Oak, Michigan, feeling much better than she had on her first visit almost a month earlier.

That visit was the culmination of almost two years' treatment for a malignant glioblastoma, one of the fastest-growing and least treatable of brain tumors. Her case began with severe headaches in May 1994, and much of her tumor was surgically removed in July 1995 at Beaumont Hospital in Royal Oak. This was followed by intense chemotherapy during which Mitzi Jo almost died of sepsis (a toxic condition resulting from the spread of bacteria) and pneumonia in November 1995.

By January 1996, chemotherapy or no, her tumor was back, almost as large as it had been before surgery. This time, it was almost the shape of an hourglass, with distinct upper and lower lobes. By the time Mitzi Jo arrived for her first visit with Burzynski on April 2, 1996, an MRI scan taken at Beaumont showed the tumor measuring about 4.5 centimeters in height and 2.2 centimeters wide at its broadest axis.

But more than a month later, another scan at Beaumont showed the tumor was half as large and fading with the antineoplaston treatments. "This latest MRI scan looks pretty good," Burzynski reported, showing the pictures to Mitzi Jo. "The lower part of your tumor has decreased greatly. But the upper part is only slightly smaller. Sometimes one part of a tumor requires more medication than another. I think we should increase your dosage a bit because now we have to work on the upper part, and that's the best way to do it. You are fortunate that you are a young woman, too, because we find young women are better able to tolerate higher doses than other people."

Mitzi Jo smiled broadly, clearly delighted with the MRI scan interpretation. And she readily agreed to try increasing her antineoplaston dosage. The first stop: a return to the waiting room couch, where nurses carefully monitored her response to the more intensive medication.

There she joined Sydney Seaward, William Boyd and Krystyna Pataluch, each reclining on different sofas, each surrounded by supportive friends or family members, each confronting his or her hopes and doubts.

Introduction

The Beginning and Its Logical Conclusion

Clouds were thick, black and threatening in east Texas one early December evening in 1976 as Dr. Stanislaw Burzynski and his close friend Carlton Hazlewood sped up Interstate 45, their separate cars covering the more than 250 miles between Houston and Dallas in less than four hours. They barely slowed down as they rounded a cloverleaf and headed northwest from Dallas on Texas Highway 199, homing in on the small town of Jacksboro and the one-story Jack County Hospital.

The two men believed they were on a lifesaving mission, carrying ice chests loaded with new and promising medications Burzynski called antineoplastons. The word came from neoplasm, the scientific term for a cancer tumor. Antineoplaston simply meant "anticancer." This wasn't the place or the manner in which Burzynski had intended to conduct the first human trial of antineoplastons, peptides he believed capable of stopping many cancers in their tracks. But the weather demanded it. Tornado warnings were up that night, and all flights were grounded at the Dallas-Fort Worth International Airport. It was an inconvenience for Burzynski and Hazlewood. It was also one more major difficulty for Emma Avadassian and Billy Bryant to surmount. Both were cancer patients being escorted by relatives to Houston, where they were scheduled to become the first people infused with Burzynski's new, and as yet unproven, medications.

Burzynski's plan had been to admit both patients to the modern Twelve Oaks Hospital, where he was a staff physician. He had earlier been refused permission to try his medication on patients by both the Baylor College of Medicine and the swank Park Plaza Hospital, near his suite of offices in south-west Houston. The threatening weather changed that plan.

Now things looked grim for Emma and Billy. Both were stranded at the Dallas airport, with no prospect of a flight to Houston in the next few hours. Both were frail and had been diagnosed with terminal cancer. Their scheduled trips to Houston were the last resort for each. Neither figured to survive long if forced to wait out the delay at the airport.

The 55-year-old Avadassian, accompanied by her husband, had already undergone two courses of radiation and chemotherapy. Nevertheless, her cancer had spread throughout her pain-racked body. Small tubules inside her kidneys and the ureters leading away from both kidneys were blocked because of scarring produced by massive radiation treatments. Back in Pennsylvania, her doctors had told her she'd never survive the flights to Dallas and then Houston. When American Airlines canceled her connecting flight from Dallas, it seemed her doctors would be proven correct. Her husband feared she might expire right beside the gate.

Billy, 13, was in equally fragile condition, suffering from cancer of the bone. Accompanied by his father, Billy had flown from his family's home in central Florida after undergoing months of fruitless chemotherapy. Oncologists at the University of Florida at Gainesville predicted he wouldn't live long enough to reach Burzynski.

Both patients learned about antineoplastons from an Associated Press story that detailed Burzynski's claim that antineoplastons—chemicals refined and purified from human urine—had shrunk laboratory-grown cancers in the test tube and petri dish. Fully aware that the treatment had not yet been approved for human trial by the FDA, they were desperate enough to give it a try.

The foul weather was keeping them from their appointments in Houston, where Burzynski eagerly waited, medication at the ready. The moment the doctor learned of his patients' plight, he was on the phone to Hazlewood, holder of Baylor professorships in pediatrics and molecular physiology. Both men took pride in being unconventional thinkers. They had met and become fast friends during Burzynski's six years as a research associate and assistant professor at Baylor. Years earlier, Hazlewood also had introduced Burzynski to his uncle Dr. William Mask, a former Navy doctor who practiced general medicine in rural Jacksboro and was medical director of the county hospital.

From their first meeting, Mask was impressed by Burzynski and his antineoplastons. "I went to Houston every month or so during the mid-'70s to keep in touch with Carlton and Stash [Burzynski's nickname] and to discuss what Burzynski was doing with the antineoplastons," Mask recalls. "Meeting him was the first time I ever talked to anyone who made any sense at all about cancer. He wanted to check the blood and urine of cancer patients to see what was different in cancer victims and those who didn't have the disease. He had told me he was finding peptides in the blood and urine of healthy people, but not in cancer victims. And he showed me how some of the peptides he was working with in test tubes had strong antitumor activity. All that made a lot of sense to me. I even watched him purify and sterilize the chemicals he was extracting from human urine."

So Mask was receptive when his phone rang that stormy December night. The caller was Hazlewood. Two cancer patients on their way to becoming Burzynski's first antineoplaston patients were stuck at the Dallas airport. Could they be admitted to Jack County Hospital if they could get there? And would Mask approve using antineoplastons on them as soon as Burzynski could reach them? The answers were yes and yes.

Twenty years later, Mask vividly remembered how Emma and Billy were treated at his hospital. "Burzynski used two different antineoplastons on Emma," he said with a distinctively Texan twang. "She responded to the treatment real well. It was just a week or so before she was well enough to travel to Houston for more treatment."

Unlike most of Burzynski's later patients, who received antineoplastons via catheters inserted into their upper chests by a vascular surgeon, the first patients got their medicine through intravenous drip feedings and injections into their muscles. "With Emma, her kidneys quickly became the main problem," Mask explained. "Soon after she arrived, her left kidney shut down completely because of radiation scarring on the ureters. I called in a urologist to insert a catheter, and pretty soon we were able to get both kidneys functioning. When I went to see her after she was transferred to Houston, she was still having more trouble with her kidneys than with her cancer." After Emma died in mid-February 1977, an autopsy showed the cause of death was a kidney infection. Said Mask, "She was eating and gaining weight right 'til the end. It was the kidneys and the aftereffects of the radiation that got her. The antineoplastons helped a lot with her pain. She was a lot more comfortable after she started on them."

Billy Bryant also reached lack County Hospital, where Mask quickly saw that his Ewing's sarcoma (bone cancer) had spread to his lungs, chest and abdomen. But after a week on antineoplastons, he was well enough to be driven to Houston. "I saw his X-rays after he'd been in Jacksboro just a couple of days," Mask remembered. "They definitely showed a shrinking of that little boy's bone tumor." About a month later, the youngster had regained enough strength to go home to Winter Haven, Florida, where he continued to take antineoplastons and thrived for several months.

Billy's father, a chemist for Florida's state citrus commission, was so pleased with the treatment that he began to help Burzynski by collecting urine from citrus orchard workers, freeze-drying it and shipping it to Houston. Burzynski would then isolate and sterilize the useful peptides it contained and dump the rest. By mid-1977, young Billy's cancer was in remission; he was doing so well on antineoplastons that he stopped taking them. His cancer soon returned, and he once again visited the Gainesville oncologist who had earlier pronounced him terminal. By now, Burzynski had a few other cancer patients and was having difficulty finding enough urine to make antineoplastons for all who wanted the treatment. So Billy's dad acquiesced when his son's oncologist suggested a new round of chemotherapy. Billy died later that year.

Even though Burzynski had lost both of his first patients, Mask had seen enough to convince him that antineoplastons work, with virtually no negative side effects. "I thought this was really miraculous stuff," he declared with obvious relish. "I still do. If this stuff is as good as I think it is, they'll have to close down the M.D. Anderson Hospital [a Houston facility that is one of the world's largest cancer centers] and turn it into a TB clinic. You had to have seen those first two patients to truly understand how I feel. It was even better because none of us were really sure if there'd be negative side effects. We knew these peptides were highly acidic, so we didn't know what the reaction would be. Imagine how pleased we were when there wasn't any."

So convinced was Mask that when his son's father-in-law developed bladder cancer about six months later, he recommended forgoing the standard treatments and starting on antineoplastons right away. Robert Steed, a Wichita Falls businessman who had become close friends with Mask after their children married, called his friend the day he was diagnosed. "I talked to his urologist right away," said Mask. "We agreed to get him down to Burzynski in Houston, and Stash treated him for three cancer tumors, all very close together. They had infiltrated the bladder wall."

After two weeks of intensive intravenous treatment, Steed carried a supply of antineoplastons home and began giving himself injections. Three months later, his urologist checked him over and pronounced his cancer in remission.

Recalled Mask, "That doctor was flabbergasted. Bob kept taking the shots for another nine months, and after he'd been on them for a year, he decided to quit. Less than three months later, there was blood in his urine again. So he went back on the shots and his cancer disappeared again. He took the shots for another year and then he lived normally until 1995, when he died of a heart attack. He was 65 when he died. In his whole life, he had no radiation and no chemotherapy." The last statement is a key fact because Burzynski's critics often claim that his successes are merely due to delayed effects of standard therapies. Steed, however, was a cancer cure who never touched any conventional therapy.

In early January 1997, exactly 20 years and one month after that first frantic trip to Jacksboro, Dr. Stanislaw Burzynski became a criminal defendant in U.S. District Court in Houston. The charges: contempt of court, insurance fraud and interstate commerce in an unapproved drug. The indictment obtained by the FDA contained 75 allegations.

In almost every way, Burzynski's presence in the courtroom was the ultimate result of those first antineoplaston treatments given to desperate, usually terminally ill patients. For once Burzynski had opted to try to help them without approval of the FDA but with legal permission from Texas state authorities, he had set out on a course that would inevitably land him in the dock. His story would eventually take on the elements of personal vendetta, industrial betrayal and apparent dishonesty at the highest levels of America's scientific institutions.

From the moment he set out for Jacksboro, Burzynski was thumbing his nose at the entire American medical establishment and the FDA in particular. The latter is not something to be done lightly, as a former special assistant to the agency's commissioner noted in a December 1995 letter to The Washington Times. "There is a rewards-and-punishment system at FDA and...retaliation is very much a way of life," wrote James G. Phillips. "Companies that complain about FDA to Congress or the media routinely suffer retaliation."

As a small private practitioner and businessman, Burzynski wanted to develop and bring to market a new drug, and to do so completely on his own without involving the FDA or anyone else. This is the sort of action the FDA considers an end run around its usually useful anti-snake oil regulations. The normal drug approval process, though, is so convoluted and complex that it usually can be accomplished only by pharmaceutical companies, which spend an average of more than $400 million testing and retesting their products before they are FDA-approved. Most ordinary research scientists and the universities for which they work sell or license their patents to drug companies. The companies then pay for testing the products and bringing them to market. This may allow scientists to win Nobel Prizes, but it lets pharmaceutical houses take the lion's share of the profits.

Burzynski, however, was different. An inveterate optimist, he was convinced that his antineoplastons were safe and effective, and that desperate cancer patients should have them as soon as possible. He left establishment medicine, believing no government should interfere with his work. He also believed that he should control the profits from his own discoveries. Operating on a shoestring, often short of cash during his early years, he nevertheless continued to publish the results of his experiments and his treatment of patients. As time passed and no one could disprove Burzynski's claims, the hackles of organized medicine rose. He became the target of campaigns on both the legal and laboratory fronts, with the government trying to put him out of business on the one hand, and authorizing clinical trials of the drug he had developed on the other hand. In 1983, the FDA attempted to get an injunction to shut him down. A federal judge refused to issue such a sweeping order. By 1988, Burzynski had already been hauled before two federal criminal grand juries. Both refused to indict him. By 1991, he had three Investigational New Drug (IND) permits to test his antineoplastons on humans. The National Cancer Institute began a three-site clinical trial of antineoplastons in 1993, then tried in midstream to change the parameters of the trial and bias it against the drug. This happened less than four months after the first patients were signed on to the trial, not enough time for most cancer doctors even to hear the trial had begun, let alone inform and sign up many suitable patients.

And in 1995, 12 years after the FDA declared war on Burzynski, on its fourth try at an indictment, the government finally managed to procure formal charges against him. Never mind that by the time his case reached court in early 1997, Burzynski had received from that same government 69 IND permits for use of antineoplastons in humans. Those permits meant that all Burzynski's patients were finally included in federally approved clinical trials. They meant he was treating patients no differently than before, but what the FDA had pronounced illegal in 1995, it now was formally sanctioning.

This official inconsistency neither deterred nor delayed the criminal trial. The FDA's enforcement wing had promised in 1983 that if it couldn't shut down Burzynski then, it would never stop trying. And small things like IND permits issued by another wing of the agency wouldn't sway it from that determined course.

As the trial opened, it quickly became clear that this was merely the newest front in the long campaign to squelch Burzynski's drug. In fact, federal prosecutor Michael Clark made it plain that he would fight to keep the jury of four men and eight women from ever hearing about the entire question of whether antineoplastons work. And U.S. District Judge Simeon T. Lake 3rd was forced to go along with the prohibition, because the federal Food, Drug and Cosmetic Act gives the FDA the sole authority to rule on the safety and efficacy of new drugs. Only Congress can change this law. "This is not a congressional hearing to reform the Food and Drug Administration," Lake remarked on the trial's first day. "Whether or not any patient or former patient believes Dr. Burzynski's drug is effective is not going to be an issue. We are not going to hear evidence of whether any drug or treatment offered by [Burzynski] is effective or not."

At the same time, Lake told the panel of 49 potential jurors initially summoned in the case that "you will be resolving important issues." But he did not tell them what important issues would be left for them to decide, if effectiveness were to be left out.

But effectiveness was the only issue that interested the scores of Burzynski patients who paraded outside the courthouse on opening day, filled many seats in the courtroom daily during the trial and raised more than $700,000 for their doctor's defense. The patients held views similar to those of Robert Steed, whose 1994 testimony before the Texas Board of Medical Examiners left no doubt that he believed antineoplastons had saved his life while causing him a minimum of side effects. JUDGE LAKE: SOMEDAY THIS COULD BE YOUR LAST HOPE, read signs carried by the picketing patients, some in wheelchairs. Others, like 15-year-old former malignant melanoma patient Jessica Kerfoot of Arlington, Texas, wore small tags with their names and the simple notation CURED.

Inside, it was as if the patients, their experiences and their strong beliefs did not matter. Never mind that Burzynski had treated more than 2,500 patients over the preceding 20 years, most of whom had been pronounced terminally ill by other doctors before they made their way to him. Never mind that at least 300 of those patients were still alive, weeks, months or years after other doctors had told them to go home to die. This was all irrelevant. "Of course, the jury will be instructed to make its decision solely on the basis of what they hear in court and my instructions," Judge Lake declared on opening day.

Prosecutor Clark attempted to stick with this edict, one for which he had long fought, as he presented his opening statement. But he couldn't completely do it. For in the midst of his statements, he also mixed some references to Burzynski's drug. He told the jury that the "seminal question in this trial is whether the defendant has created a scheme to defraud and whether the U.S. mail was used to carry it out," Hearing this, even the most dense of jurors couldn't help but wonder whether the drug worked and why people took it. Wasn't the question of whether or not the drug worked central to deciding the issue of fraud?

Yet Clark pushed on, seemingly oblivious. He said the FDA "tried to work with Dr. Burzynski to try to get his patients into approved trials." But he didn't mention that after Burzynski applied, the FDA needed six years to approve his first IND permit—a process that is normally rubber-stamped quickly when applications come from drug companies. Clark said, "This country treated Dr. Burzynski well when he came from Poland, but when it came time to play by the rules, he left [establishment medicine]." He did not mention that Burzynski's early efforts to get approval for tests of antineoplastons ran into the classic Catch-22: The Baylor medical school refused him permission because he had no IND permit, and he couldn't get it because he didn't have a green light from Baylor.

As the trial began, there was no doubt that Burzynski had made mistakes in judgment and tactics. One occurred when he failed to patent a primitive early version of antineoplastons made up purely of the chemical phenylacetate. He made another when he allowed representatives of a drug company two months to examine all aspects of his operation before finalizing a deal with him. The firm quickly took advantage of the absent patent and began developing phenylacetate on its own as a cancer drug.

In his opening statement, Clark implied that Burzynski was plotting a fraud scheme from the moment he ventured out on his own, abandoning academia and treating desperate patients without permission from any establishment medical agency. "This case is not about Dr. Burzynski's character," Clark said. "We all realize good men can do bad things. This case is about a man who decided not to obey the laws of this country. The FDA tried to work with him."

But Clark ignored the truly seminal questions in this case, the ones some members of the original jury panel raised during the voir dire process: Should patients with terminal illness be permitted to seek whatever treatments they want? Should doctors be permitted to provide any treatments they think will help, even if those treatments don't yet have federal approval?

From the start, prosecutor Clark tried to confine the trial to narrow issues of semantics: Was it interstate commerce when a patient picked up antineoplastons from Burzynski and carried them home? And was it mail fraud when Burzynski wrote the codes for chemotherapy on insurance forms for patients who received antineoplaston therapy? Clark, of course, didn't mention that every insurance company in America and Canada had copious knowledge of Burzynski and the nature of his treatment.

Unfortunately for Clark, his issues were not those that brought the press and public to the trial. It was the larger questions that interested everybody else. And it was the larger issues that caused some to wonder whether Burzynski's trial would serve notice on the FDA that its days of pandering to large pharmaceutical corporations and discouraging smaller operators might soon end.

The Tori Moreno Story

Saving a tiny 'One-Eyed Jack'—With Help from
Antineoplastons and a Book About Them

> *"This child is very unusual. There is clear-cut involu-*
> *tion of her tumor due to this treatment."*
>
> —Statement of Fred Epstein M.D., Director of the Institute
> for Neurology and Neurosurgery, Beth Israel Medical Center,
> New York, and professor at Albert Einstein Medical School,
> in a telephone interview on January 21, 2000

> *"I am forever grateful to Tom Elias for his contribution*
> *in helping me help my little daughter live."*
>
> —Electronic mail from Roman Moreno, February 14, 1999

The summer of 1998 started as the most bucolic and happy of times for Kim and Roman Moreno. They'd been married just over a year, their first child was on the way, both had arranged leaves from their jobs as Los Angeles County sheriff's deputies to see their new infant through the first few months of her life.

Roman and Kim needed some good times, too. Both had weathered some difficult times before finding each other while working as guards in the Sybil Brand Institute, the main women's jail for Los Angeles County and the second-largest women's penal institution in America. Both had good reason to hope and wish for a long and stable marriage—and all signs pointed in that direction.

Both Roman and Kim were born and grew up in Southern California, in and near Long Beach. Roman's parents split up in the late 1960s, when he was barely two years old. For awhile, he lived alternately with his mother and father. But by the time he was eight, Roman and his sister and two brothers were living exclusively with their father, a longshoreman who worked the docks of Long Beach and San Pedro. He moved them to nearby Cypress. But Roman remembers that "I never had a great relationship with my father." So the moment he graduated from high school, he joined the Army, serving as a sharpshooter in a reconnaissance unit stationed near Fairbanks, Alaska. "I didn't mind being far from home at all," he remembers, "but I would have preferred Europe."

After that kind of duty, it seemed natural for Roman to become a policeman once he completed two years of junior college. "I liked the mental and physical challenge," he says. "The idea of chasing people, driving fast perfectly legally and taking bad guys off the street—these things appealed to me. I saw a lot of crime when I was little and living in the north part of Long Beach, on the edge of town right next to Compton. By the time I was six I knew what a Crip was."

But before he could take part in any car chases, he had to serve guard duty for awhile. That's where he met Kim, who joined the sheriff's department a couple of years before he did. Roman supervised one dormitory room of 100 prisoners; she was in charge of the whole floor—six big dorm rooms.

Kim was divorced. She'd been married to another deputy sheriff and already had two children, a boy and a girl. But the romance in that marriage died out after three years filled with bills, 100-mile round-trip commutes and long shifts that kept her and first husband Ron apart almost all the time. She was available when she met Roman in 1996, and they hit it off after he talked his way into a New Year's Eve jaunt to San Francisco with Kim and some friends.

They were married in May of 1997 and Kim was pregnant four months later. It was a perfectly normal pregnancy until Kim reached full term. "It was pretty normal," remembers Kim. "I didn't have any complications. Yeah, I guess it was a little harder than my first two, because I was about 10 years older. But I worked up until a week before Tori was born. I saw no reason to get amniocentesis, but I did have several blood tests because I'm Rh negative and I have a thyroid deficiency. There was no problem. I did have an ultrasound at the very end. They told me it showed Tori would be in breech. But she kept rotating around and around, so eventually I had a Caesarian section. I've wondered since then about the sonogram they did. It did not show Tori's brain stem. I saw the report later, and it said the view was blocked. That never triggered anything in my mind until afterward."

Neither did the fact Tori was in position to become a breech baby, her head refusing to enter the birth canal. Later, doctors would tell Kim that the birth canal might have been too tight for the fetal Tori's comfort, because of what was growing in her head.

But no one noticed anything wrong with Tori at birth. She seemed completely normal for her entire natal hospital stay, even if Kim had experienced a brief "bad feeling" when nurses first told her the baby was in a breech position. "My baby book, which I read all the time, said hydrocephalus—water on the brain—was one possible cause for being the breech position."

But any feelings of foreboding dissipated quickly after Tori was born. "She looked perfect," said Roman. Adds Kim, who worked as a medical assistant before older daughter Cassie was born, "It wasn't just that she looked so darling. Her scores on reflexes, coloration and body proportion were all 9.9 out of 10. In the hospital, there was no hint of anything wrong."

Meanwhile, Roman was flying high. He'd had doubts about the pregnancy at first. "I was still adjusting to the idea of marriage when Kim got pregnant," he says. "But by the last three months of the pregnancy, I was completely turned around. And when I saw Tori, it was instant love and adoration. Plus, Kim went into labor on Father's Day in 1998, June 21, so I had hopes this would be a real daddy's girl."

But big trouble lurked in the wings. There were a few early hints, but nothing even a doctor could have recognized without the benefit of a brain scan. "In retrospect, we both remember that from the time she came home from the hospital, Tori's left eye would stay open when she cried," Roman remembers. "We called her 'one-eyed jack,' and sometimes chuckled a little. But when she was five or six weeks old, we noticed a real problem with her eyes. She had trouble tracking things."

Kim noticed something else: "When she was on the bottle, her lips were almost never completely sealed on the nipple. The left side of her face was affected. It got worse over the week or so after we first noticed." By now, says Roman, "You could put your finger on her eyeball and she wouldn't blink. But just looking at her, you still couldn't tell anything except when she was crying. And we looked at her a lot. We were kind of enchanted with her. At least I sure was."

After a week or so of seeing this seeming abnormality, Kim and Roman acted. They took Tori to her pediatrician, Dr. Albert Lee of the Harriman Jones Medical Clinic in Long Beach, not far from their home in Garden Grove. "At first, he couldn't even see what I was talking about, just looking at her," says Roman. "But then she started crying and he could see just what I meant." As it turned out, there was good reason for Tori to cry, but even at this point, no one else was very alarmed.

Lee told the anxious parents he didn't think there was a serious problem, but nevertheless set up an appointment for Tori the next day with neurologist Dr. Perry Lubens. The Morenos saw him on August 11, 1998, and still didn't suspect anything serious was wrong, even after Lubens examined Tori, rang bells and shook rattles in her ear. "At first, he saw nothing," recalls Kim. "Just like Dr. Lee. He asked me, 'Are you a first-time mom?' I thought he was implying I was anxious and putting something on Tori. But I'm definitely not a first-time mom and something was wrong."

After examining Tori a bit longer, Kim remembers, Lubens concluded that "There's something going on in there, possibly a slight hemorrhage. We need an MRI scan to see what's going on. But I don't think it's life-threatening." It was the first time anyone had mentioned any possibility of something serious.

Very anxious by now, the Morenos showed up for the magnetic resonance imaging procedure at Long Beach Community Hospital at the appointed hour of 9 a.m. the next day. Miserable as it made her, Tori had been given nothing to eat or drink overnight. Acting fussy, Tori wasn't allowed to stay with her mom or dad during her MRI. The parents had to stay in a waiting room nearby.

The next thing they saw was tiny Tori on a gurney, being transferred to the pediatric intensive care unit. No one told the instantly anxious parents why. "At that point, I didn't feel anything," recalls Kim. "I thought maybe because she's an infant and they put her to sleep for the MRI, they're doing this because they want to make a space for someone else. I knew the ICU was the only pediatric specialty unit they had in this hospital."

But once they reached the ICU, trailing behind Tori's gurney, the parents quickly got an inkling something was wrong, possibly something serious. "Do you guys know why you're here?" the duty nurse asked in a querulous voice. Kim and Roman shook their heads. The nurse sighed. "You know, she has to be able to suck from a bottle before she goes home."

The parents remember every word and every detail of this time with the clarity of police officers trained to take accurate witness statements for possible use in court. Within five minutes after they and Tori reached the ICU, nurses closed the sliding glass door sealing off the cubicle housing Tori's crib and a couple of chairs. "But not before I heard them whispering and mentioning Tori's name. Then I heard them page Lubens just before they closed the door," says Kim. "At that point I told Roman, 'Something's up.'"

He nodded in agreement. But both parents were still just intensely curious, not yet as horrified as they soon would become. "I was concerned when I learned about the MRI," says Roman. "But I felt it might be something minor—until they dropped the bomb on me. Our frame of mind had been that our daughter has a weak eye muscle, and then all of a sudden she's strapped onto a gurney."
Thirty minutes after overhearing the nurses' whispers, Kim remembers, "I went out into the hall and heard a nurse ask someone on the telephone, 'Who's going to tell them?' That's when I started feeling the ground start to give way under me," recalls Kim.

Within minutes, the nurses handed Kim a telephone and she was speaking with Dr. Lee, the longtime family pediatrician. "He asked me if I was sitting down and if my husband was with me," she remembers. "Then he said, very simply, 'We did the MRI to see what was going on. The MRI shows Tori has a tumor in her brain stem.' He told me it might be inoperable, but they had contacted a neurosurgeon and that a surgery team was being assembled. Tori was going to be transferred by ambulance to Long Beach Memorial Hospital, he said, because they have a cancer center there and they have more experience. He said we could expect surgery in the morning."

Kim was devastated. "I dropped the phone and left the room and went and cried in the hallway. He was telling me they were going to cut my baby's head open."

"My wife doesn't panic," says Roman. "She is really tough, used to handling stress, and I had just heard her break down on the phone and become incoherent. So I thought the doctor had given Tori a death sentence. Kim finally got a few words out, and then I picked up the phone and got on with Dr. Lee. He made it crystal clear to me. He said anything involving brain surgery with an infant is extremely serious and dangerous. I could never get any odds of survival out of him. He did say it had to be brain surgery or Tori would die. He said she had a very rare tumor and could die at any time. He said it was surgery or nothing." But it was clear that Kim had read the doctor right: He thought he was handing the Morenos a death sentence for Tori.

So, too, did the hospital staff, from the grim-faced, whispering nurses to the MRI technicians who'd been forbidden by hospital rules from telling the Morenos what they must have seen the moment they scanned Tori's brain.

Later, some oncology staffers at Long Beach Memorial would tell Roman that Tori's was "the worst glioma they had ever seen." In fact, it was an aggressive, fast-growing

Grade 4 brain stem glioma. There is no cure for this tumor in conventional medicine. The best doctors can hope is to remove all or most of the tumor—if it is encapsulated, or wrapped in a membrane—and wait for its almost inevitable regrowth within weeks or months.

"At first, I asked Dr. Lee if there was nothing else they could do besides brain surgery," says Kim. "He said there was not. Then I couldn't take it any more, and I went in the hallway and cried and wandered while Roman talked to him a while longer."

"They clearly thought at the beginning that the tumor was encapsulated," says Roman. "They didn't realize right away that it was deep inside the brain stem and inoperable. But we never found out who made the first diagnosis, who read the scan first."

The parents didn't have time to ask that sort of question. Tori was quickly transferred to an ambulance for the 10-minute ride and placed in another pediatric intensive care unit. It was now 8 p.m., four hours after Lee had given the Morenos his news, and nurses told the parents Tori would be monitored overnight, with surgery early the next day. Both parents slept in their daughter's small room, more scared than they'd ever been.

But no one turned up in the morning to take Tori to surgery. "For hours, we waited and nobody wanted to talk to us. We wondered why. Was there something wrong with us?" says Roman. Finally, at 10 a.m. neurosurgeon Clarence Greene came in. An unpretentious man, he immediately taped Tori's MRI films on the window of the room and said, "I'm sorry, there's nothing I can do for you. I was under the impression the tumor was at the base of the brain and at least a portion could be removed. But her tumor travels throughout her brain stem and is intertwined with normal tissue. If you were to go in, you couldn't tell what was brain tissue and what was tumor. She wouldn't make it off the operating table."

"He was confident, definite and clear-cut," recalls Roman. "He acted as if there were nothing debatable about it. He was all business and he was gone in five or seven minutes. But he did say he would refer us to an oncologist who deals with other forms of treatment."

Tori's parents were even more devastated than the previous day. "We had no clue about brain tumors," remembers Kim, who would soon learn a lot. "Neither of us knew anything."

And no physician seemed to want to deal with them or offer them any help. "We sat there all day and all night without hearing from any doctor of any kind," says Roman. "That's a very long, cold night sitting in an ICU. We didn't eat all day and all night, because we wanted to be with Tori and we didn't want to risk missing it if a doctor finally came to talk to us."

But they had to tell some family members. "My two kids were in Kansas, where my parents now live," says Kim. "I had to call there. I told my dad and he told my mom and they were in the car the next morning driving out to California to help us. They told my son Jake 'Tori's in the hospital, we have to get out there.'"

But a few phone calls and the emotional support of family and friends didn't do much to relieve the tension in Kim and Roman. "That may have been the worst moment of our lives, at least up until then," says Roman. There was much more to come.

More than 48 hours after Greene rendered his opinion, almost three days after Lee told the Morenos that Tori might die "at any time," they finally saw an oncologist.

Entering Tori's room accompanied by Lee, Dr. Ramesh Patel immediately said neither he nor any of his colleagues were sure what to do for Tori. "We have little experience with a child this young with this type of tumor," Roman remembers Patel saying. He promised to contact pediatric brain tumor experts around the nation on her behalf, and he mentioned the possibility of chemotherapy. "It was clear they were stunned and didn't know what to say to us," recalls Kim. Later that night, Tori was taken from the ICU to Memorial's pediatric oncology unit.

"We sat the rest of that day without anyone telling us anything," says Kim. "Patel came back the next afternoon. We were pretty angry by then. Roman and I had started talking about chemo. I expressed the feeling that unless they could give us some good odds of success with it, I wasn't going to kill my daughter with chemotherapy. Roman and I agreed on that."

So when Patel took the Morenos to the hospital's conference room, the couple was ready. "They put up Tori's films on their fluorescent light-board and at last showed us what was what," Kim remembers. "They said it was horrible. Patel's colleague, a woman, said 'We are in this profession to help children and save lives. Very few times in your career do you come across a situation where you can do nothing. This is one of them.'"

But the doctors soon mentioned the possibility of specialized baby chemotherapy, saying they thought Tori could tolerate it. "I asked what it would do for her," says Kim. "They said it might slow the tumor down, but would not stop it or shrink it. The extra time, they said, would be about a month. I asked flat out, 'Will chemo help my daughter?' They said no. And I said, 'Then why do you offer it?' Their answer was, 'Because some people just can't handle doing nothing.'"

The Morenos remember Patel as the most certain that Tori would die very soon. "Our last two visits with him were about how to let her die," remembers Kim. "He told us not to do cardiopulmonary resuscitation on her when her breathing stopped and he suggested that I not call 911 because that would only prolong Tori's agony."

As each of their meetings ended, the Morenos refused chemotherapy for Tori, and the doctors finally estimated she could live no longer than six weeks, and might be dead in days, if she had no treatment. "They didn't want to tell us that," says Roman, his memories of the moment extremely sharp. "I had to force it out of them."

In the end, the Morenos agreed to take Tori home and give her the steroid drug Decadron to reduce the swelling around the tumor. "I asked them again, if we took her home, was it possible she could die at any moment?" says Roman. "They said yes. Patel also said she might become paralyzed before she died, as the tumor grew. But the next day, we took her home."

It took the Morenos about a week to mobilize energy and determination enough to start seeking alternatives other than merely watching the towheaded Tori die. "We started looking in bookstores and on the Internet," remembers Kim. "My sister LeAnn signed us onto a brain tumor list-serve and one of the e-mails was a letter from a father of a little girl from San Diego who had just started onto a treatment by a Dr. Stanislaw Burzynski. Her first MRI after the treatment showed it was dissolving the tumor from the inside out in a kind of doughnut effect.

"We looked at that and thought about it and the next day we called the Burzynski Clinic and they told us Tori wasn't old enough for their clinical trials. So we started looking at books about brain tumors. We found Dr. Fred Epstein of Beth Israel Hospital in New York on a list of the top pediatric neurosurgeons in the world. We sent him Tori's scans and he called us back and was very much a gentleman. He said he agreed with Dr. Greene that Tori's tumor was inoperable. And he said he knew of no other experimental remedies that might be helpful."

Epstein, the director of Beth Israel's Institute for Neurology and Neurosurgery, confirmed this. "This tumor was clearly inoperable," he said in an interview more than one year later.

"We also got a second opinion at this time from specialists at the City of Hope Medical Center in Duarte, Calif.," Roman recalls. "They fully agreed it was a terminal case and that Tori had only a very short time to live. The only thing different that they offered was an oral form of chemotherapy, which Tori could take at home instead of being in the hospital. But they also said she wouldn't live any longer than if she had regular chemo—which we knew would extend her life only a little. So we said 'No, thanks."

So it was back to the bookstore for Roman Moreno, who soon found and bought a copy of the first edition of The Burzynski Breakthrough. "I also read up on shark cartilage and laetrile," Roman remembers. "But I read The Burzynski Breakthrough in full." That's when things began moving quickly. "In the book, I found out about Ric Schiff (See The Crystin Schiff Story) and I called him." Roman hit it off immediately with Schiff, another policeman. "He's an encyclopedia of knowledge on childhood brain tumors and how to deal with them," Roman says. "I told him the Burzynski Clinic had told me Tori didn't qualify for one of their trials because she was under six months old. He said to call the Food and Drug Administration and he told me who to call there to get a compassionate use exception. I called. Ric also told me to talk to our local congresswoman. I went and talked to Loretta Sanchez (D-Calif.). Ric gave me Tom Elias' phone number, and he also told me a lot about Dr. Burzynski's treatment. At the same time, I got back in touch with the Burzynski Clinic, and they also requested a compassionate and sent letters at the same time Sanchez did. Within two days, the FDA told me I needed two letters from qualified doctors saying the tumor was inoperable. We got one from Dr. Epstein. We told him we were going to go to Dr. Burzynski, and he didn't mind at all, the way we'd been told most doctors do. We also got a letter from Dr. Greene. The letters were faxed to the FDA, which issued a compassionate use exemption the next day, the first Thursday in October 1998. I still don't know why they acted so fast. Maybe it was because she was just three months old and had absolutely no viable options."

Two days later the Morenos took a four-hour flight to Houston to consult Burzynski. In the interim, their story was aired on five Los Angeles television stations, which invited viewers to send tax-deductible contributions to help pay for her treatment to a special fund set up within the county sheriff's department.

"We knew we'd run into financial problems and would probably need public donations," says Roman. "Blue Cross had told us they would not pay anything for this treatment." In fact, Blue Cross representatives testifying at the 1997 criminal trial of Dr. Burzynski in Houston repeatedly testified it was their policy to pay nothing for treatment with Burzynski's antineoplaston medications, no matter how successful the outcome of treatment. That weekend, the Morenos also searched frantically for a local doctor who would agree to monitor Tori's treatment after she returned home from Houston. Eventually, Lee agreed to help. "Patel said he wanted no part of Dr. Burzynski," says Roman. "He told me Dr. Burzynski is not part of any nationally recognized oncology group [ed: a statement that is not correct] and he told me we were wasting our money. He gave me literature about medical quackery. And he told me he didn't know much about Dr. Burzynski. I told him if I were him, I'd be embarrassed to say I didn't know about antineoplastons." In a telephone interview in February 2000, Patel reiterated that he knows nothing about antineoplastons and thus did not want to work with a patient taking them. "I know nothing about it," he said.

"I had a very heated conversation with two other oncologists in the Harriman Jones group," Roman continues. "They also told me they didn't want to be involved in any way with Dr. Burzynski. With Lee, I didn't ask him to agree with me about going to Burzynski. It was a decision me and my wife should make. He finally said that he's responsible for watching Tori's progress, so he would do it."

Eventually, the Morenos would name Patel and the Harriman Jones group as codefendants in a lawsuit against Blue Cross. But that was still in the unpredictable future.

So was Tori's fate on antineoplastons. Burzynski's clinical trial using antineoplastons against brain stem gliomas indicated she would have about a 65 percent chance of responding to the medication, if complete remissions, partial remissions and stable disease with no tumor progression are considered responses (See Appendix: charts). But at three months, Tori was the youngest patient Burzynski had ever encountered.

"Tori would have qualified for an almost automatic compassionate use exception because of her Karnovsky test scores," he remembers. The Karnovsky test measures physical abilities and responses. "If a patient scores 50 or lower on this test, the usual life expectancy is two months to four months. Tori qualified on the Karnovsky basis, but I thought it best to ask the FDA specially because she was so young. This was a very risky case and she was in danger of dying at any minute when she arrived. Our protocols for the clinical trials have a minimum age of six months."

That didn't stop Burzynski from approaching his tiny patient optimistically, when he saw her that Tuesday. She had spent Monday visiting a vascular surgeon to have a Hickman catheter inserted into her chest. "I can't promise you I'll save Tori's life, but I am confident we have a good chance," he told the Morenos during his first examination of Tori. "I have a good chance if there's enough time." Consistent with his usual policy of openness—so long as patients consent—the examination was videotaped by the CBS television station in Houston and parts were shown that night on the local news programs in both Houston and Los Angeles.

But Burzynski plainly felt somewhat ginger about Tori's case. "When he first saw her MRI scans, he told us it might be too late," Roman remembers. "He looked at one scan and said, 'I cannot believe she is not paralyzed." Another doctor had told the Morenos that Tori's brain stem had somehow manipulated itself into a position that did not paralyze her, allowing her to buy some time.

Burzynski started Tori on a small dose of antineoplastons to test whether she would be allergic to them. The dose was gradually increased over the 10 days the Morenos remained in Houston. Then they went home, scheduled to return three months later. As they flew home, they didn't know if the trip and the treatment now being constantly pumped into a vein in her chest were doing Tori any good.

But soon after they got home, the parents started noticing changes for the better. "Within a week of our getting back, Tori's eyes started tracking things more normally," says Roman. "She started sucking properly on a bottle. Her eyes lost some of their droopy look and her left eye started blinking. "We noticed these things even before the first MRI scan taken after treatment started—in December 1998—showed a 23 percent reduction in the size of the tumor.

Pediatrician Lee did not respond to attempts to interview him, but he told the Morenos after the MRI results came in that "Something's obviously working." "You could see a sense of excitement in him, but he had a conflict of interest and I didn't think he could talk to us freely," says Roman. "Harriman Jones, which he's part of, has a huge contract with Blue Cross of California and they had refused to cover the treatment, so he can never say much about the success of this treatment."

Patel, meanwhile, displayed no excitement at all on hearing that Tori had survived the death sentence he pronounced. "Maybe the tumor was benign," Kim recalls him saying. "It was the surgeon who read the scans, not me. I don't know precisely what kind of tumor it was."

But Patel conceded he had never seen a patient who had no chemotherapy or radiation survive more than a few weeks with a tumor like Tori's. "I never saw a patient who had no treatment in which a tumor involuted," he said in the February 2000 telephone interview. But he was unwilling to give any credit to Burzynski or his antineoplastons and displayed no interest in learning about them.

"I know there was some kind of treatment given her," he said. I have know idea whether that did it or it happened spontaneously." This, from a man who stated in the same interview he had never before seen a remission in a case like Tori's.

Tori's cheeks were still puffed out and swollen from the Decadron she was taking to reduce swelling in her brain. But the Morenos at last felt their daughter might make it. "We still faced the fact that Burzynski doesn't cure everybody," says Kim. "But we learned that his patients do better if they've never been poisoned with chemo and radiation—and Tori never had either. We're told his response rate is more than 75 percent when the immune system is free of the effects of chemotherapy. And with a 23 percent reduction after two months, we began to feel she had a chance. But Dr. Patel was still sure she'd die. 'Don't worry about an autopsy,' he told me once. 'I will sign the death certificate without one.'"

Tori wasn't anywhere near to dying. She stayed on the antineoplastons and began to develop like a normal child—laughing, crying, crawling and charming almost everyone who met her. Eventually, Kim and Roman took her back to visit Lubens, the neurologist who first saw the need to have Tori's brain scanned. By now, Tori was a bouncy baby, just over one year old. "He rang bells, saw her reactions to them and other stimuli, and said, "She's doing great. Obviously, her body knows what to do to fight this. Lots of children with brain tumors survive and do well with brain tumors for many years." Kim and Roman quickly noted the difference between this and the prognoses Tori had gotten many months earlier from Lubens, Patel, Greene, Epstein and their colleagues. They also noted that Lubens looked briefly—"less than five minutes," deputy sheriff Kim reports—at four different scans of Tori's tumor which had been taken at regular intervals over the preceding few months. He said he saw no difference in the tumor size.

This contrasts sharply with the words of Epstein, to whom the Morenos sent scans several months after Tori started antineoplaston treatment. "This child is very unusual. There is clear-cut involution of her tumor due to this treatment," Epstein would tell an interviewer. Momentarily disturbed by what Lubens said, Roman quickly checked for statistics on brain tumor remissions with the National Cancer Institute and the American Cancer Society. Both told him there are no such statistics, because remissions are almost unheard-of.

But Lubens persists in his view. Like many other oncologists, he poo-poos the obvious results of antineoplaston treatment even when they stare him in the face. Given the opportunity to explain why he persists in this attitude, Lubens displayed the same unwillingness that Patel did when it came to discussing anything about antineoplastons. "I'm interested in non-fiction, not fiction!" he exclaimed, and slammed down his telephone on an interviewer in February 2000.

And yet, the Morenos say he was one of the more constructive doctors in helping them through the earliest moments of their ordeal. "He came to Memorial after we'd gotten the terminal diagnosis for Tori and were waiting for the Decadron prescription to be filled," Kim remembers. "He wanted to console us. He is by-the-book; he's not a rebel; he goes with the system."

But the Morenos still had a little skepticism about whether the treatment was helping their daughter, or whether, as Lubens said, she was simply "adjusting" to the tumor's presence. "We had been warned by the doctors who gave us the quackery material that Dr. Burzynski would try to take all our money," Kim says. "So we sent Tori's scans to two neutral doctors at a different hospital who were not affiliated with either Dr. Burzynski or with Blue Cross, which we were suing by then. They told us there was a definite decrease in tumor size and whatever medicine Tori was on was working."

So the Morenos kept Tori on the medication, even though her first chest catheter became infected and another one had to be inserted in her abdomen. By September 1999, one year after Patel and others had given her a death sentence, her tumor was reduced by 70 percent.

Even so, by FDA standards, Tori cannot be identified as a responder to antineoplastons. The FDA demands that only tumors which see a 50 percent reduction within any six-month period of treatment can be described as responding. Tori's did not diminish that much in any six-month period. The FDA calls her condition "stable disease." But a tumor that was growing fast and which authoritative neurosurgeons and radiologists at institutions as diverse as the Albert Einstein School of Medicine and the City of Hope predicted would kill Tori within days or weeks was more than two-thirds gone less than one year after antineoplaston treatment began.

Meanwhile, the Morenos eventually called off the aggressive fund-raising campaign with which they raised more than $50,000 to help pay Tori's expenses. They settled their lawsuit against Blue Cross, signing an agreement that prevents them from disclosing the amount paid to them. But it was enough to assure there would never be interruptions in Tori's treatment.

Kim and Roman insist Tori will stay on the medicine until Burzynski thinks it's time to stop. And they're keeping a careful scrapbook so that when Tori learns to read, she'll understand what Kim and Roman already know— she's a miracle, saved by antineoplaston treatment and a book that helped her parents find out about it.

CHAPTER 1

The Criminal Trials: Efficacy Becomes Obvious

Defendant's request for a jury view is a thinly veiled effort to expose the jury to the specter of Dr. Burzynski in his act of saving lives. Permitting such a visit will certainly infect the jury's consideration of the real issues with irrelevant, prejudicial, and misleading concerns regarding whether antineoplaston works and the unfortunate fate of Dr. Burzynski's patients.

—From a court memo filed by Assistant U.S. Attorney Michael Clark on Oct. 11, 1996

It could have been a trial for the ages, one that would have finally settled any scientific doubts about whether antineoplastons are effective against cancer. It could have settled vital questions about the federal government's intrusions into individual decision making, especially the efforts by the FDA to regulate what measures desperate cancer patients can take in an effort to save their own lives. Those were the issues the world cared about when Dr. Stanislaw Burzynski went on trial in Houston in January 1997 on 75 charges of contempt of court, interstate commerce in an unapproved drug and insurance fraud. This was a case that could have rivaled in importance the Scopes monkey trial, in which Charles Darwin's theory of evolution was debated.

U.S. District Judge Simeon T. Lake 3rd, who presided, clearly realized all this. "This trial will be one of the most interesting we have ever heard in Houston," Lake declared as *voir dire*, the questioning of potential jurors, began. But then Lake set about systematically trying to prevent the jury from hearing any of the interesting issues vital to the case.

Instead, Burzynski's first criminal trial devolved into a mundane insurance-fraud case. Time after time, Burzynski's lawyers tried to shoehorn the issue of efficacy—the question of whether antineoplastons work—into the trial. Time after time, chief prosecutor Clark and Judge Lake tried to push those issues out of Lake's marble and mahogany-paneled courtroom. The issue of whether antineoplastons work was formally banned both from this trial and the much shorter one that would follow. "Whether or not any patient or former patient believes Dr. Burzynski's drug is effective is not going to be an issue," Lake told the jurors. "We are not going to be hearing evidence of whether any drug or treatment is effective or not." But like a friendly and persistent camel in the Sahara Desert, the efficacy issue again and again poked its nose into the big tent of the trial, eventually getting both humps in despite repeated attempts by Lake and Clark to push it out.

Their efforts to sidestep the issue became almost comical at times. And they eventually had to fail. "The jurors apparently took to heart the issue of efficacy, even though many thought Burzynski had broken the law," Clark said after the jury in the first trial deliberated 35 hours and was unable to come to a unanimous decision on even one count. In fact, jurors reported being split 6-6 on most of the charges against the doctor.

How did the prosecutors try to keep efficacy out? Let us count the ways. First, they filed their October memo opposing a defense request to take the jury on a tour of Burzynski's clinic and the plant where he manufactures antineoplastons. The memo revealed for the first time in the government's 15-year campaign to squelch Burzynski and his medication that high officials realized Burzynski had been saving lives. Defense attorneys wanted to stage a tour to show jurors that Burzynski was not, in fact, a greedy profiteer but that most of the money he took in was reinvested in his business, where he employed more than 120 persons.

Next, prosecutors tried to erase from the jury's memory any mention of anything that related to the safety or effectiveness of antineoplastons. Typical was the questioning of reluctant prosecution witness Clay Levit, a high school teacher from Austin, Texas. Levit testified that in 1994, he received a telephone call from a distant acquaintance named Dennis Kojan, who suffered from non-Hodgkin's lymphoma and lived in Sebastopol, California. Levit testified that Kojan had told him it was illegal for Burzynski to ship antineoplastons to him, but said Kojan was in desperate need of the medication. Kojan asked Levit to drive to Houston, pick up the medicine and ship it to him in California. Levit said he agreed and made the drive to Burzynski's clinic at least seven times, perhaps 10. "I viewed this as a matter of human mercy," Levit said.

Obviously, the government saw it differently. Four times after Burzynski was indicted in November 1995, Levit was interviewed or subpoenaed by federal agents. Under cross-examination by defense attorney Michael Ramsey, Levit said he never understood why FDA rules allow shipment of foreign-made unapproved drugs to points in America but forbid interstate shipment of those made in the United States. Now Assistant U.S. Attorney George Tallichet blundered. In the courthouse hallway before Levit's testimony began, Tallichet, the prosecution's hyper-energetic version of a pit bull, had said he expected

Levit would provide "comic relief." But the jury clearly wasn't responding to Levit that way. So on his re-direct questioning, Tallichet asked Levit why he had repeatedly performed an act he thought might be illegal. "Dennis told me this medicine was the only one that was working for him," Levit explained. Instantly, Tallichet was on his feet protesting the testimony of his own witness. "Objection!" he shouted. "That answer is non-responsive."

Actually, it was the efficacy camel pushing its nose into the tent. Lake responded by ordering the jury to disregard Levit's statement. But the statement had been made, the jury heard it, and it was to be just one of many similar statements by witnesses.

Lake's decision to keep efficacy out of testimony was made long before the first trial began. "Arguments about effectiveness have nothing to do with this case," he said in a November 1996 interview in his chambers on the ninth floor of Houston's federal courthouse. "Anyone's opinion of whether Burzynski saves lives is relevant only if and when the case gets to sentencing. We have only three basic charges here: violating an injunction, mail fraud and selling an unapproved drug in interstate commerce. Whether antineoplastons are effective or not is not relevant to the counts of contempt and mail fraud. On the violations of the Food, Drug and Cosmetic Act, the government must prove that these are unapproved new drugs, but nothing about whether they work or not."

That represented an evolution toward the prosecution in the judge's thinking. In another interview in July 1996, after reading scores of letters from Burzynski patients, Lake had demonstrated that he fully understood all the implications of the upcoming trial. "The real parties in interest here are the patients and the FDA," Lake said. "If antineoplastons work and [Burzynski] is not allowed to use them, who is harmed? If it's a placebo, who is harm visited upon?" This understanding that effectiveness was really at the heart of the case never stopped the legalistic Lake from trying to eject the issue. Still, he never lost sight of his realization that Burzynski's patients had a major interest in the outcome of the case, even if he would see to it that their testimony was sharply restricted.

And about a month after Levit testified, it became clear that at least some jurors understood that prosecutors were trying to hide something and that the judge also was trying to keep them from understanding a key factor. This was plain from the response of jurors while defense lawyer Richard Jaffe questioned Dr. Barbara Szymkowski, a Polish-trained M.D. working as an intake interviewer for Burzynski. As Jaffe asked her how she interviews prospective patients, the bespectacled Szymkowski explained that she especially pays attention to people with brain tumors, "because antineoplastons work so well against brain tumors." Before Szymkowski could utter another word, Assistant U.S. Attorney Amy LeCocq struggled to her feet as fast as her seven-months-pregnant body would permit. "I object," she protested. "This is irrelevant." As Lake sustained the objection, juror Anthony Batiste, a short, trim engineer whose shirts were consistently so starched they could have stood up in a corner of the courtroom, clapped a hand over his mouth and barely managed to suppress a loud guffaw. At that point, it seemed obvious that at least some jurors understood what this case was really about.

"I was still going to vote guilty, but I knew what was going on," Batiste said later. "I was laughing because the efficacy issue was out of the bag, and there was obviously no putting it back." Added juror Darlene Phillips, who started the trial as an alternate and wound up occupying seat No. 11, "It became so obvious what the government was doing, after a while. It was like they were saying, 'Tell the jury anything, but Lord, don't let them see that the drug works.' But the fact that patient after patient after patient came on the witness stand looking healthier than we did, that said a lot to me."

The ultimate outcome of the first trial, with six jurors adamantly voting for acquittal on all counts and six determined to convict on at least some counts, demonstrated that the jury had differing notions about what the trial meant. From the first day, Jan. 6, 1997, it was clear that the FDA wanted this trial to serve as a vehicle to jail Burzynski and send a warning to any scientist who might try to bring a drug into wide use independent of the FDA's jurisdiction and its approval process. Each day, the FDA's top enforcement lawyer, Robert Spiller, the same man who in 1983 signed what became the agency's declaration of war on Burzynski, sat in the third row of spectator benches, carefully transcribing by hand virtually every word spoken. Each evening, he met with prosecutors, who nevertheless repeatedly proclaimed their independence from the FDA. At every courtroom break, they consulted him. But Spiller refused to say even one word about why the FDA had pursued its long-term campaign against Burzynski and his antineoplastons. "Can't say anything about this case," he often remarked. Neither Spiller nor anyone else at the agency would comment on the fact that the very conduct it was trying to declare illegal at trial was now fully sanctioned—by the FDA itself—a contradiction and confusion never understood by the jurors. The FDA contended that because Burzynski knew his patients were taking his medication home to other states, his actions constituted interstate commerce. Even in its carefully cherry-picked charges against the doctor—all involving desperately ill patients who eventually died—the FDA never accused Burzynski or his employees of shipping anything over state lines. This, Burzynski realized, would have been a violation of the 1983 injunction that allowed him to operate in Texas but not across state lines. "I do not have a police force," Burzynski often said. "I cannot force my patients to stay in the state of Texas."

In closing arguments, defense attorney Ramsey would use what Burzynski partisans called the "candy bar defense" to explain the absurdity of the interstate-commerce charges. "If I buy a candy bar in Houston and take it to Louisiana before I eat it, the commerce is all in Houston, not in Louisiana," he said. "It would be the same if my wife in Louisiana asked me to buy a candy bar for her while I was visiting Houston and I brought one home to her. The commerce would all be in Houston, where the money changed hands. How is this different?" And what the jury never heard, of course, was that because Burzynski was given IND permits by the FDA as a result of congressional pressure after his indictment, by the time the trial began he was able to ship as much of his drug as he wished over any and all state lines.

"This amazes all of his patients," said Steven Siegel, one of the leaders of the Burzynski patient organization, which staged daily demonstrations, on the sidewalk outside the downtown courthouse regardless of the weather. "He is on trial for doing something that he is now fully permitted to do. It makes no sense."

With the FDA clamming up, it was left to Clark to do his best to explain the government's actions. "I'm interested in the wrongful taking of money," he said during one afternoon break. "I also believe Burzynski is a pathological liar. I believe this is just an ordinary, if rather complicated, case of fraud. He introduced a drug into interstate commerce, and this was done with fraudulent intent."

From the start, Clark and the government wanted to portray Burzynski as a venal figure, victimizing patients whose mental powers were impaired by their desperation to survive and their willingness to try almost anything. The indictment claimed Burzynski made a $40 million profit over a five-year period before his indictment. Affidavits on file in Washington, D.C., reveal that as early as 1984, FDA investigators were interviewing fired Burzynski employees in an effort to find out how much money he made.

As part of this effort, almost every witness was asked how much Burzynski charged for treatment. The usual figure: $342.50 per day. But no one was asked by prosecutors to compare Burzynski's charges with those for conventional chemotherapy and radiation, which are generally more than five times as high. And when defense lawyers tried to raise this question, it was not permitted because asking would have put antineoplastons on an even plane with conventional therapies, thus implying merit.

But Burzynski managed to fend off the accusations of profiteering by revealing his tax returns and profit statements for the years 1991-95, the period covered by the indictment. Those returns showed that income from his medical practice ranged from $35,653 in 1993 to $111,339 in 1991. His overall family income, including investments and income from his physician wife and the research institute where the antineoplastons are manufactured, was much higher. Burzynski's total taxable income ranged from $400,012 in 1993 to $1.92 million in 1991.

His accountant, Russell DeMarco, testified that those

figures were "substantially less than most doctors" audited by his firm in Houston. "Surgeons in the first year of practice usually make between $400,000 and $500,000," DeMarco said. "After that, their income goes much higher." In the end, then, the government never was able to hang a "greedy" tag on Burzynski and make it stick.

Throughout the trials, Clark also insisted that his first concern was the welfare of the patients, who, he said, were being defrauded by Burzynski. Clark never explained the contradiction between that contention and his written concession that Burzynski was "saving lives." Nor did he explain why the FDA never prepared a contingency plan for treatment of Burzynski's cancer-ridden patients in case their doctor was convicted and driven out of business. "The one thing I tried to convey through the trials is that we also care about the patients," he said just after closing arguments in the first trial. "But it's not my province to tell the patients what to do if Burzynski is convicted. If we win, I would advise the patients to talk to Burzynski about getting a clinical sub-investigator to take his place." But patients believed Clark showed his true level of concern for them in one encounter on the final day of pretrial hearings, just four days before opening statements. On that day, Steven Siegel and his wife, Mary Jo, approached Clark as he sat in the courthouse coffee room with his wife during the lunch break. "What do you propose we do to survive if Dr. B. is convicted?" Mary Jo asked Clark. His response: "I'm trying to have a quiet lunch with my wife." When the Siegels persisted with their questions, Clark added that "it's up to the FDA."

But the Siegels and other patients had visited FDA headquarters in Rockville, Maryland, several times without receiving an explanation for the agency's persistent campaign against Burzynski or suggestions for alternative treatments.

Clark's often-depressed demeanor during the trials may have stemmed from the fact that he had been handed a difficult task. To convict Burzynski, Judge Lake made clear in his final instructions to the jury, prosecutors would have to prove that he willfully and intentionally created a scheme to defraud insurance companies and that he tried to deceive the FDA about whether his drug was being used in interstate commerce. The task was difficult because the facts weren't there to support it, even though the government spent more than $2 million pursuing the case in the four years leading to trial. Four assistant U.S. attorneys worked on the case full time for months. A postal inspector and an FDA field investigator spent four years trying to find evidence. Scores of witnesses were flown to Houston for both pretrial interviews and trial testimony. Sending Spiller to Houston and quartering him in the posh Hyatt Regency four blocks from the courthouse contributed at least $20,000 to the cost of the case, if Spiller's salary is included.

Starting with their first witness, prosecutors tried to prove the kind of fraudulent intent needed to convict, but they never managed to pull it off. They began their case with postal inspector Barbara Ritchey, a certified public accountant and former Internal Revenue Service agent who testified that she had spent the previous four years working to convict Burzynski. She testified that in early 1995, while she was assigned to the Health Care Fraud Task Force in the Houston U.S. Attorney's office, a friend of a Burzynski patient gave her a shipping ticket that identified a private shipping office—Postal USA in west Houston—as a place from which some of Burzynski's medication had been sent to a point outside Texas. She said that on March 15, 1995, she and FDA field investigator Sharon Miller went to the postal drop in a strip mall on Westheimer Avenue, not far from the former site of Burzynski's clinic.

"After we had been there about 20 minutes, a man named Alan Shea came in with large boxes," she told the jury. "We tried to ascertain whether he was mailing anti-neoplastons."

Apparently because of nervous behavior on the part of the Postal USA clerk, who knew the federal agents were lurking in his back room, Shea did not ship the boxes. Instead, he left the mailing facility.

"We followed him when he left," Ritchey testified. "He was driving a Lincoln Continental. He went directly to the Burzynski Clinic and went inside. Later, he exited the parking lot there, following a van driven by a man we identified as Bob Moseray, Burzynski's shipping clerk. Their cars went to another shipping facility nearby."

This time, Ritchey and Miller waited to enter until after Shea had completed his transaction. Later, she would learn that Shea was a friend of Burzynski patient John Buckley, a prostate cancer victim. Because Burzynski refused to ship his medication to Buckley or any other out-of-state patient at the time, Buckley and any others too ill to make frequent trips to Houston were compelled to find intermediaries to pick up and ship their drugs.

So the cavalcade of cars proceeded through west Houston, with Moseray's van leading the way to the alternate shipping facility and Shea following, trailed by the two federal agents. Later, Shea, a former Smith Barney stockbroker, would testify that he got involved when Buckley, a business acquaintance, telephoned him early in March 1995 and begged him to pick up some medication and ship it to him in New York state. Shaking visibly as he testified, Shea said Miller and Ritchey did not stop him from shipping the boxes but later told him he had done something illegal.

Ritchey said she and Miller waited until Moseray and Shea had completed their transaction, then went inside with search warrants and opened the boxes. "They contained plastic bags of liquid labeled Antineoplastons," she said. A few days later, she and Miller, accompanied by "at least eight other federal agents," most borrowed from agencies such as the Drug Enforcement Administration and the FBI, raided Burzynski's clinic, spending six and a half hours ransacking and confiscating files. "We took patient medical-insurance files, reports on Investigational New Drug permits, and payment records," Ritchey testified.

Those records would be used as the nub of the insurance-fraud case against Burzynski—a case even prosecution-oriented jurors felt was worse than weak. "We never even really got to the insurance-fraud charges in our deliberations," reported Batiste. "But I can tell you for sure, no one would have ever convicted him of fraud." That was also how Lake saw the fraud charges, eventually throwing them out because "the government presented insufficient evidence."

Prosecutors, however, spent millions of tax dollars pursuing those charges, including the cost of keeping Spiller in Houston for two full months, even though he played no direct role in the courtroom. They sought insurance-claim examiners from myriad companies around America, then brought them to Houston. Like Spiller, all were quartered at the Hyatt Regency Hotel at taxpayer expense.

The first such insurance clerk to testify was Karen Kelleher, a paralegal working for Blue Cross/Blue Shield of Massachusetts. She testified that Burzynski had filed several claims for services provided to cancer patient Rhoda

Coyne of Belmont, Massachusetts. She said Burzynski charged $342.50 per day, using the code number 96414 to describe his services. The number came from a code book of physicians' current procedural terminology (CPT) published each year by the American Medical Association (AMA). The number stood for chemotherapy via portable infusion pump lasting eight hours or more. Prosecutors would argue repeatedly that using this code implies a doctor is physically present at least when the infusion begins each day, even though Coyne and other Burzynski patients infused at home and were in regular telephone contact with the doctor and his staff.

This was the so-called fraud and deception Clark, LeCocq and Tallichet would try to prove. But starting with Kelleher, defense lawyers chipped away at any notion of deceptiveness. "Does the 96414 code say a physician must be present?" asked defense attorney Ramsey. Answer: "Well, no, but sort of." Did Blue Cross/Blue Shield know what antineoplastons are and exactly how Burzynski uses them? Yes, the firm's national association, based in Chicago, published a policy memo on antineoplastons in 1990, long before the period covered in the indictment. But "we at Blue Cross of Massachusetts didn't know anything about it," Kelleher said.

Next came Sharon Halstead, a claims administrator for Equifax insurance, headquartered in Charleston, West Virginia, which administered the health care coverage used by most West Virginia state employees. "The Public Employee Insurance Agency does not cover experimental or investigational drugs," she testified, after noting that Burzynski's claim for treating brain tumor patient Michael Misiti listed the same 96414 CPT code. After receiving claims for Misiti, she said, she telephoned Burzynski's insurance administrator, Cheryl Owens, and was told that none of the charges Burzynski made were for the drug itself. Like other researchers, Burzynski can't charge for experimental drugs, and Owens would testify that he never tried to. But like all others, he can charge for ancillary services, including nursing care, consultations and reading various kinds of scans. Owens, said Halstead, also insisted in their phone conversations that the use of the 96414 CPT code was suggested by the AMA itself.

Weeks later, as part of its effort to prove fraud, the government brought on Chicago-based AMA official Celeste Kirschner, chief designer of the CPT code system used by every doctor, hospital and insurance company in America. She admitted under cross-examination by defense attorney Dan Cogdell that "there is not a code for every single action of every doctor. People sometimes use the code closest to what they do if [existing] codes don't match precisely." Kirschner also told the jury that it is "common practice for doctors to charge for overhead included in their other charges." And, she said, "There is not just one single code for management of chemotherapy administration."

The upshot, when the government was finished presenting more than 30 hours of testimony from insurance clerks and executives, was that Burzynski for years consistently used the same code in billing for his services and that he consistently used his own provider number on claims even though he knew almost every insurance company in America had installed "flags" in their computers to kick out his claims and prevent him from receiving automatic payment. Whenever an insurance company asked for information about his treatment, it quickly received detailed answers, which included the fact that antineoplastons were experimental drugs. The question that arose in the courtroom was, "Where's the fraud?" If Burzynski had intended to deceive anyone, he could have varied the CPT code he used. He could have tried to use the provider numbers of one or more of the doctors working with and for him. But he did none of these things, instead continuing to file claims into a system he knew was stacked against him.

Eventually, after the jury in the first trial deadlocked and individual jurors later revealed they never even got around to seriously discussing the fraud counts, Lake felt forced to throw out the counts and did, acquitting Burzynski, on the court's own motion, of anything resembling fraud.

That left the government only with what became known as the "FDA counts" and the charge of contempt of court. But during the eight-week first trial, prosecutors were unable to make any of those counts stick despite heroic efforts. FDA investigators had fanned out across the country in the months before the trial, locating survivors of patients who had sought out Burzynski but died anyway. Carefully choosing the cases they would use, prosecutors managed to indict the doctor on 40 charges of interstate transportation of an unapproved new drug. In each case, they said, either the patient or some relative or friend of the patient picked up antineoplastons at Burzynski's clinic— much as Alan Shea had done—and shipped them or took them to an out-of-state location. Because Burzynski realized that these patients or intermediaries would take the drug outside Texas, they charged, he was knowingly introducing it into interstate commerce, a violation of both the federal Food, Drug and Cosmetic Act and a 1983 injunction handed down by U.S. District Judge Gabrielle McDonald.

The problem for the government was that it had to prove Burzynski did this with intent to deceive the FDA, a burden of proof prosecutors never came close to achieving. Instead, by threatening to prosecute survivors of dead patients, they coerced testimony from a long series of witnesses, almost all of whom painted a positive picture of Burzynski and their relatives' experiences with him.

Typical was Raymond Goulet, a computer technician who testified that in early 1993 he traveled to Houston with his wife, Christine, from their home in New Hampshire. At the time, he said, Christine suffered from a diffuse large-cell lymphoma. Other doctors gave her no hope of long-term survival. She was wheelchair-bound when they arrived at Burzynski's clinic. "My wife was so ill, I was afraid she'd die the very night we got to Houston," Raymond said.

Did Burzynski guarantee that his treatment would work? asked prosecutor Clark. No, testified Raymond. "There were no guarantees by Dr. Burzynski or anyone else. He told us it was at best doubtful the treatment could help Christine." He was not allowed to tell the jury whether the treatment helped his wife. To do so would have implied efficacy. But outside the presence of the jury, he told the courtroom that after Christine began antineoplaston treatment, her blood counts improved. She felt better and was able to discard her wheelchair. Just two weeks after beginning treatment, he said, she asked her husband to take her line dancing. She died of a streptococcus infection a few weeks later, Raymond said, adding that "there is no doubt the drug improved the quality of her life." He was not permitted to tell the jury that his wife's tumors were substantially smaller at her death than when she first went to Texas.

As for the key questions about shipping the drug, Raymond said, clinic workers "told me that if I took this home, it would be my responsibility." And he added that "someone at the clinic, maybe Burzynski, recommended that we stay in Houston." But the Goulets opted to go home with their antineoplastons. Repeated Burzynski, "I cannot force anyone to stay in Texas."

Raymond's impression of the Burzynski trials, offered in the hallway after his coerced testimony? "A witch-hunt."

Also typical was the subpoenaed testimony of Michael Smith, a self-employed writer from Pascagoula, Mississippi, and the brother-in-law of one-time breast-cancer patient Mary Ann McNally. Smith said he was living in Houston in 1993-94 when McNally arrived for treatment by Burzynski after chemotherapy and radiation treatments had failed to stop her cancer.

"When she became too ill to come to Houston, I picked up the medicine for her twice," Smith said. "I signed a release form at the clinic, promising that I would not take it out of state, then I mailed it from Postal USA." Now Smith, under cross-examination by defense attorney Ramsey, began to describe the adverse effects of conventional treatment and detailed how McNally began looking for an alternative. Lake immediately stopped Smith's narrative, ruling it was beginning to get into questions of efficacy. "This line of questioning is irrelevant," the judge declared.

But he did not stop Smith from saying that although he knew it was illegal to ship antineoplastons over state lines, "I felt if Mary Ann traveled while on the treatment, she would not herself be contraband. I never felt she was an article of commerce. And when I shipped the medicine, it was strictly to help my wife's sister, not to help Dr. Burzynski."

Of all the relatives and intermediaries who assisted patients who later died, not one would claim that Burzynski had promised a cure. Their absence of resentment impressed the jurors. "The government could not find one person to say something bad about Burzynski," said Batiste, who nevertheless voted guilty. "I think that says a lot about his character. I was willing to convict, but I understood it was just technicalities."

Once the government finished presenting relatives and friends of dead patients, the defense got its chance to bring on live ones. Burzynski's patients had been demonstrating outside the courthouse from the day the first trial began. "Save the doctor who saves lives," they chanted as they picketed the courthouse, hoping jurors headed for lunch would see them and take heed. I WAS CURED BY DR. B., read the picket sign carried by Jessica Kerfoot.

Jurors never said whether the picketing and chanting made any impression on them, but they were visibly moved by the parade of patients defense lawyers brought to the witness stand. There was Mary Jo Siegel of Pacific Palisades, California, cured of non-Hodgkin's lymphoma. There was Pamela Winningham of Princeton, New Jersey, cured of an astrocytoma brain tumor eight years earlier. There was Tracy Hall, currently on the treatment for a Grade 3 astrocytoma and looking healthy. There was Leslie Graham, a registered nurse from Largo, Florida, whose son Robbie's aggressive medulloblastoma brain tumor was almost in remission. There was Mariann Kunnari of Aurora, Minnesota, whose son Dustin was afflicted with a brain tumor in 1994 and was by then a healthy six-year-old. There was Mary Michaels of Troy, Michigan, whose son Paul was diagnosed with a tangerine-size astrocytoma brain tumor in 1988 and given only months to live. Paul, now a strapping teenager, watched proudly as his mother testified. His tumor is now the size of a pea, and he remains on the treatment. Said Mrs. Michaels, "Dr. Burzynski did not force us to choose between moving to Texas and losing our son. We chose to go back to Michigan, and we took the medicine with us. He had nothing to do with it. The clinic always refused to ship it and made us come back to Texas to get new supplies." All were asked if Burzynski had "victimized" them when they were desperate, as prosecutor LeCocq charged was the doctor's standard practice. "No," they all declared. Some managed to say before prosecutors could object that they believed the government was victimizing them by putting their doctor on trial.

Each of the patient-witnesses was allowed to tell the jury when he or she began treatment. They were not allowed to describe how antineoplastons affected them. Efficacy. But the message got across. "Those witnesses were positively precious," said juror Phillips.

Complained Clark after the first jury deadlocked, "The defense got the best of all worlds. They got to bring in the patients and imply that the stuff works, but we could not bring in experts to question its effects." What he did not note is that this was the clear-cut result of the government's own strategy of keeping efficacy out of the trial, a strategy born of the fear that no jury would convict Burzynski if it felt there was even a small chance that his antineoplastons are effective.

Defense lawyers gave Clark ample opportunity to question their implication that antineoplastons work. As the trial ended, they even tried to put into evidence a report from Dr. Robert E. Burdick, a Seattle oncologist and faculty member of the highly respected University of Washington Medical School. Burdick's letter, filed with Judge Lake and protested immediately by prosecutors, offered a summary of his evaluation of both conventional treatments and of 17 brain tumor patients who were undergoing antineoplaston treatment as of April 1996. "It is very rare, currently, to ever get a complete remission or cure in a patient who has a malignant brain tumor, using our standard modalities of surgery, radiation, and chemotherapy .... As a rough estimate, neurosurgeons do well to cure one in every 1,000 brain-cancer patients they operate on. Radiation therapy slows the growth of adult tumors, gaining perhaps one month of life, and again may result in a cure in only one in 500-1,000 patients, those cures being in the pediatric age group. Similarly, chemotherapy research, despite 30 years of clinical trials, has not resulted in the development of a single drug or drug combination that elicits more than an occasional transient response in primary brain tumors."

Against this dismal background, Burdick said, he reviewed Burzynski's cases. Of the 17, he reported, there were seven complete remissions, one patient having a second complete remission after he'd discontinued antineoplaston therapy and his tumor then regrew. There were nine partial remissions of 50 percent or more, and one case of stable disease. Summarized Burdick, "I am very impressed with the number of complete and partial responses that I have seen here, compared with the number of responses that I have seen in my personal experience. The responses here also are far in excess of any prior series of patients published in the medical literature...the response rate here is an astounding 81 percent, with an equally astounding 35 percent complete remission rate. Such remission rates are far in excess of anything I or anyone else has seen since research work on brain tumors began. It is very clear the responses here are due to antineoplaston therapy and are not due to surgery, radiation, or standard chemotherapy."

Lake's response, after taking Burdick's letter under submission for one day, was that it was irrelevant. In short, he said again, it did not matter if the drug worked or how many lives it could save. All that mattered was whether Burzynski had violated the FDA's rules. With that ruling, he deprived the world of a major opportunity to have experts on both sides debate the effectiveness of antineo-plastons, subject to cross-examination. This, of course, would have required finding experts willing to testify that the drug does not work, a more difficult task.

The eventual 6-6 jury split in the first trial, then, reflected accurately the two strong schools of thought that ran through the courtroom throughout that trial. On one side were the legal purists, who felt that if Burzynski violated the letter of the law in the slightest, even if he hurt no one and stole nothing, he must be convicted simply to uphold the law. On the other were those who believe that choice and hope are more important than technicalities.

No such split occurred two months later when Judge Lake convened a new jury in mid-May 1997 for Burzynski's second criminal trial. In fact, aside from the courtroom, the judge and the cast of lawyers, the similarities were few between the two trials.

Where Burzynski faced 75 counts and a possible 300-year prison term in his first trial, this time there was only one charge: contempt of court, the one offense for which there are no federal sentencing guidelines. Punishment for contempt is strictly up to the judge.

There was only one charge against Burzynski this time because Lake had thrown out all fraud counts after the first trial for lack of evidence, and because prosecutors by their own admission were simply unprepared for a full-blown trial the second time around. LeCocq was out on maternity leave, so Clark filed a request in early May for a continuance until September 1997. Clark's memo conceded that prosecutors had not even ordered transcripts of the first trial in time to read them before the second trial. Lake refused any delay, insisting that the second trial go forward precisely on schedule.

One reason the prosecution was unprepared may have been an ongoing investigation of the Houston U.S. attorney's office by the Justice Department's Office of Professional Responsibility. One charge under investigation: that someone in the U.S. attorney's office gave Aetna Life Insurance secret 1990 grand jury testimony for the company's use in one of its civil suits against Burzynski. Later, that investigation would end inconclusively.

Even before the second trial began, Clark put out signals indicating he knew his case was weak. For weeks before the trial date, he tried to negotiate a settlement, finally offering to drop all criminal charges if Burzynski would plead guilty to one count of civil contempt of court and pay a $250,000 fine. But Burzynski would have no part of any settlement. "I don't want to admit to anything that makes it look like I did anything wrong at all," he said. "I did nothing wrong. I was always very careful to obey every court order."

Clark dropped all 40 of the interstate commerce charges against Burzynski on opening day of the second trial. He opted to proceed on the contempt count alone, with Burzynski again accused of violating the 1983 injunction that forbade him from placing antineoplastons into interstate commerce.

"The heart of the case was the contempt, anyway," Clark said. "I saw no reason for a protracted trial."

When the second trial began with *voir dire* of prospective jurors on May 19, 1997, Clark had more reason for pessimism. "The FDA is like the Gestapo," declared one potential juror. "Why isn't the FDA on trial instead of Dr. Burzynski?" asked another. Forced to spend two of his six peremptory challenges on this pair, Clark could only look on helplessly as Burzynski's legal team shaped the jury to its liking.

"I could see right from the start this would be an uphill battle," Clark would say later. "It concerns me as a government employee to see a trend toward government bashing, and this was part of it."

Once the two sides began calling witnesses, the differences between this trial and the earlier one became pronounced. Rather than taking up more than five weeks with dull prosecution testimony, Clark and his assistants used just two days this time. The defense needed only one. Some of the witnesses were the same. Clark again led off with postal inspector Barbara Ritchey; jurors had difficulty keeping straight faces as she described following shipping clerk Bob Moseray and Alan Shea while they caravaned through west Houston.

For his part, Moseray appeared as a defense witness this time. He clearly bested prosecutor George Tallichet in one exchange. You received special training for packing glass bottles [of antineoplastons] into boxes, didn't you?" Tallichet asked. "No," responded the ever dignified and unflappable Moseray. "It was quite simple. One would just put them in the boxes. It was so easy, even you could do it."

At trial's end, Clark argued once again that Burzynski was a conniving businessman and that it made no difference whether his drug worked or not. "None of us is above the law," he said. Defense lawyers countered by noting that there was nothing in the 1983 injunction to prohibit Burzynski from treating out-of-state patients. Since he never shipped the drug out of state, they argued, he never violated the order.

The jury agreed with that argument completely. "A felony finding when the doctor's license could have been taken away wasn't fair," said juror Stephenie Shapiro, a Houston attorney. "I found the government's behavior offensive. A lot of people felt it was. This was a Big Brother issue."

Where the first jury needed 35 hours to reach its final split, this panel required less than three to acquit. Even Clark appeared relieved when the verdict came in on May 27, 1997. "I knew going in we would have a difficult time and we did," he said. "Now my job is done at last. I don't see that it would accomplish anything to go after him anymore."

Burzynski, resolving to continue working within the IND protocols he won as a condition of bail, indicated he would be careful not to invite more legal woes. "This is the end of 14 years of war," he said. "It's the beginning of the end of the war on cancer."

Postscript, Spring 2000

Three years after it put Burzynski on trial, the FDA was still refusing to say why.

"I am not inclined to be interviewed on that subject," said Robert Spiller, still serving as one of the agency's chief enforcement lawyers. Spiller and other FDA officials had been asked to explain why the agency spent more than 14 years and approximately $15 million pursuing Burzynski. But Spiller remained as silent as he had during the criminal trials. At that time, he insisted that federal law precluded him from talking about the case, because it was still under litigation. But by the early portion of 2000, there were no longer any legal disputes between Burzynski and the FDA. There was no longer any legal reason for FDA silence. Nevertheless, Spiller refused absolutely to say anything about the many years and the taxpayer dollars he wasted trying to jail Burzynski.

Others in the FDA were just as closed-mouthed. Larry Bachorik, a line public information officer who handled all inquiries to the agency at the time of Burzynski's trials, had become chief of the FDA's information office three years later, reporting directly to the commissioner. "The entire rationale is in the indictment," he said. In other words, the same flimsy charges that judge and jury threw out were all the FDA had to offer in the way of explanation.

The agency also refused several requests for information about what Burzynski would have to do in order to get his medication approved. "We have nothing more to say than what's in the indictment and the press release we issued at the time," Bachorik said.

Meanwhile, for years, whenever the FDA was asked about Burzynski, rather than referring prospective patients to his agency-authorized clinical trials, the patients were given copies of criticisms of Burzynski printed in 1998 by The Cancer Letter, a newsletter on cancer-related subjects (see postscript to Chapter 7, Answering the Critics, for detail on those critiques). But the FDA never sends out Burzynski's answers, also printed in The Cancer Letter. "I wasn't aware he had answered," said Bachorik. The rebuttals, of course, were contained in the same issue of the newsletter than carried many of the critiques. So the FDA seems as determined as ever to sabotage antineoplastons and Burzynski's clinical trials.

For Judge Lake, the Burzynski trials were long over by

the spring of 2000. For Michael Clark, who joined a private law firm in Houston shortly after the trial ended, they were also in the past. But, plainly, not for the Food and Drug Administration.

The Pamela Winningham Story

Thank God for Sally Jessy

Eat, drink, and be merry–get your life in order. You have six weeks to six months to live.

–Statement of a University of California-San Francisco Medical Center neuro-oncology resident to Pamela Winningham, April 1988

Every day, as she and her husband, Scott, commute together to their jobs in Princeton, New Jersey, Pamela Winningham thanks her lucky stars that her sister's mother-in-law liked to watch the syndicated Sally Jessy Raphael television talk show. The distant relative happened to be tuned in one day in the spring of 1988, when Dr. Stanislaw Burzynski and some of his patients appeared on the program. Later that day, Pam's sister telephoned her with the exciting news that there might be someone who could do something about the growing brain tumor that had precipitated Mrs. Winningham's apparent death sentence.

By the time she heard about Burzynski and his already controversial antineoplaston cancer medication, Pam Winningham had endured unsuccessful surgery for an astrocytoma tumor so tangled in her brain stem that it was impossible to remove it without killing her or doing other major harm. She underwent two months of twice-daily radiation treatments targeted directly at the tumor. But she declined to try massive chemotherapy because her doctors said the chances that it might do much good were slim, and she knew it would subject her to months of miserable side effects.

Pam, then a 35-year-old school psychologist, and her Ph.D. economist husband got their first hint of a serious problem in 1987, when she began to complain of double vision a few weeks after the couple moved to San Francisco from Los Angeles, where Pam had worked in inner-city public schools. "I found it hard to focus when I would try to read," she recalls. "Instead of seeing just one word, I'd see a shadow on top of it. It was annoying, because Scott and I read a lot. But I didn't think it was a serious health problem, certainly not anything that involved my survival. I just thought I needed new glasses."

She would soon learn that her situation was far more serious. "I went to an ophthalmologist, who said this was not an eye problem," Pam remembers. He sent her to a neurologist, who immediately ordered an MRI scan of her head. The scan was performed on June 30, 1987, the couple's wedding anniversary. They were teenage sweethearts at Granada Hills High School in the suburban San Fernando Valley section of Los Angeles.

"Things started to happen very quickly once that scan was ordered," Pam remarks. The couple, with their seven-year-old daughter, Lynn, lived in a rented apartment less than a block up a hill from the California Medical Center, where the test was done. "I vividly remember walking down the block from our place to get the MRI report," Pam says. "I wasn't really worried. Later, I thought of that as my last carefree walk. They just threw this on me."

"You have a brain tumor," the neurologist said, declaring that her double vision was not caused by her eyes. She was immediately referred to Dr. Charles Wilson, a brain surgeon at the University of California-San Francisco.

Looking back, both Pam and Scott believe they might have spotted clues about this tumor 13 years earlier, when both were graduate students at the University of Wisconsin at Madison. "I had something like the flu and later had a palsy in my face; I couldn't smile with the right side of my face and had trouble blinking," Pam says. "I was hospitalized briefly at the time, and I had a CT scan, but nothing showed up. The only thing I know for sure is that since then I've always had kind of a crooked smile. So we sometimes think this started way back then and just slowly grew until it caused my double vision."

Pam's normally sharp memory becomes briefly short-circuited when she tries to recall her first visit to Wilson's office, so husband Scott's recollections kick in as the couple tries to comprehend all that happened that day and immediately after. "Wilson told her, 'You have a tumor in your brain stem. We don't know what grade it is, how fast it's growing or if we can remove it.' He wanted to do immediate exploratory surgery," Scott explains. "He said he wasn't sure what he'd find, but once he was inside her head, he could see what was there and decide what to do about it. He held out the hope that he could remove the tumor, but he said that if he couldn't, the surgery would still be useful, if only because he could at least take a biopsy, and we could determine exactly what was going on."

The couple considered their options for two tortured days before deciding to accept that recommendation. Their daughter had just finished first grade and "we were in a state of shock," Scott recalls. "All I could tell Lynn was, 'Mom's sick, she needs an operation.' I was real concerned, but I guess I was naive. I don't recall thinking she would die. For sure, we didn't know much about what was happening to us."

"I didn't think I'd die, either," Pam says. "But I sure was glad when my parents flew up from L.A. to help take care of Lynn."

Her surgery on July 14, 1987, exactly two weeks after the MRI scan, revealed the alarming reason for her double vision. "They couldn't take the tumor out, but they did take a biopsy," Scott notes. The verdict: Pam had a slow-growing Stage 2 astrocytoma. Such tumors account for about one-sixth of all brain cancers, according to American Cancer Society (ACS) statistics. The ACS Textbook on Clinical Oncology indicates that just 32 percent of all low-grade astrocytoma victims who don't seek treatment can expect to survive more than five years. Sixty percent live that long if they undergo partial removal of the tumor and then radiation therapy. If surgeons can remove the entire tumor, the five-year survival rate is nearly 100 percent. But virtually none of Pam Winningham's tumor could be removed and it wouldn't retain its slow-growing description for very long.

"The doctors told me after surgery that radiation was the best thing they could offer, that my tumor was so entwined in my brain stem that they couldn't do much with it," she says. "They told me, 'You need to do radiation treatments, or you will die.'" Adds Scott, "Wilson told us there were no guarantees about the radiation, but that he was optimistic it would help."

So Pam resolved to try that therapy, waiting only long enough to recover from her surgery before starting treatment in September 1987.

Unlike some brain tumor patients, Pam was not subjected to full-brain or spinal-column radiation. She received hyperfractionated treatments twice daily, with beams targeted directly at her tumor. "They shaved the back of my head and tattooed dots near my ears as targets to shoot at," she recalls. "It did not debilitate me completely [the way] it does some people. I was able to drive myself to the hospital and back for the treatments twice a day for eight weeks."

But the treatment appeared to accomplish nothing; it actually may have stimulated new tumor growth. Pam's first MRI scan after the radiation indicated that her astrocytoma was still growing, maybe faster than before. "They counseled Scott and me to wait," she says. "We were told there is sometimes a delayed effect from radiation, which my reading about that type of treatment confirmed."

So the Winninghams waited and hoped. But nothing much happened, except more tumor growth. The following spring, in April 1988, she had a follow-up MRI scan and met with radiation oncologist William Wara, who announced that the couple had waited long enough—the radiation obviously was not working.

By this time, Pam's tumor was about the diameter of a quarter, roughly double its size when first diagnosed. It was now that the UCSF resident—whose name Pam never knew—told her it would be a good idea to get her affairs in order and enjoy the rest of her life. "I said, 'Excuse me...what did you say?' and he told me, 'You have six weeks to six months to live.'"

Meanwhile, Wara and other doctors were urging the Winninghams to try chemotherapy, even though such medications have never been shown to be very effective against brain tumors. "By now, Scott and I had studied a lot about cancer treatments, and we knew what could happen in chemotherapy," Pam points out. "I wasn't willing to do it."

Scott was a bit more hesitant about refusing. "My impression was that nothing had worked yet and that this would probably not work, either," he says. "But I felt it might at least extend things, and I might have my wife a little longer."

Pam, who normally weighs 122 pounds and exercises regularly to stay in top shape, says, "I wasn't willing to do this. From what was happening to me, I already knew how complicated side effects from drugs could be. I'd been given the corticosteroid Decadron as an anti-inflammatory to reduce the swelling in my brain after surgery and during the radiation; it made me constantly hungry. I gained 35 pounds right away, and I found that I wasn't able to get off the drug. It's highly addictive stuff. Every time I tried to go off it or cut my dosage, I got excruciatingly painful headaches. It left me feeling and looking cushionoid. I was bloated and felt really sluggish all the time. About all I could do in any one day was shower, blow-dry my hair and make dinner. The rest of the day, it left me just plain lethargic, and I'd sleep and listen to the radio. So I wasn't going to try these other chemicals, which were much more toxic, especially when I knew there was only a small chance they would help me."

Despondent and resigned to her fate, Pam and her husband decided he would quit his job so they could leave San Francisco and return to Los Angeles to be near their families during her final months. But just before they left the Bay area, she learned about Burzynski.

"At first, all I knew from what I heard about the Sally Jessy show was that this doctor was somewhere in Texas and that he was supposedly curing cancer patients," Pam says. Scott tried to learn more. By coincidence, his boss in the financial-consulting firm where he then worked was helping the American Cancer Society manage some of its funds, and eagerly consulted some of the society's executives about Burzynski and his reputation. "At least one of them trashed him as a fellow who was not highly thought of," Scott remembers. "This guy said Burzynski was probably a quack."

But the Winninghams were desperate, so Scott told his wife he would do whatever she wanted, spend whatever it took. Before moving back to Los Angeles, the couple flew to Houston to check out Burzynski. "I was so weak and lethargic from the Decadron that by the time we got there, I had to lean on Scott physically in order to walk. And by then I had really severe double vision. But I found that if I lowered the Decadron dosage, I was in incredible pain."

The Winninghams, skeptical after what they'd been told about Burzynski, nevertheless agreed to rent an apartment in Houston for two weeks, figuring it would take that long to determine whether Pam should make a serious commitment to use Burzynski's antineoplastons. Neither was much impressed by their first look at the doctor or his clinic.

"It was a dinky little clinic on the outskirts of town," recalls Scott, referring to the quarters Burzynski used during the mid- and late-1980s. "There were a lot of sick people in that waiting room. It was not a very optimistic scene." The couple's first meeting with Burzynski was brief. "It took only about 10 minutes," Scott says. "He told us what he would do, but he never promised to cure Pam's tumor. He just seemed matter-of-fact about the whole thing and acted as if he didn't have any doubts at all that the tumor would respond to his medication. He seemed very confident. I was not."

As Pam puts it, "We were scared, and Scott was just extremely skeptical the whole time."

"I figured all this was probably a complete waste of time and money—a lot of money—but we might as well try it, because there was nothing else left to do," Scott says.

Pam adds, "It was a bit traumatic that they wanted so much money up front. We almost walked right out when they asked for a $5,000 payment. Of course, they had told us about that when we called. But it still did not feel right."

Scott remembers, "I didn't like the looks of it. But I did ask for all the literature I could get on antineoplastons. I looked at as many of Burzynski's papers as I could find, and I was impressed that he'd used the standard tests and controls when he tried his stuff on laboratory animals. I also looked up his name in the telephone book, and we went to see where he lived. I had hoped that the whole picture would be nice, that he was not a fly-by-night sort of guy. As it turned out, he lived in a regular house in a nice neighborhood, not the kind of big and flashy place where you'd expect to find a guy who was making a fortune off some kind of scam."

Within days, the couple began to think of Pam as a Burzynski patient despite their continuing skepticism. Scott took Pam first to a vascular surgeon for insertion of a catheter in her chest. Then they visited a local imaging center so Burzynski would have a record of the exact size and shape of her tumor before he began treatment. An MRI scan there confirmed that her tumor had continued growing in the month or so since the last pictures were taken in San Francisco.

"The whole process was well organized and very professional, even down to the way they set up temporary housing for us," Pam explains. "They wanted to monitor me for the first two weeks to see how I was tolerating the medication, whether there were any allergies. Mostly, I slept during that time. But I had absolutely no side effects."

"We didn't notice anything new happening right after she started on the treatment," Scott says. "We took the drugs home to California, and pretty soon we began a routine of going back down to Houston for more antineoplastons every two months." In fact, the MRI scan she underwent after starting the treatment, in July 1988, showed a significant reduction in the swelling around her tumor, but no difference in tumor size from the scan taken at UCSF in April. But because there were no side effects and the tumor appeared at least to have stabilized, the Winninghams decided to stick with the treatment. Two months later, their patience was rewarded.

"The lesion is now measured at 1.8 x 2.1 x 2.2 centimeters," read the report from the Houston Imaging Center after Pam's September 1988 MRI. "This represents a decrease in the size of the tumor compared to the previous study. This is estimated as a 30 to 40 percent decrease in tumor volume."

"My reaction was sheer joy," beams Pam. "Suddenly I had some reason to hope that I would live. It was wonderful. Something was finally working." That was also when Scott's skepticism ended. "I began to believe there was really something here," he says. "My feeling was reinforced by the next scan a month later."

The report on that MRI, taken in October, states that "the lesion is measured at 1.6 x 1.8 x 2.0 centimeters. This is estimated to be a change of 20 to 30 percent in overall volume of tumor [since the last scan]."

Pam's astrocytoma was gradually disappearing. By the following January, there was no sign of tumor. The formal report on an MRI scan taken that month states that "since the previous study, this region [where the tumor was located in the brain stem] has undergone a marked decrease in size....This suggests that the lesion may now consist of scarring or even old hemorrhage."

More than two years later, Pam's scans and records were among the seven cases reviewed by National Cancer

Institute experts on a one-day site visit to Burzynski's clinic. That team also found no more sign of tumor on her scans and concluded "there definitely was a tumor response" to antineoplastons in her case.

For the sake of certainty, Pam has had new MRI scans taken every January since then. All have shown something, most likely scar tissue, where her tumor once lurked. She stayed on antineoplastons more than a year after the landmark January 1989 scan that revealed her tumor had all but disappeared. "Dr. Burzynski gradually reduced the dosage of the antineoplastons to wean me from them," Pam says. "I got the feeling he wanted to be very sure the tumor wouldn't come back before he stopped the medication altogether."

As her treatment progressed successfully, Pam and Scott recall, their feelings about Burzynski grew more positive. "He really turned us around. It got so we looked up to him," Scott says. "We respected him."

Adds Pam, "I'd look forward to going down there and seeing him. Look, he was getting results. I was improving. So it was really very reassuring whenever we'd see him."

She also enjoyed the moral support she got from Burzynski's office staff. "When the first positive MRI report came in, the whole office exploded in cheers for me," Pam remembers. "That felt very good."

The Winninghams add they're grateful to Burzynski for helping Pam leave Decadron behind. "I tried again to go off it in the fall of '88, as the positive MRIs began to come in," she says. "This time, I could do it. And I lost all that weight. I was no longer the Pillsbury doughgirl."

"Suddenly I had my wife back," Scott says. "When I met her, she was the original surfer girl. And now she's got that body back."

Within a month after her MRIs began showing tumor reduction and she began to lessen her dependence on Decadron, Pam started to regain her old energy. She and Scott—who had not worked since he quit his job when the family left San Francisco—had been living off their savings for months, but Pam found work that fall in the Los Angeles city schools, her first full-time job in two years. A year later, the family relocated again, this time to New Jersey, where both went to work for the same financial-consulting firm.

Only one residual ill effect remains: The palsy that first afflicted Pam's face during the 1970s and became most severe at the height of her tumor growth has not completely disappeared. She still can't smile with the right side of her face, and she had gold implants placed into her eyelids to help her blink. Doctors have told her that this remaining problem was likely caused by the combination of surgery and radiation therapy she underwent, which probably created permanent nerve damage.

But neither she nor Scott cares much about that. Not when they think about her new life without a death sentence. "It's such a wonderful feeling to be alive these many years after they told me I'd be dead," Pam said in the fall of 1996.

Added Scott, "I feel like I got my wife back from the grave." Both he and Pam are convinced beyond any doubt that the antineoplastons saved Pam's life. "I cannot understand any other reason for Pam's being here and being healthy," says her husband. "So we will do anything we can to help Burzynski anytime he has a problem. I feel the government has been after him for years for violating technicalities—which I don't even think he did. They don't seem to be interested in whether his stuff works or not. And that means the government isn't really interested in protecting patients; it wants to protect its own power."

Postscript

PRINCETON, N. J., midyear 2000—From the deck of a cruise ship steaming up Alaska's Inside Passage in the spring of 2000, the world looked sweet to Pamela Winningham, whose doctors once told her in April 1988 to go home and prepare to die from her "incurable brain tumor." "There's surely a sense of appreciation I didn't ever have before," she says. "Imagine...I was supposed to be dead 12 years ago."

Instead, Pam and her husband Scott have seen their daughter Lynn graduate from high school in Princeton and enroll at the elite Yale University, taken cruises on luxury ships, made jaunts through Ireland and testified at the criminal trial of Dr. Stanislaw Burzynski. Pam has been totally clear of cancer since going off antineoplastons in 1989, as verified through MRIs taken every year, most recently in January 2000.

"The bottom line is I'm still here and healthy, with no deterioration in my health at all," she says. "I'm still working at an economic consulting firm in Princeton, still doing whatever artistic things I can. I've taken pottery classes at a community college for seven years and now I'm starting to study stone sculpture. I walk two miles at lunchtime with a friend four times a week. I have Dr. Burzynski to thank for all that."

And if anything went wrong, if a new brain tumor should suddenly appear? "If that happened, I'd go back on antineoplastons right away. There would be no hesitation at all."

Chapter 2

Youth and Discovery

Gray was the dominant color in the Polish city of Lublin during the years after World War II, just as it was in the rest of Poland and all around the Communist bloc. Ruins dotted the city, marking the spots where one of every five buildings had been leveled by the Nazis who occupied it during the war. They had herded Jews from the city and small towns in the surrounding countryside into the walled Old Town in the city center, instantly creating an overcrowded ghetto. Later, when the ghetto's occupants were murdered or taken to death camps, the Germans turned about 20 percent of the city into rubble, devastating Lublin's medieval gingerbread heart.

Born in 1943 in the midst of this maelstrom, the young Stanislaw Burzynski was nevertheless isolated for a time from some of the hardship that surrounded him. His mother's family lived in an old part of Lublin, on Krolewska Street, or King Street, which acquired its name because Poland's medieval monarchs often traversed its length on their way to the landmark castle in the middle of the old city. The ornate family house, built around three inner courtyards, served as the local Roman Catholic bishop's palace in the early 1800s. Designed in a Baroque Renaissance style, its three-story facade bore elaborate lattice sculptures around all the windows and delicate cornices under its eaves. Before the war, Burzynski's grandmother used its plentiful space to operate a private high school for girls. In the early 1940s, she gave her daughter and son-in-law and their family an apartment there.

But Burzynski's parents preferred to spend most of their time during his early years in a country house his mother's family kept on the edge of the great Stary Las Forest outside Lublin. The forest, with its thick woods of beech, oak and pine, would later play a role in his discovery of antineoplastons. In Burzynski's toddler years, though, it provided a climate of refuge for his parents—refuge both from the political storms raging around them and from most of their relatives.

Burzynski's father was never truly accepted by his mother's relatives. "My father's father was a blacksmith. He was orphaned when he was a little boy during one of the many insurrections against the Russians, who after 1812 occupied the country around his hometown of Boratya, in the province of Podolya, which is now in the Ukraine," Burzynski remembers. "My father met my mother at the university, where he was studying classical Greek and Latin. He wanted to teach in the university, but because he came from a poor background, he had difficulty finding the right place to teach. Poland was a very class-conscious place. Eventually he found a position in the Jewish high school in Lublin, but the rich Poles, including my mother's family, always treated him like a poor relation. So I grew up in a climate of nonacceptance by many relatives on my mother's side. The house outside town was a place to escape all that. It had a large garden, with meadows nearby and a river we children could play in."

Burzynski's early childhood was marred by his father's arrest by the Nazis, who objected to his efforts to keep teaching Jewish students after the locked, walled ghetto was created. For this transgression, he was imprisoned in the former royal castle for two years during the occupation.

Even that, however, was not as bad for the Burzynskis

as the events that abruptly ended young Stanislaw's early childhood in the late 1940s. The Iron Curtain descended over Poland. Suddenly the old family mansion was no longer family property. It belonged to the state, which divided it into many apartments, turning them over to peasants and workers left homeless by the war. The Burzynski household was allowed to remain in a small apartment, but soon the family was sharing its kitchen and bathtub with newcomers.

"We quickly learned that one woman who lived in the house with us was a government spy," Burzynski says. "This was dangerous because my brother Zygmunt was in the anti-Communist underground. Meanwhile, the Communists continued using the royal palace as a prison, just as the Nazis had. My father was taken there again for a time for providing underground education. He was ultimately released, but he could never again get a proper teaching job."

Although he came from a line of rural blacksmiths and thus had proletarian roots, no position Burzynski's father held lasted long once the local Communist bosses learned that he had married into a wealthy family with property inside and outside Lublin. Eventually, he would be relegated to giving private lessons in Greek and Latin, as well as teaching a variety of subjects in public high schools. Meanwhile, many of Zygmunt's friends were killed in prison. "We lived in constant fear because we knew it could happen to anyone at any time," Burzynski recalls.

"So," he declares, "the idea of fighting a government was nothing new to me when I began having difficulties with the Food and Drug Administration."

The young Burzynski was forced to fight almost every day in the years immediately following the Communist takeover of his family's home. Though he attended a top-flight elementary school—it was a demonstration school for the local teacher's college—his classmates were a self-conscious mix of rich and poor. And he found no respite at home. "There was something like a class war all the time at school. At home, the school for wealthy girls my grandmother had run was suddenly turned into a school for retarded children. The courtyards of the house were filled with quarrels and drunks. I had to fight someone every day in my backyard and at school. There was a fight at every break, and this persisted through the fourth grade."

Burzynski insists that the fights were no fun for him, but the feeling that he should never duck one stayed with him as he grew into adulthood. Before his trial began in January 1997, he admitted he had had many chances to move his clinic and his antineoplaston manufacturing operation to Mexico and avoid the need to do battle with anyone. "But I want to beat the bastards...if I win, I win big," he explained.

His spirit was also shaped by watching as older brother Zygmunt became a fighter in the resistance. "The last battle Zygmunt fought was in the forest near Lublin in 1948," Burzynski says. "He was shot in the neck and very soon afterward he died of meningitis. The idea of fighting people in authority became natural to me. I learned that you must never let them defeat you in your own core." But little Stanislaw, who had by now acquired the nickname Stash, was more academic than his brother had been. His biggest battles would be fought in laboratories, courtrooms and the pages of academic journals, not in open fields and forests.

The young Burzynski's need to fight physically came to an end as he sped through the Lyceum Zamoyski, Lublin's finest secondary school, and went directly to medical school—the usual European route. There he quickly became involved in medical research, working as an assistant to chemistry professor Irana Krzeczkowski and biochemist Janina Blaut. Soon he developed a special fascination for peptides, chemicals built from amino acids in human and animal blood and urine.

Both his professors were conducting experiments with chromatography, a technique for separating molecules and analyzing the peculiar makeup of each. "It was a special art to do this right," Burzynski says. "When you would analyze amino acids, you'd get a bunch of stripes, looking a little like a supermarket bar code. Each stripe represents one amino acid. If you mix 20 amino acids and you do the process right, you will get 20 stripes."

Within months, Burzynski was analyzing the amino acids in organic fluids, starting with those that made up the peptides in wild mushrooms he found while wandering through his beloved Stary Las Forest. "This was great for me," he says, smiling, many years later. "I would go to the forest and find various kinds of mushrooms. Then I would analyze how they produced different chemicals. It was wonderful training. My professor hoped to use what we learned to develop new kinds of mushrooms for agriculture. I found some mushrooms with highly toxic peptides, but some of these also had strong antibacterial action. I wanted to detoxify these to see if they could become antibiotics. But this would have required many more mushrooms than I could find in the forest, and a lot of money. There was no money. So I began to be interested in other peptides."

From mushrooms, the young researcher moved to blood and urine samples, again trying to see how different individuals manufacture different chemicals. "If you analyze blood, for example, you can compare its stripes with the ones from other laboratory samples you have already identified. And based on the intensity of the stripe, you can tell how much of each component is present," he says. Burzynski began by using paper chromatography, in which the stripes appear on special paper. Later, he performed variations on the technique, using glass slides or test tubes instead of paper.

It wasn't long before he noticed some stripes that neither he nor anyone else could identify. They appeared when blood was analyzed; they had first been reported as early as the 1940s by English researchers. Many of the same stripes also appeared when urine was analyzed. "These were not amino acids, but nobody had bothered to identify them. Nobody cared what they were," Burzynski remarks.

His curiosity was quickly aroused and soon grew intense as he prepared to write his doctoral dissertation in 1967. At first, he intended the thesis to compare the amino acids of healthy persons with those in people with kidney disease. The dissertation, completed in 1968 and bound in green cloth, still enjoys a prominent place on a shelf beside Burzynski's heavy mahogany desk, beneath the large photo of Mount Everest he faces whenever he sits in his office. And Burzynski dearly enjoys its topic as much today as he did in 1968.

"I needed an interesting subject for my doctoral thesis," he recalls. "And there were those unidentified stripes staring at me. So I took the subject of amino acids and kidney disease to see whether the blood and urine of kidney patients would produce the same stripes we got from other people." But he was afraid to allow the stripes to remain completely unidentified. "I thought I would be asked about them during my oral exam, when I had to defend my thesis before distinguished professors. If your thesis is defeated or destroyed, you don't get your doctorate—and I wanted very badly to get my doctorate."

Soon Burzynski established that the mystery stripes were evidence of peptides of some kind. These chemicals, some also known as phenylacetates, are built from complex combinations of amino acids. The more Burzynski analyzed the unidentified stripes, the more complex and puzzling they seemed to become. "I soon found that these stripes were not homogeneous," Burzynski says. "From just three spots that I examined closely while doing my thesis, I found more than 39 individual peptides. I knew these were peptides because when I broke them down further, the components were amino acids. And I knew that there were still more peptides to be identified if I could only do more work."

For Burzynski, this was a tedious and difficult task, a chore that for many months yielded no clues about its ultimate potential importance. Later, he would learn that one of the 39 mysterious chemicals he was studying had been investigated by a Rockefeller University team as part of a Nobel Prize-winning research project that developed new forms of chromatography. This substance was primarily made of the chemicals phenylacetate and glutamine, also known as phenylacetylglutamine (PG). "All of my tests for these substances were chromatographic," Burzynski remembers. "In Poland we had good equipment for some of this testing. But we had trouble getting the chemical reagents we needed to do the work. When we wanted dansyl chloride, for example, it had to come from Merck Pharmaceuticals. That meant it had to come from the West, and there was always trouble getting anything in from the West."

As he worked with available laboratory supplies, Burzynski began seeing patterns. He believed that he would have to come to America to have any real chance at identifying the substances he was trying to analyze. "I thought that I could come to America, identify these things and then go back to Poland. I did not expect to stay in America," Burzynski explains. That was because, despite the oppressive society around him, the expropriation of his family's home and the difficulty in getting laboratory supplies, Burzynski was having fun.

"Research in Poland was a joyous experience," he says. "There was never any interference with my work. The politicians weren't interested in science as long as it didn't threaten them. I had the complete cooperation of my teachers, too."

Within months of his decision to seriously study the unknown stripes, Burzynski observed that some seemed to appear less frequently when he tested samples of blood and urine from cancer patients. "To confirm this, I collected samples from many cancer patients and from many others who came to the hospital that was associated with the medical school," he says. Another finding that fascinated him, but one he never researched further, was that there were abnormally high quantities of the unknown peptides in the blood and urine of patients with primary kidney diseases— persons whose kidneys were damaged, but the damage was independent of any other disorder. "We saw that one peptide accumulates to a great extent in primary kidney failure patients," Burzynski adds.

That finding would become interesting more than 25 years later, when researchers at Johns Hopkins University and other centers found both the gene and the mechanism that spur polycystic kidney disease (PKD). This illness, which afflicts approximately 600,000 Americans, causes fluid-filled cysts to form in otherwise healthy kidneys. The cysts expand at a pace that varies from person to person, replacing healthy tissue as they grow and eventually making kidneys look something like large blocks of bloody Swiss cheese.

When he first observed that cancer victims have a dearth of the peptides he was examining, Burzynski and other researchers already knew that cancer tumors grow because their cells multiply but do not die off, as most normal cells do after they divide. Burzynski theorized that the substances he studied might be one factor that triggers the process of normal cell death, known as apoptosis.

Decades later, in 1994, other researchers would discover that the cysts in PKD victims expand via the process of apoptosis. Normal cells, they found, die without replicating themselves, and fluid fills the void they once occupied, eventually developing into cysts that are easy to detect by touch or via ultrasound.

In short, if Burzynski is correct, the same substances whose absence allows cancer tumors to grow out of control can promote the death of kidney cells when they are present in excessive amounts. That conclusion, Burzynski says, is logical in light of his early finding that PG "accumulated in a most spectacular way in patients with kidney failure." At the time, Burzynski was also aware that Zygmunt Hanicki, dean of the medical school in Krakow, Poland, had found that patients with primary kidney diseases like PKD rarely suffer from cancer. This is a finding that no one has tried to replicate, but Burzynski says it suggested to him that "there was a correlation between kidney failure, cancer and these stripes I was seeing. It raised my curiosity about these peptides and cancer, and I wanted to explore this further."

Just as Burzynski was arriving at these conclusions, politics intervened. One of the two youngest people in Poland with both M.D. and Ph.D. degrees, he was aggressively recruited by the Communist party, with the promise of permanent security in a prestigious university position if he joined. But he remembered his brother Zygmunt's death at the hands of those same Communists. He remembered how his mother's ancestral home had been taken over by the government and partitioned into a rabbit warren of small apartments filled with people he regarded as interlopers.

The doctor would not be swayed. "I also knew that the government at the time was trying to suppress Polish science, at least when research in any way threatened Communist principles. They wanted a completely docile population where no one had any independent thought. Ultimately, they wiped out the middle and upper classes in Poland.

"But the irony was that at the same time, they wanted to keep all those people inside the country, and they made it very difficult to get a passport."

Burzynski's refusal to join the party soon branded him as the very sort of independent thinker who was anathema to Polish authorities. As they did with many dissenters and free thinkers, the government sought to quash his independence by drafting him into the army. Burzynski received orders to report for duty on Sept. 4, 1970. Enter Marian Mazur, a member of the Polish Academy of Sciences who was known as the "father of Polish cybernetics." Mazur took an interest in the research being done by the young Burzynski, research he knew would end abruptly if Burzynski were drafted and sent to North Vietnam to aid the Vietcong, the fate of many Polish draftee doctors.

Burzynski still is not certain, but he believes it was a telephone call from the influential Mazur to the Polish foreign ministry that produced a passport for him. He left Poland less than a week after the passport arrived.

It wasn't a moment too soon. Only hours after his airplane left Warsaw for New York, military police came to the Burzynski apartment in the family's former mansion, seeking the promising young doctor. Their purpose: to abduct him and induct him. Burzynski would not return to Poland for decades.

He arrived at New York's John F. Kennedy Airport on Sept. 4, 1970, the very day his draft notice had instructed him to report to the Polish army. He carried just $20 and chromatographic documentation of the 39 peptides he had singled out. He spent $13 on taxi fare to the apartment of an uncle who lived in the Bronx. "Then, just a few days later, I got a message from the medical school in Lublin. I was fired from my position as a researcher." The same notice told him he could no longer have any position at the medical school in Lublin or any other Polish medical school. "Now I couldn't go back under any circumstances. So I started to look for a job in the States."

His first job interview, at the Baylor College of Medicine in Houston, produced immediate results. "At the time, a scientist named Georges Ungar was working on brain peptides in the university's department of anesthesiology," Burzynski says. "Anesthesiology had a lot of money in those days, especially at Baylor. That was the time of pioneering heart-transplant surgery, and Michael DeBakey and Denton Cooley, two of the pioneers, were both at Baylor. They had large amounts of grant money, some of it going toward research in anesthesiology. Ungar and his department chairman thought peptides had an impact on transmission of memories, and I thought this was a fascinating project."

Equally important, Ungar agreed to allow Burzynski time and laboratory space to continue his own peptide research.

The Theresa Kennet Story

How Could This Be a Spontaneous Remission?

We have re-examined the lymph node biopsy and again confirm the diagnosis of malignant lymphoma, follicular...the present bone marrow biopsy shows involvement by malignant lymphoma.

–From the text of a Stanford University Hospital pathology report on Theresa Kennett, dated Aug. 8, 1984

Twelve years after that straightforward and bleak report confirmed her worst fears about the huge abdominal lump she felt every time she touched her midsection, Theresa Kennett had been completely clear of cancer for more than seven years. But she never received a single dose of radiation or one drop of conventional chemotherapy. Few cancer patients have ever been more determined to survive than Theresa, who was 35 when her diagnosis was confirmed at Stanford in August 1984. No establishment doctor could give her any reliable assurance that the traditional treatments would cure her. So she felt free to explore almost every alternative therapy available.

The timing of Theresa Kennett's disease could not have been worse. That summer of 1984 should have been the happiest of her life, and for a while it was. She had an interesting, secure and enjoyable job, a devoted husband and a brand-new baby named Zia. Theresa, a San Franciscan who delights in the diversity and open-minded quality of her scenic city, had worked for seven years for a privately funded conflict-resolution agency called the Community Boards Program. As area coordinator for the Bernal Heights neighborhood, the San Francisco State University graduate trained volunteers to peacefully settle disputes over property, parking, noise and myriad issues that arise between neighbors. "I loved the job because I loved bringing all the different kinds of people together," she says. "There was a real satisfaction in helping make the city a better place."

She and her newspaper-photographer husband, David Butterfield, had been uncertain for 10 years about whether they wanted a child. But when she finally became pregnant, it was as if a great burden had been lifted from Theresa's shoulders. "It was a tremendous relief, and I had a great pregnancy," she remembers. "I loved being pregnant. And when my baby was born, there was an immediate bond I had never felt before."

Zia was born at home with help from a midwife, not an unusual birthing method in open-minded San Francisco. But Theresa's moments of joy at the birth were not to last long. Days after Zia's arrival, Theresa made a routine postpartum checkup visit to her midwife, who felt her abdomen and found a large lump. The midwife's first guess was that it was a hematoma, a large clump of partially clotted blood that would dissipate within weeks. Theresa waited, somewhat worried. After two weeks, when the lump showed no signs of dissolving, she visited the same family practice doctor who had checked her over before she became pregnant. At that time, she had complained to him about only one minor ailment: alternating constipation and diarrhea, which had persisted for a few months. "Don't worry," the doctor told her on that visit. "It's probably just stress from your job."

When he saw her again and felt her new and obvious symptom, the doctor wasted no time referring her to a surgeon. "I had no idea at the time that it could be cancer,"

Theresa says. "But I admit I was just a little bit nervous," She visited the surgeon less than one week later, in July 1984. He immediately ordered a CT scan to learn the precise nature of her lump.

"I remember being in the basement of St. Mary's Hospital and being really nervous before the scan," she says. "My breasts were full of milk, and I wanted to get home to feed Zia." But she was going nowhere. Soon after the scan, the surgeon emerged from a back room with bad news. "I'm afraid you have cancer," he told her flatly.

"The first thing I thought was, 'My God, I've got to be here for Zia now. I can't die now.'" Moments later, her family doctor reentered the room, wrapping his arms around her to console her. But neither he nor the surgeon gave Theresa any idea of what lay ahead. They said only that they wanted to perform a biopsy on the lump. So the next day, Theresa became a St. Mary's inpatient. Her mother, stepfather, natural father and grandmother all flew up from Southern California to be at her side, along with a sister who lived nearby. "I remember my step-dad holding my hand. I knew they all thought I was going to die, even though no one said anything. That's what I thought, too."

Theresa soon underwent surgery; doctors found that her cancer was widespread, involving her spleen, all the lymph glands in her abdomen and her bone marrow. Pathologists at nearby Stanford University Medical Center would later confirm that finding. "All they took out in that surgery was one lymph node," she reports. "They were going to take out my spleen because they thought that's where the big tumor was. But they decided there was no point when they saw how widespread the cancer was."

With the exploratory surgery done, her family practitioner gave her the word: "It's too bad you have this kind of lymphoma," he said. "If it were the fast-growing type, we could do a lot for you. But this is the slow-growing type that doesn't respond well to treatment."

That reality also had a positive side. Because her lymphoma was slow-growing, she would have time to seek out available treatments.

Now Theresa met her first oncologist, a man who entered her hospital room and promised that as soon as she recovered from surgery, she would start chemotherapy. Most heartbreaking to the new mother, he instructed her to stop breast-feeding her baby immediately because of the impending chemotherapy.

Theresa recovered quickly from her operation, and her constant efforts to walk the hospital corridors soon exasperated the good-natured nurses trying to keep tabs on her progress. While she recovered, she decided to delay chemotherapy and seek another opinion at the renowned Stanford hospital. Less than two weeks after the exploratory surgery, she presented herself to Stanford oncologist Norman Rosenberg, who gave her two options. One was to do nothing but wait and watch the disease's progress, leaving it undisturbed until it began to spread more rapidly. The other was to take the same course of chemotherapy that had been proposed at St. Mary's, a combination that included the powerfully toxic drugs Cytoxan and vincristine. Among the potential side effects of those drugs: nerve damage, palsy, severe constipation, nausea, darkened skin and nails and missed periods. If she opted for the chemotherapy, Kennett would also have to choose between taking a high dose intravenously or a low dose over a longer period.

"They warned me that my lymphoma might speed up at any time, but they also said it might be indolent for a time," she remembers. "If it speeded up, they said I'd have a year to live at the most. They really didn't recommend any of those choices but only offered them all. So I chose to do nothing and be monitored every month at Stanford."

She did so for six months, watching while her largest tumor, located behind her spleen, grew rapidly at first and then slowed. Now her stomach was distended as much as in a normal six-month pregnancy. But Theresa would not remain passive. Her will to live—and vigorously—was too strong.

While making regular observation visits to Stanford, she began to seek alternative treatment methods. The least invasive of these and the first she tried was visualization. "I met a woman who said she had healed her liver cancer with visualization alone," she recalls. "She would close her eyes for hours and visualize her tumor as spaghetti-like and then see herself pulling a gigantically long strand of the spaghetti out of her liver. So I immediately started visualization."

It did no good. Repeated scans of her tumors showed that they were still growing slowly. But Theresa wanted as little to do with Stanford and St. Mary's as she could manage. "I see now that I was gradually opting away from the conventional chemotherapy," she says. "Part of it was the atmosphere. The sense in that clinic at Stanford was so hopeless that I didn't want any part of it. Plus, they kept telling me the chemotherapy would only temporarily reduce my tumors. And I had done some research on the toxic effects of chemotherapy. Basically, I felt I needed an intact immune system and that chemotherapy would destroy any hope I had of ever having quality of life. I saw other patients come out of chemotherapy, and they were sick as dogs. They couldn't eat much, and they felt terrible all the time."

Theresa was soon forced to leave her job. "I figured I

had only a short time to live, and I wanted to spend it with my daughter."

And she continued her search for an alternative therapy. She took a three-week trip to Tijuana, Mexico, where she lived in a cancer clinic, eating only carrots, beets and juiced vegetables. She tried a macrobiotic diet, eating cooked seaweed, adzuki beans and root vegetables such as yams. She did ozone therapy, taking intravenous doses of the common atmospheric gas. "It was like shooting up air," she laughed later. She tried laetrile and high doses of vitamins A, E and C. At one point, she overdosed on vitamin A and suffered nausea, pain in her liver, ringing ears, yellowed and peeling skin, loss of all her hair, dry eyes and dry mouth. All are classic symptoms of extreme overdoses of vitamin A, which researchers say can be an effective treatment for some kinds of leukemia but is useless against all other cancers. "None of this changed my tumors a lot. They were still growing slowly, according to the scans I got at Stanford," Theresa says. "So after a while, I stopped getting the scans. I just didn't want to know. And I still didn't want to go back to a conventional doctor, even after it took me four weeks to recover from the vitamin A overdose. I was very stubborn and probably pretty stupid and rash."

Eventually, more than two years after her initial diagnosis, her abdomen still grossly swollen, she found her way to an Oregon-based nutritionist who knew about Dr. Stanislaw Burzynski and the success he'd had with antineoplastons. "So from Oregon I called Burzynski's clinic, and after I described my case, they said they would take me. I had them give me the phone numbers of some other patients and I called them right away, too. The reports I got were good, so I got on a plane immediately."

After all her fruitless efforts, Theresa's expectations

were low when she arrived in Houston. She expected a seedy storefront clinic with dirty equipment and uneducated workers, the conditions she had encountered at almost every alternative-medicine treatment stop. But she was pleasantly surprised.

"God, what a difference!" Theresa sighs, remembering her relief. "It was far and away more professional than any other alternative clinic I had gone to. In Mexico, there was always an atmosphere of fear and secrecy. Here, everything was open. The first thing Burzynski did was explain the chemistry of antineoplastons. He told me exactly what the treatment would be like. But he did not make promises of a sudden, miraculous cure, the way Jimmy Keller did before he gave me vegetable juices and shots of DMSO in Tijuana. Burzynski didn't even tell me how long it would take if the medicine worked."

Theresa started her antineoplaston treatment with oral medication, taking 21 large capsules daily. "That didn't seem like very much to do, not after some of the things I had tried. Burzynski told me I would probably feel fine while taking them because these are compounds that occur naturally in the body. He said little about side effects, and he explained that antineoplastons seem to block replication of cancer cells. This made a lot of sense to me."

In December 1986, with her tumors having steadily grown since her original diagnosis almost two and a half years earlier, she carried a large bag filled with bottles of antineoplaston capsules home to San Francisco. "I took both types Burzynski uses, the A10 and the AS2-1," she says. "I had been exhausted for months, constantly tired and without energy, and I remember the first day I took the medicine: I came back from running an errand and I was astounded to find that I wasn't tired at all. I'll never forget that because it was so radically different from how I had been feeling. It seemed like a miracle. So I can say for certain that the antineoplastons had a big impact on me right away."

One other thing Theresa points out: There was barely a mention of price. Whereas Burzynski usually charges patients about $340 a day for the therapy, he charged her almost nothing. "The nutritionist in Oregon who sent me to him told me he was expensive," Kennett remembers. "But I told her Dave and I were struggling, and she suggested I tell Burzynski I had never had chemotherapy or radiation."

This was important to him because critics of Burzynski's system of treatment often claim that patients who respond to his therapy with tumor shrinkage are merely exhibiting a delayed response to earlier chemotherapy or radiation. Such a claim could never be made about Theresa. She related to Burzynski her full history, including her financial woes. He responded by treating her; his office sent monthly statements but never insisted on payment. "I paid what I could, and they never bothered me," Theresa says.

She stayed on antineoplaston capsules through the summer of 1986, then underwent a new CT scan at Burzynski's suggestion. "There was no change in the tumors, even though the quality of my life had been much better," she says. For Burzynski, this was the indicator he needed to increase her antineoplaston dosage, which could only be done intravenously. It would be inconvenient for her, but she was willing. "I was going to stay the course with this treatment. It was the only thing I had tried that worked. He was the first doctor and this was the first treatment I could put my faith in. Even if it didn't cure me, I was going to stay on it because it gave me energy and a decent quality of life for the first time since my daughter was born. But I still wanted to get rid of the tumors."

So she began intravenous infusion of antineoplastons. This was not an easy step for Theresa, who had now spent two years resisting the notion of radiation and chemotherapy. "I was pretty nervous about the idea of a catheter sticking in my chest for a long time," she explains. "And I wondered how I would handle giving myself this intravenous drip. The mechanics of loading the bags with fluid and sleeping with an IV going all night were really intimidating, too."

But Theresa did it. She hung the IV bags from a curtain rod in her bedroom and loaded up an eight-hour supply of antineoplaston solution before going to bed each night, transferring the fluid from glass bottles to plastic bags. "My dose was 1,000 cc's every day," she says. "I still didn't have to use an IV all day long, the way some patients do."

She did this for six weeks and then underwent another CT scan. For the first time in more than three years, her tumors were reduced. They were 10 percent smaller, and Theresa was elated. "For the first time since Zia was born, I figured I might live. So I stayed on it, no matter how inconvenient or how much work it might be. I could hardly believe it was true that something that was not making me feel horrible was actually working. It was like a little man from a flying saucer had landed—I was that amazed. On some level I had come to believe that absolutely nothing would ever work." She reported only one negative side effect. "I started to smell like a bag lady," she laughs. "But after a while, I got to love the smell. It was the odor of getting well."

Theresa continued infusing herself with 1,000 cubic centimeters daily, taking monthly trips to Burzynski's clinic in Houston and getting CT scans every two months. After she'd been on the intravenous medication three months, her tumors were 30 percent smaller. Even when a scan after five months showed no further progress, she stayed with it, and the tumor shrinkage soon resumed.

By now it was mid-1988, and Theresa's husband had met physician Paul Volberding, the pioneering AIDS specialist who founded the world's first AIDS clinic at San Francisco General Hospital. Because so many AIDS patients also suffer from lymphomas, Volberding had become an expert on that type of cancer, and he readily agreed to take an oversight role in Theresa's care so she wouldn't need to consult Burzynski constantly at long distance. She brought Volberding copies of her CT scan results, both new and old, and he confirmed that her tumors were steadily shrinking. "I asked him what he thought and he said, 'I don't know why it's happening, but I think it's great;'" she says.

Volberding knew then that Theresa was regularly infusing antineoplastons into her bloodstream, and he knew shrinkage of her tumors had not begun until she started that therapy. Years later, he remembered her case in detail. "She did have a Stage 4 non-Hodgkin's lymphoma and has done extremely well," he admits. "But spontaneous remissions do occur. They are not common, but they do happen."

In fact, spontaneous remissions—in which cancers disappear on their own without treatment—are very rare. "We don't keep statistics on them," said Joanne Schellenbach, chief of media relations for the American Cancer Society, whose annual publication Cancer Facts & Figures is generally accepted as the definitive statistical report on cancer in America. "There just aren't enough to keep track of them. The rate is far less than 1 percent."

As Volberding kept marveling at her so-called spontaneous tumor reductions, Theresa continued to visit both him and Burzynski for almost another year. Long before she stopped the antineoplaston therapy, her tumors had shrunk to the point where they could no longer be felt. "Just before Zia's fifth birthday in 1989, I took an MRI scan and Dr. Volberding said he saw no disease. I couldn't feel anything anymore, either. I stayed on the IV for two more weeks just to be sure, and then went back on the capsules for four more weeks. I haven't taken it since, and I've been in remission all that time."

Her cancer was gone, but by then, so was her husband. "Of course, our sex life had been destroyed while I had cancer," Theresa says. "I became asexual. Then, later, I was so angry, I wasn't interested in sex. Dave was understanding for a long time. But we were different kinds of people and this kind of stress just made it more obvious than it had ever been. Finally, I asked him to leave, and he moved out."

Meanwhile, like other established cancer doctors who have watched their patients' tumors disappear while on antineoplastons, Volberding refused to credit Burzynski's medication for the disappearance of Theresa's tumors. "It can be hard to prove whether a change in a patient is due to a therapy or to the variable nature of the disease," he said. But Volberding does not dispute that Theresa's tumors began to shrink only after she started taking intravenous antineoplastons.

"A lot of Burzynski's therapy doesn't fit into the best current thinking," Volberding noted. "For instance, the idea of adjusting the dose to the size of the tumor isn't the way we handle most chemotherapy. We do it to some degree that way with radiation."

Would he send other patients to Burzynski? Volberding

was noncommittal. Theresa is not. When Burzynski was indicted almost seven years after she had last seen him, she sprang into action as a key member of Burzynski's patient-support group, using the energy she believes antineoplastons revived in her. "I hadn't wanted to think about my cancer anymore," Theresa says. "I'd gotten away from that whole world. But when I heard what they were trying to do to Burzynski, I went to Washington with the other patients and lobbied congressmen and senators and spoke at a press conference.

"I did all those other treatments and nothing happened. Then I started on the antineoplastons and my tumors shrank. What else could have caused it? I can't be a spontaneous remission because the timing is too precise. I was scared the moment they indicted Dr. B. What if he were put out of business and then my cancer somehow recurred? What would I do?"

Postscript

SAN FRANCISCO, midyear 2000—"Paul Volberding is still scratching his head over me," chuckles Theresa Kennett. "He still can't explain my recovery—my remission—any other way than by attributing it to antineoplastons, but he's reluctant to do that."

Theresa's remission remains complete 16 years after her initial diagnosis, 14 years after she began taking antineoplastons. "I'm 50 years old and I have no health problems at all any more," she says, with sheer delight and immense life-force in her voice. "I get MRI scans every year and they've consistently been clear as a bell."

That allows her to continue her very full life. Theresa completed a master's degree in counseling from the San Francisco School of Psychology in late 1999 and immediately began working with elderly persons in their homes. And she's never stopped promoting the treatment that she's quite sure saved her life. "I spent two years in the late 1990s running a cancer alternative therapy hotline, trying to answer people's questions and telling them as much about Dr. Burzynski as I could," she says. Now she's no longer the main voice callers hear when they phone, but she's still as enthusiastic about the treatment as ever. "It's a crime that more people can't take advantage of it. Think of the lives that could be saved, like mine was."

Best for all for Theresa, there's new romance in her life, a "wonderful new man, a writer I met in 1997. You put it all together, and I'm doing as fine as anyone could."

Best place to encounter Theresa: At one of the poetry readings she now organizes around her city.

CHAPTER 3

The Baylor Years

One current concept hypothesizes that polypeptides, called antineoplastons, are produced by normal cells and act in the regulation of neoplastic cell growth .... Cancer cells lack these regulators and can be controlled by supplementing them with the proper peptides.

> —Concluding sentences of "Polypeptides That Inhibit
> Human Breast Cancer Cell Division," Journal of Cancer,
> Chemistry and Biophysics, 1979

There was strong synergy from that moment in 1970 when the young Polish refugee Dr. Stanislaw Burzynski joined the research team of Dr. Georges Ungar at the Baylor College of Medicine. Ungar needed someone sophisticated in the art of separating peptides from human blood; Burzynski needed a sophisticated laboratory in which to advance his work on the blood peptides he'd stumbled upon in Poland. These naturally occurring chemicals had not received a name or much attention from earlier medical researchers.

"Ungar was also a refugee," Burzynski recalls. Originally from Hungary, he had been educated at the Sorbonne in Paris and at England's Oxford University before coming to Baylor. There he became head of the anesthesia research laboratory, performing research to prove that memories are carried in peptides in the brain. If that was true, Ungar reasoned, it meant that transferring peptides from one brain to another could also transfer memories from one organism, or one person, to another.

"I knew all about him from his publications," Burzynski says. "That was why he was one of the first people I sent a letter to after I came to the United States. We were comfortable together immediately. When he hired me as a research associate, I was thrilled. He had the best equipment for chromatography, the process I had used in isolating peptides. Now, when I joined him, I was suddenly considered an expert in the field, even though it was tough at first for me to understand people." It was English, not science, that Burzynski now had to master.

From the start, Burzynski had an understanding with his boss: He would spend half his time on Ungar's projects and the other half on further identification and refinement of the 39 peptides he had brought with him from Lublin. This arrangement created no problems for several years, because Burzynski pursued his own work quietly and it did not quickly draw attention from or foster jealousy in his fellow scientists. Burzynski got help in his first few years from Dr. George Georgiades, a friend working nearby in the world-famous M.D. Anderson Tumor Institute; Georgiades was then trying to isolate the leukemia virus.

As Burzynski grew more conversant with the peptides he had first found in Poland, he discovered that substances which at first appeared to produce only three stripes in primitive chromatography tests could be broken down not just into 39 fractions, but also into 119 distinct substances.

Early on, Burzynski had suspected that some of these peptides might possess anticancer properties. In Poland, he'd observed that chromatographic tests of blood from prostate cancer patients usually showed almost a total absence of the chemical that normally produced one of the initial three mystery stripes. At Baylor, Burzynski began to test his intuitive theory that at least some of the peptide fractions he had isolated might stunt the growth of human cancer tumors.

His thinking had been influenced by Marian Mazur, the Warsaw cybernetics professor whose telephone call to Polish authorities was probably the key to Burzynski's escape from Poland. Discussing his work with Mazur while it was still in its early stages, Burzynski began to believe that cancer is the result of a biochemical "programming error" as much as it is the product of inadequate immune-system responses. Living cells multiply out of control to produce a cancer tumor, Burzynski thought, because whatever triggers normal, healthy cell reproduction and death is either turned off or not present.

Early in his stay at Baylor, Burzynski tested his theory in the laboratory by introducing peptide fractions refined from his own urine into tumors produced by well-established lines of cancer cells grown in Georgiades' laboratory at M.D. Anderson. "I found that at least some of these peptides had anticancer properties," Burzynski explains. This was also when he coined the term antineoplaston for some of the peptides he found. Because neoplasm is the Greek term for a cancer tumor (literally, it means "new growth"), antineoplaston simply meant "anticancer."

But Burzynski soon saw that not all of his peptides had an impact on cancer cell cultures. "Most had no anticancer activity. Those that did were quite specific. We had one we called Antineoplaston L, which worked against some leukemias. And we found one that worked only on osteosarcoma. We called it Antineoplaston O. But we also found one that seemed to have a broad spectrum of anticancer activity. We called this one Antineoplaston A, and we concentrated on it. Antineoplastons L and 0 have been sitting on the shelf ever since.

"Our idea was to concentrate on the group with the broadest range of effectiveness. This seemed to us the most practical and productive way to proceed. We knew then and we know now that other antineoplastons exist, and we would work with them if we could. But we have had neither the time nor the money."

When Burzynski says "we," he is almost always including his wife, Barbara Scope Burzynski, a fellow M.D. and Polish immigrant—whose name appears as a co-author on several of his papers. They met in a laboratory at Baylor, have never been apart for more than a few days and occupy offices side by side at his west Houston clinic.

Over the next 15 years, the broad-spectrum Antineoplaston A would be broken down into smaller fractions known as A1, A2, A3, A4 and all the way up to A10. "A10 became the first one we were able to make synthetically," Burzynski says. "Once we had that, we studied metabolites of A10, the substances produced when the human body processes the original A10. We discovered that when you metabolize A10, you get another fraction we called AS2-5. And when you metabolize AS2-5, you get the chemical phenylacetate. Of all the antineoplastons we tested, this has the least anticancer activity." Ironically, almost two decades later, it would also be the first antineoplaston put into a large-scale clinical trial approved by the FDA and funded by a major maker of pharmaceuticals.

His early findings led Burzynski to apply for a research grant from the National Cancer Institute (NCI), then in the budding years of what President Richard Nixon called the war on cancer. Burzynski applied in cooperation with scientists from M.D. Anderson, planning at first to work with Georgiades as his chief co-investigator. At the last moment, however, Georgiades pulled out. Burzynski turned to Dr. Ti

Lee Loo, then vice chairman of M.D. Anderson's department of developmental therapeutics. With Loo as a powerful ally, Burzynski saw his grant funded in 1974 and got a raise, a promotion and an expanded staff. Both the NCI and M.D. Anderson would support Burzynski's work until 1977. And the grant would produce steady progress in antineoplaston research, with Burzynski, Loo, Ungar and Georgiades joining as co-authors of academic papers that carried such promising titles as "Biologically Active Peptides in Human Urine" and "Antineoplastons: Biochemical Defense Against Cancer."

During this time, Burzynski also pursued Ungar's theories about peptides as memory transmitters. But progress in this area was slower, if only because the sheer amounts of peptide produced in the brain are so much smaller than those which occur in blood and urine. "To get less than one microgram of brain peptide, we needed to train and kill 8,000 rats," Burzynski says. "These rats were trained to be accustomed to the sound of a bell. When the animal was exposed to an unfamiliar sound, we would get a startled response. But we elicited no reaction if it heard a bell or another sound that was repeated often.

"To prove that you can transfer memory chemically by using peptides, we had to sacrifice the rat, take its tiny amount of peptide fraction and then inject it into another rat that had never heard a bell before. It worked. But it required a huge number of laboratory animals. We would kill 300 to 500 rats a day with a kind of guillotine and then instantly place their brains on dry ice. It depressed me terribly to kill all these poor animals. But in the process we learned to fractionate the peptide responsible for transmission of this memory, called ameletin. We also saw that these peptides were attached to the ribonucleic acid [RNA] in the brain cells."

Burzynski's findings on brain peptides reinforced his theory that peptides were key factors in controlling cell growth. He also got reinforcement from another Baylor researcher, Dr. Carlton Hazlewood.

They'd met when Burzynski had been at Baylor less than two years. Working with his colleague Ungar, Hazlewood, a tenured professor of molecular physiology, set out in 1971 to organize an international conference on the physical and chemical state of ions in water, both in living and nonliving systems. "At the time, Russian scientists were very interested in my theories of the cell, and I wanted them to come to the conference," Hazlewood remembers. "I needed someone who could write letters to Russians in Russian. So I had two or three meetings where Burzynski helped me. Each time, I would ask what he was doing, and he'd say he was studying peptides. I became interested because in my work, I was beginning to think there must be some substance of low molecular weight that is constantly manipulating living cells. Burzynski's peptides fit that description. Eventually, we became friends."

Hazlewood was most interested in the apparent conunctions of their work. "I was beginning to believe that a peptide might be involved with the workings of the cell. Then Burzynski told me these peptides might have some anti-cancer activity. We began to work together." Hazlewood soon introduced Burzynski to his uncle, country doctor William Mask, who later said he came to regard Burzynski as "a little Polish genius."

During Burzynski's last year or so at Baylor, he and Hazlewood began working on an experiment that employed antineoplastons against well-established laboratory cultures of breast cancer. Their findings, published in the peer-reviewed Journal of Cancer, Chemistry and Biophysics, would not appear until 1979, years after Burzynski departed Baylor to set up an independent clinic and research institute. "Urinary peptide fractions...were found to be cytotoxic or cytostatic for human mammary cell cancers in culture depending on dose," their paper said. In other words, antineoplastons had stopped the multiplication of some cancer cells in their tracks and killed others. Hazlewood and Burzynski reported that the response of breast cancer cells to treatment with peptides derived from urine varied among the three peptide fractions tried. One of the peptides employed—dubbed G9—killed virtually every cancer cell it encountered, demonstrating an effectiveness rate at least eight times better than one of the other peptides. Success also depended on dose. If too little antineoplaston was applied, it could have little or no effect on the cancer cells. This result led Burzynski and Hazlewood to conclude that "there is a neutral to slightly acidic group of medium-size polypeptides in normal human urine that can act as growth controllers of several types of cancer cells."

Seeing this, Burzynski began to believe that the human body contains a biochemical defense system that operates parallel to the immune system and is just as important. "I began to see that the body doesn't have just one line of defense," he says. "You could say the immune system is the first line of defense. If it is working, it destroys invaders when they approach healthy cells. The biochemical defense system is like a second line of defense. If invading cancer-causing substances cause cells to become abnormal or malignant, it acts to switch them back to normal."

Influenced by Mazur, Burzynski equates this process with computer programming. "Cancer is really a disease of cells that are not programmed correctly. Antineoplastons simply reprogram them so that they behave normally again."

Before they even tried to go public with this concept in their breast cancer paper, Burzynski says, he and Hazlewood agreed that antineoplastons should be tried against laboratory cultures of several other cancers besides the breast cancer culture used for the formal report. They were tested—and they succeeded in vitro, in test tubes and petri dishes against a combination culture of osteosarcoma and leukemia cells, against malignant melanoma, against colon cancer and against HeLa cells from cervical cancer. Burzynski wanted to try antineoplastons against brain tumors, too, but "cultured cells of brain cancers were almost impossible to get," he says.

The breast cancer paper should not have come as a total surprise to cancer researchers. Years before it saw print, Burzynski had given the scientific community notice of what he was discovering. At the 1976 meeting of the Federation of Associations for Experimental Biology (FACEB) in Anaheim, California, he presented a paper reporting that peptides found in urine apparently had the power to change cancer cells back to normal cells. That paper sparked an Associated Press article that appeared in dozens of newspapers, bringing Burzynski's work into the public realm for the first time.

"Everything Burzynski was saying made sound scientific sense to me," says Hazlewood. "But he began to come into conflict with the scientific priesthood, just as I am. I have an unconventional view of the cell; he had an unconventional view of how cancer works. What's more, what Burzynski claimed was testable. The first big test, reported in the paper we co-wrote, was consistent with his idea that the peptides he calls antineoplastons work by turning cell division on and off. But the acid test of the utility of this stuff is the treatment of a person with cancer."

Before Burzynski could even think about any human test, he had to try antineoplastons on animals. This was primarily to make sure the compounds would not be toxic, because Burzynski already suspected the peptides he was refining from urine were not only tumor-specific, but also species-specific. In other words, an antineoplaston that could shut down the growth of one type of cancer might have no impact on another. And one that worked on some form of human cancer might not have any impact on similar tumors in other species.

That's just what Burzynski found in his mid-'70s experiments on rats, chickens and other animals. Although human antineoplastons were almost completely nontoxic, they did not stop the progress of most animal cancers. This finding was consistent with Burzynski's view that healthy members of every species manufacture their own peptides. The finding would create difficulties years later, when Burzynski sought wider acceptance of his antineoplaston therapy.

By the end of 1976, the doctor felt ready to try his antineoplastons on human patients for whom all other treatments had failed. Because he had passed the Texas medical licensing exams in 1973, Burzynski believed he was qualified to administer that trial himself. But, for the first time since he had left Poland, he would run into major bureaucratic obstacles. Like any other researcher wanting to try an experimental treatment on living humans, Burzynski needed permission from the institutional review board of any hospital where he would use that treatment. Such boards are usually drawn from hospital staff doctors.

"I tried to get permission from Baylor," Burzynski says.

"But I was turned down by the institutional review board, mainly because I did not have an Investigational New Drug permit from the Food and Drug Administration. But this was a Catch-22. Because in order to have an IND, I first needed the blessing of this same board. I spent months filing and re-filing papers to get their permission."

By this time, Burzynski had set up a private general practice in an office building adjacent to the Baylor-affiliated Park Plaza Hospital near downtown Houston. There he sometimes tried to treat terminally ill cancer patients, and when he did, he was haunted by the thought that he might be able to help them but could not because of bureaucratic rules. "I would go to bed at night thinking about how this or that patient was sure to die unless something intervened," he explains. "And I would think that I already knew what the intervention should be."

When Baylor turned him down, Burzynski tried the Park Plaza institutional review board. He was refused there, too. But Burzynski also had an affiliation with the independent Twelve Oaks Hospital, a modern 380-bed facility just west of downtown Houston. There, at last, he received permission to test his discovery.

This was where Emma Avadassian and Billy Bryant were headed before dangerous weather detoured them and Burzynski to Jacksboro and the Jack County Hospital headed by William Mask.

Meanwhile, Burzynski's safe academic haven at Baylor was also in turmoil, an upheaval caused more by internal politics than by resentment of his peptide research. Ungar had been ousted from Baylor in 1976, and the school had recalled a 70-year-old retiree and installed him as head of its anesthesiology lab. Burzynski saw the shifts as part of a power struggle between the eminent, pioneering heart surgeons Michael DeBakey and Denton Cooley, whose joint presence at Baylor was one large reason the anesthesiology department had never lacked for research funds during the 1970s. "I took over Ungar's research," Burzynski recalls. "But the new boss of anesthesiology was Lawrence Schumacher, a DeBakey ally who knew nothing about peptide research; he didn't like me."

Soon, Burzynski was being told to give up his lucrative private practice—the same practice that served as his vehicle for testing antineoplastons. Citing the publicity from his FACEB appearance in Anaheim as their reason for becoming more interested in him, Baylor's new leaders asked Burzynski to become a full-time member of the Baylor Cancer Research Center. As an inducement and a sort of welcome gift, he received a new $30,000 research grant from the university. But there was a catch: He would have to give up his private practice, and the laboratory space and financial support he and Ungar had enjoyed would also be reduced.

Despite the enhanced prestige, secure salary and tenure that could have been his had he gone along with the proposed changes, Burzynski hesitated. He didn't like the idea of subjecting himself to the authority of an institution. As long as he had a private practice, he believed he could use whatever medications he thought most effective, subject only to the consent of his patients. He believed then, as now, that hierarchies stifle innovation. "Most medical breakthroughs," he told author Ralph Moss during a 1980s interview, "have happened because there was some lack of suppression by the supervisors of people doing innovative work."

Burzynski likes to cite insulin as an example, his face lighting up with a wide grin as he notes that this lifesaving drug was discovered by a graduate student while his boss was on vacation.

In the end, Burzynski refused to be tempted to join any large establishment. By late 1977, he was operating entirely on his own.

The Crystin Schiff Story

If Only Her Daddy Had Known About Antineoplastons

Christmas Day, 1992, dawned happily in the home of Ric and Paula Schiff on their oak-studded, 20-acre ranch outside tiny Clayton, California, beneath the eastern slope of Mount Diablo near San Francisco. The couple's four-year-old twin daughters, Crystin and Gwendolyn, scrambled into the living room and began unwrapping presents, squealing with delight over the dolls and other toys beneath the tree.

It was also a festive time for Ric and Paula. "Life was good. We were riding the crest then," Ric recalls. The youngest sergeant on the San Francisco police force, Ric had won the department's gold medal of valor for saving lives when he was one of the first two policemen on the scene after the Cypress Avenue freeway overpass collapsed in the 1989 Bay Area earthquake. His heroism in the frantic rescue effort was portrayed in a larger-than-life-size oil painting on display in the rotunda of City Hall. Just 31, he was due that spring to take the lieutenant's exam. "I felt like the golden boy of the San Francisco P.D.," Ric says. Paula, meanwhile, was pregnant with the Schiffs' fifth child.

Further cause for satisfaction was the Schiffs' autumn victory over Waste Management Corp., which had planned to build a toxic waste dump on vacant property just across the road from the family ranch. The company had backed down after years of opposition from the Schiffs and a few neighbors. Once that threat was over, Ric and Paula had refinanced their ranch, hoping to give themselves a little financial ease.

As the twin girls ate breakfast that morning, their father

noticed that Gwendolyn was by far the cheerier, even though both had gotten exactly the gifts they wanted. This was a puzzle to Ric, because both his daughters had equally pleasant dispositions.

"Her mom and I looked closely at Crystin," Ric remembers. "She was whining and unhappy and complaining that her food didn't taste good. Her pupils were dilated. I looked at Gwennie's eyes and found they were not looking similar at all. Then, after a while, Crystin just became lethargic."

Ric didn't wait to see if the problem would fade on its own. Ever the vigilant policeman, he acted immediately, calling the girls' pediatrician. "He diagnosed the problem as a throat infection and prescribed an antibiotic," Ric says, shaking his head regretfully.

This was the first in what would prove to be a nightmarish series of encounters with conventional medicine for Crystin Schiff, who would not get anything approaching long-lasting relief until her parents learned of Dr. Stanislaw Burzynski.

For Crystin Schiff did not have a mere throat infection. Although she at first appeared to respond to the antibiotic, two weeks after she began taking it, her baby-sitter reported to Paula that something was seriously wrong with the tow-headed girl. Crystin's vision was almost gone, and she could walk only sideways. Every time she tried to take a step straight ahead, she stumbled. When her father asked her to come to him from across the room, she walked with her head turned completely to one side.

This time, there was no mere call to a pediatrician. "We rushed her to John Muir Hospital in Walnut Creek," Crystin's father says. "They immediately did a CT scan. I knew there was a big problem even while the scan was being done. I could see the doctor's face as she watched it proceed. I saw her hands go to her cheeks, and I knew it had to be a brain tumor.

It had cut her field of vision to about 10 percent of normal. In fact, they found a tumor the size of a small tangerine in Crystin's brain. Then we rushed her across the Bay to the University of California Hospital in San Francisco for brain surgery."

Ric stayed in his daughter's hospital room overnight before and after her surgery. "She woke up afterward and looked up at me and she could look at me straight again," he remembers. "Later, we learned that her field of vision was back to about 75 percent of normal. Right away, she asked if they got the 'owee' out. I said yes, even though her surgeon had told me they didn't get it all. She said, 'OK, let's go home.' The bottom line was that they had taken the big nodule out, but it was only part of a tumor that grew all around her spine and brain."

Crystin Schiff had a malignant rhabdoid tumor, a cancer so rare that only 25 other cases were then available for reference in formulating her treatment. Only seven were well documented. All 25 of the known cases had proven terminal, leading to death within four months to a year after the diagnosis.

"I wanted the doctors to tell me the best way to get through this, to help me do this in a way that wouldn't ruin my life and my family's," Ric says. "I read everything I could find on the disease and learned that the tumor spreads like thick maple syrup around the spine and in the brain. Then it gets thicker and thicker or it forms a growing nodule. This time, it had formed a nodule in her brain that was pressing on her eyes. That was causing the dilation."

Quickly, Crystin's case went before the regional tumor board, where specialists discuss the best way to handle tough cases. "They looked over the CT scan and the surgical records and advised me to 'take her home and let her die.' They said there was no hope for her. The only alternative was to go after very heavy chemotherapy, with all the side effects it brings—hair loss, nausea, loss of balance, the works. We were told that even by being this aggressive, we would only be buying time. They told us the treatment would likely kill her. They eventually were proven correct about that one point."

One member of that tumor board was Dr. Michael Prados, a UCSF neuro-oncologist who has written or helped author more than 30 academic papers on the treatment of brain tumors. He knew that two previous UCSF brain tumor patients, Jeffrey Keller and Pamela Winningham, had tried antineoplastons and that both had survived years longer than anyone had expected. But Prados, like the others on the tumor board, did not tell the Schiffs about Burzynski.

"We asked Prados the same question we asked the other doctors: Is there anything else you know of, other than chemotherapy or radiation?" Ric says. Prados, like the other doctors the family asked, said no. Eventually, this would lead the Schiffs to sue him. "We assumed that these people were oncologists and therefore they study cancer," Ric continues. "We were wrong. None of them could tell us about anything except the types of therapies they themselves used. The harder I would push them to try to think of something else, the more enthusiastic they became about their chemotherapy and radiation. They would say, 'Maybe Cryssie will be the one in a thousand who makes it.' And I immediately would become optimistic; I'd think, 'Oh, she has one chance in a thousand, but at least it's a chance.'"

Years later, Prados continually refused to discuss

Crystin's case. "I won't talk about that," he said in one telephone call. Asked why, he replied, "I won't talk about that, either."

Ric and Paula weren't about to give up on their daughter. Nor were they ready to try alternative therapies. There would be no laetrile for Crystin, no trips to clinics in Tijuana. Her parents launched her into the full-scale conventional cancer treatment, side effects and all.

The treatment knocked out her cancer—for a while. Between January and April 1993, Crystin's brain absorbed 6,000 rads of radiation, as much as people less than one mile from the atomic bomb explosion at Hiroshima. Her spine got an additional 4,000 rads. At the same time, she received heavy chemotherapy. Among the side effects were impaired vision and balance. Crystin had trouble walking and couldn't run. Her skin had second-degree burns from the radiation. "It was large-scale radiation dysfunction," her dad says. "Her central nervous system problems were familiar to all the doctors at UCSF, and they were consistent with the damage she had suffered." She also became so infused with toxic chemicals that her parents had to wear rubber gloves to change her diapers. But her tumor disappeared.

Nobody thought this was permanent. After all, no one had ever been cured of a malignant rhabdoid tumor. "They only gave her so much radiation and chemotherapy because they thought she would surely die, anyway," Ric points out. "They knew exactly what was happening: You give a little girl 6,000 rads of radiation to the brain and 4,000 to the spine and she won't live long. She will lose her ability to swallow easily. She will lose her gag reflex and won't respond when things are swallowed the wrong way and go into the lungs. She will develop various sarcomas. The bones in her spine will be stunted."

But Ric and Paula didn't know all that until much later. As they took Cryssie for her treatments, they still hoped that she would live a normal life, even though, as Ric remembers, "Every doctor told us the tumor would come back, that these always do." So he and Paula began looking for something different for their daughter. "We found Burzynski and his antineoplastons in a book about options. I know something about fraud. I've worked the bunco squad," the police sergeant says. "I wasn't going to buy just anything."

But the Schiffs wanted Crystin to live, and without the horrific side effects they had seen debilitate her during the seven months of her conventional treatment. By now her parents had learned about some of Burzynski's successes in treating brain tumors. Once again, they asked advice from Prados. He told them antineoplastons don't work. Further, he told them, phenylacetate—the principal chemical component of Burzynski's medication—is toxic and could do more damage to Crystin. And he labeled Burzynski a fraud who would simply take advantage of them. Later, he wrote the Schiffs a letter urging them not to try any alternative therapy. By then, though, Ric had spoken to patients experienced in the antineoplaston treatment. Against Prados' advice, he and Paula took Crystin to the Burzynski Clinic in Houston. Their hope: that the antineoplastons could prevent the otherwise certain reappearance of her tumor and that Crystin would eventually overcome the damage done to her by radiation and chemotherapy.

"TWA flew us down to Houston on a compassionate fare, and Westin hotels put us up," Ric recalls. "I looked around the clinic and I talked to some more Burzynski patients just to be sure it wasn't phony. I sensed that they all felt the stuff was working for them. Then I paid Dr. Burzynski $6,000 up front, and Cryssie was on the anti-neoplastons. After that, it was $3,000 a month. We spent a total of $30,000, including $23,000 from a self-insurance plan at my wife's employer." That, he says, was a mere drop in a bucket compared with what Cryssie's course of conventional chemotherapy and radiation had cost: a total of more than $800,000. "After a while, we realized we just couldn't afford it. So some friends and I contacted Senators Barbara Boxer and Dianne Feinstein and Representative Nancy Pelosi. They got us a compassionate Investigative New Drug permit. That let Burzynski ship the stuff to us, instead of our having to go to Houston every month. We were lucky one other way: Crystin had already had what they call a 'broviac' tube installed for her chemotherapy." That tube carried other drugs into a blood vessel near her heart and could also be used for the antineoplastons, which are usually pumped directly into a large vein in the chest. The broviac tube spared Crystin the need for the vascular surgery most patients undergo when they have similar tubes installed at the start of antineoplaston treatment.

Against the advice of every doctor they consulted, the Schiffs kept Crystin on antineoplastons until December 1994. "Everybody at UCSF said, 'Don't do it. Don't believe in it. It won't work;" Ric remembers. "But we stuck with it. And every time we showed up for an MRI and it turned out to be clear, we were thrilled, but it was obvious the doctors at UCSF were not. As time passed, they seemed more and more nervous. This is something I can recognize. I hunt human beings for a living, so I was watching these people with all my experience coming into play, and they didn't like the idea that her scans were clear."

About a year after she began taking antineoplastons, in

the summer of 1994, Crystin began to seem as if she were on a roller-coaster ride. She would make progress and walk well. Then she'd fall back. She would start to see better, then she wouldn't. She had problems with her kidneys and difficulties metabolizing and absorbing food. "Each time there was a problem, Prados would say it was due to the toxicity of the phenylacetate," Ric says. Crystin also suffered from ultra-low sodium levels and had two seizures during the last eight months of her life. But her tumor had not reappeared as of mid-November 1994, when her entire body was subjected to an MRI screening.

Shortly after that MRI, the family stopped her antineoplaston treatment in December 1994, hoping the tumor was permanently gone. It was not.

"Almost immediately, she started having more seizures and becoming more sensitive to seizure medication," Ric remembers. "It was almost like she was morphined out."

Crystin became sluggish. Her blood tests showed that she had severe liver and kidney damage. Then, when she had another MRI on Dec. 22, her tumor was back and widespread in her brain. "So we know for certain that antineoplastons prevented her tumor from recurring and that taking her off them was what brought the tumor back," Schiff declares. The parents again saw the tumor begin producing negative effects in their daughter, including dizziness and impaired physical abilities. She had difficulty keeping her balance while walking; her eyesight was again constricted.

Now the Schiffs were in a quandary. They were near bankruptcy. Eventually, they would formally file for relief from their debts. Their health insurance was not covering Burzynski's treatment and would only pay for CT scans and MRIs (about $2,000 per screening) if they were ordered by a physician. The Schiffs were forced again to deal with

Prados and other oncologists at UCSF.

"I distinctly remember Prados coming in when Cryssie had her problems after going off the antineoplastons," Ric says. "He had a little smile and he told us, 'You've obviously got a recurrence.'"

Immediately, Prados and other doctors at UCSF urged the family to submit Crystin to another course of radiation and chemotherapy. The Schiffs refused, opting instead to restart their daughter on antineoplastons. But they knew they would need repeated scans to monitor how she was doing on the treatment, and they did not have the money to pay for them unless they could get a doctor's approval. That's when Ric Schiff was forced into what he calls "a deal with the devil."

"I had asked Burzynski how soon we could expect to see results; he said Cryssie would need to be on the treatment for at least three weeks before any improvement was likely to show," he remembers. "So I asked Prados what he had. He mentioned several toxic chemotherapies and he seemed to be getting excited about using them on Cryssie. We arranged an MRI for three weeks later and I agreed that if there was no change in the tumor, she would take one of his toxic chemotherapies. You can imagine how I felt, knowing what toxic chemotherapy and radiation had already done to my daughter."

But after three weeks, the regrown tumor was 25 percent smaller. "I never heard anything from Prados again," Ric says. "Once the tumor had been reduced by 25 percent, he just stayed away." Cryssie stayed on antineoplastons. Nine weeks later, another scan showed that the tumor was gone. And later that year, Prados ironically become a lead investigator in a 16-hospital clinical trial of pure phenylacetate—of whose alleged toxicity he had warned the

Schiffs—as an anticancer drug. Still later, radiologist Dr. James Barcovich of UCSF confirmed that the MRIs taken three weeks and nine weeks after the Dec. 22 exam showed Crystin's tumor first reduced and later gone. "But no doctor at UCSF would ever ascribe that tumor remission to anything but residual radiation effects. They simply didn't want to give any credit to Burzynski or his antineoplastons," Ric complains.

Crystin would stay on antineoplastons for the rest of her life, a span cut radically short because of the aftereffects of the radiation treatment she received when her tumor was first diagnosed. "When Cryssie died, the hospital demanded an autopsy," Ric remembers. "I knew they wanted it just so they could fuck Burzynski over if there was a tumor present. But I thought about it and soon realized I wouldn't be helping anyone if I didn't allow it."

The family had taken Cryssie's body from the hospital after she died, but Ric brought it back the next morning for the medical examination. He demanded the autopsy procedure be full and look over every part of her body. "I spent hours looking at the slides from that procedure with her pediatric oncologist, Dr. Byron Smith, and the radio-oncologist, Dr. William Wara. The bottom line is that at the time of her death, there was not a cancer cell in Cryssie's body."

Ric's vivid memories torture him every day. "I can't escape it," he says. "I make my living being suspicious, but I can't think of any reason other than the antineoplastons that would have eliminated Cryssie's tumor so fast the second time. That tells me we killed her because of our lack of knowledge about Burzynski and antineoplastons the first time the tumor arrived. I know I tortured my daughter. I know I threw my training out the window. And the only person who can forgive me for it is dead. Yes, Prados and the other doctors are responsible, too. But my share of the responsibility is pretty big. If I had been trying to fix a car, I would have gotten out every Chilton guide I could find, but with my daughter, I just accepted what I was told. Nothing else can change that or replace Cryssie."

Not even the fact that he has since helped two other children with malignant rhabdoid tumors find their way to Burzynski can assuage Ric's self-blame. Parents of both these children contacted Ric after Cryssie's case was publicized by the Scripps Howard News Service and in the Health & Healing newsletter published by Dr. Julian Whittaker. "Those kids are doing great on antineoplastons, and Cryssie could have, too, if we had taken her there first. But we didn't," he says.

Crystin's death from pneumonia was the result of her repeatedly swallowing food into her lungs, a problem her parents attribute to her radiation treatment. The Schiffs are convinced that if they had known about Burzynski and his antineoplastons before starting Crystin on conventional radiation and chemotherapy, if her doctors had properly informed them of that option, she would be alive today.

"Of 52 cases of that disease that have been documented, no one died cancer-free, just Cryssie," Ric testified in a February 1996 hearing of the House Commerce Committee's Subcommittee on Investigations and Oversight. "She didn't die of a terminal illness. She died of my inability to care for her properly, and she died from bad advice. And she died because there is a government institution that disseminates false information, at least a portion of it, and it is not looking out for the welfare of the people."

So Ric blames the FDA, which has tried for more than a decade to drive Burzynski out of business. "The job of the FDA is to tell us whether something is safe, not to keep us from finding out about something," he asserts. "I believed it when the doctors told me that Cryssie had no chance other than radiation and chemotherapy. Because I didn't know enough, I turned to doctors who didn't know enough either, or wouldn't tell me what they did know. If I had questioned everything, maybe we would have used less radiation and not fried her brain, and she'd still be alive, on antineoplastons, and playing happily today."

Postscript

SAN FRANCISCO, midyear 2000—For Ric Schiff, much of the last three years has been sheer frustration. "I talk to people continually whose children have brain tumors," he says. "Of 100 percent I talk to who should go to Dr. Burzynski for treatment, about 80 percent don't go. Their oncologists are willing to do almost anything to keep them from going. Even when the doctors have already told the parents chemotherapy won't help and can't help, the minute they hear that someone is about to go to Dr. Burzynski as a last resort, those doctors almost always say, 'OK, we'll try chemotherapy.' They don't seem interested in cures, only in promoting their present types of treatment, as destructive as they are. But of the 20 percent who resist all that talk and do go to Dr. Burzynski, more than half are cured."

There has also been frustration on the legal front. With financial help from Dr. Julian Whitaker of the Health & Healing Newsletter, Ric and Paula sued Dr. Michael Prados, charging he repeatedly refused to take advantage of opportunities to tell the Schiffs about antineoplastons even though he knew of the success Dr. Burzynski had in treating Pamela Winningham (see The Pamela Winningham Story) and one other patient. The suit was dismissed on a legal technicality in 1999, and Ric appealed. But because of a California law limiting medical malpractice judgments to $250,000, he has no hope of recouping the tens of thousands of dollars he's spent pursuing Dr. Prados and several other doctors who gave Cryssie the immense radiation doses that apparently led to her death.

"The money was never the point in my suits," says Ric. "The point is to expose these people and their activities. Dr. Whitaker calls what these doctors do 'pure evil.' It is. But celebrities go on staging huge fundraisers for them and their so-called research. It is very frustrating."

Yet Ric can take some satisfaction from lives saved because he sent them to Dr. Burzynski and from his role in keeping the Burzynski Clinic in business. Ric's testimony in Dr. Burzynski's first trial was among the most effective, in part because Judge Simeon T. Lake 3rd allowed him to testify on areas where other patients were barred from talking. "It was almost like he looked at me and saw I was a policeman and that was good enough for him," Ric smiles. "To my amazement, I found myself testifying as an expert witness on chemotherapy and radiation. So in almost five years of campaigning, at least we've kept Dr. Burzynski out of jail and his clinic operating."

It won't bring Cryssie back, but it's much better than nothing.

CHAPTER 4

On His Own and Curing Cancers

For Dr Stanislaw Burzynski, the year 1977 was every bit as exciting and daring as 1970, the year he came to America. With a mere $5,000 in the bank, he left his research position at the Baylor College of Medicine to strike out on his own. While working part time for another physician, he opened his own clinic.

The lure of independence was so strong that he turned down an offer from the University of Tennessee's medical school in Memphis. Burzynski's former mentor, Georges Ungar, had moved to Memphis after his position at Baylor became politically untenable; he wanted Burzynski to help him continue his work on brain peptides. Initially invited to give a series of lectures in Tennessee, Burzynski was soon offered a tenured joint appointment in biochemistry and oncology.

Just as the doctor was agonizing over what to do, the Polish scientist Marian Mazur suddenly reappeared, turning up in Houston to lecture at Rice University and bedding down at Burzynski's home. This wasn't a complete accident, but decades later, Burzynski still believed the timing of Mazur's arrival was predestined. "Since he helped me so much in Poland, I had wanted to do something for him," Burzynski says. "I had some friends at Rice whom I convinced to invite Mazur to speak on cybernetics, as well as give him a nice honorarium. He showed up suddenly, like an angel, just when I had to make a decision that would affect the rest of my life. At that time, it seemed as if Mazur always showed up at the key moments."

Mazur argued that Burzynski should strike out on his

own, that he would be better off independent of any and all academic bureaucracy. "I had also discussed this with Carlton Hazlewood and a few others," Burzynski says. "They said I would need partners to make it on my own. But to have partners is to give away a lot. Mazur's advice was that if what I had was good, income from patients alone would be enough to support me. I liked that idea."

So Burzynski rented two offices and a garage in a low-slung building on Westline Drive in West Houston and began seeing patients. To make ends meet, he also worked part time as an internist in the medical practice of Dr. Rhey Walker, seeing patients with a variety of ailments. But in his own clinic, he saw only cancer victims. From the beginning, there was no shortage of patients, mostly because of the Associated Press coverage of his presentation at the 1976 FACEB convention. "The story circulated around the world," Burzynski recalls. "It was in newspapers, it was covered on radio and TV, and I was flooded with telephone calls. Locally, I went on the Nancy Ames television talk show in Houston. It all meant that people became interested, and my patients came from many places, just as they have since."

But when he opened his tiny clinic, Burzynski couldn't have known that that's how his life would work. "For me, it was like crossing the Red Sea. Just a year or so earlier, I never even dreamed I would do anything like that: going into business for myself. In Poland, academic people despised business people. They felt that if you left the university voluntarily, you were crazy. And, you know, to do it without any money or assurance of patients, it really was crazy. I never would have done it without the advice of Mazur."

Burzynski pushed ahead into a practice that would

shortly become one of the most controversial ventures in American medicine. "From the $5,000 1 had, I made a down payment of $600 for the first month's rent," he remembers. "In the garage, we set up freeze-dryers and a manufacturing facility." The makeshift garage laboratory would prove crucial to Burzynski's early success, since he brought along from Baylor only enough antineoplastons to treat 10 patients for a few months. He would soon need much more. But in those early years, human urine was the only source for the necessary peptides.

"I started making them on my own," Burzynski says. "I took a loan for $30,000 and ordered a large freeze-dryer. Then the operation began to grow. So we soon needed more and more urine." It came from many sources. Employees of Twelve Oaks Hospital set up refrigerators on every floor and collected their urine for Burzynski. Through several priests he befriended, Burzynski arranged for students at St. Mary's Roman Catholic Seminary in Houston to collect their urine. The nuns at the Villa de Matel convent also con-tributed. And whenever there was a mass or any other gath-ering at Houston's main Polish-American Catholic church, all urine produced also went to Burzynski. For a while, he even collected urine from inmates in the Texas prison sys-tem. In most of these places, collection systems were set up in the rest rooms, with the liquid ending up in a central con-tainer. In return for their cooperation, Burzynski regularly made donations to the outfits that kept him supplied.

The doctor and his early assistants were forced to spend several hours each day driving around Houston collecting urine. They brought it back to the garage on Westline, where it was immediately dumped into the nine freezer chests that were always on hand. "We ran pipelines from the freezers to our filtration machinery, and we usually had enough urine," Burzynski recalls. "But we needed about 30 liters [approximately 10 gallons] for each patient for each day of treatment. So we needed a constant stream. It was killing us, forever driving around and picking up urine."

His schedule also weighed on him. He served as chief chemist, saw patients, wrote academic papers and, for the first two years, worked in Dr. Walker's practice. And he was forced to think about hiring and firing technicians and secretaries. "I had no experience in business," Burzynski says. "Like any other Polish academic, I despised business. But I learned fast, as I had to write hundreds of pages of instructions for our technicians, because from the earliest time, we knew the Food and Drug Administration would not leave us alone forever. I had had a nice life with a good salary and none of these worries. But all of a sudden, I needed to think about money." So he began asking patients for an initial $2,500 deposit, to be refunded if and when their insurance companies paid their claims. Soon he began to cure some patients, which made all the struggles feel worthwhile.

Burzynski treated his first group of patients with intramuscular injections of the original broad-spectrum peptide he called Antineoplaston A, which contains the chemical phenylacetylglutamine. The results were reported in a paper titled "Antineoplaston A in Cancer Therapy," published in late 1977 in the peer-reviewed journal Physiological Chemistry and Physics. There, Burzynski reported that the majority of the patients in his first group of 22 achieved either significant tumor reduction or stabilization. Four of the 22 saw their tumors completely dissipate, two others achieved reductions of 50 percent or more, and only four cases ended with the cancer progressing during the months of the study. Because Antineoplaston A was so broad-ranging, that first group included patients with a variety of tumors, including breast cancers, lymphomas and brain cancers.

But this did not satisfy Burzynski. Working with high-performance chromatography in his garage laboratory, he broke Antineoplaston A down into five fractions, dubbed A1 through A5. "A2 seemed to be the most active, and we published the results of a Phase 1 study of its toxicity in a journal in Switzerland in 1978," Burzynski recalls. "Our response rates improved as we made different antineoplastons, each one a fraction of Antineoplaston A. When we tried A2 on 15 patients, only one had progressive disease. We had complete responses in cases of breast cancer, liver cancer, chronic leukemia and brain tumors. I tried to get this published in America, but it was rejected by the journals here. I suppose the first study was published easily in this country because I was still close to my time at Baylor. I was not yet a complete outcast. But I soon became one."

A2, then, was almost completely nontoxic and apparently quite effective—but no one in the cancer-research community cared. Even when Burzynski presented his findings at the quadrennial International Cancer Congress in Budapest in 1984, they received no attention from other American cancer researchers.

The process of branding Burzynski an outcast began in 1978 while he was still deeply involved with his study of how to break Antineoplaston A into fractions. It started with an investigation by the Harris County (Houston) Medical Society's board of ethics. Burzynski was charged with concocting an unapproved medication and giving it to his patients. After repeatedly summoning him for questioning, Burzynski's fellow doctors instructed him not to give any more interviews to the press, a rule he complied with for almost two years. But Burzynski did not allow this to interfere with his operation, and patients continued to seek him out at the rate of about 30 per year. He is unsure of the reason, but he never heard from the board of ethics after April 1980.

In 1979, he told New York health writer Gary Null, who was then putting together an Our Town magazine article titled "This Man Could Save Your Life, But He Can't Get the Money to Do It," that he would never give up treating patients with antineoplastons. "I'm going to fight no matter what they do," Burzynski had said, sounding as if he realized what might lie ahead, "because I'm doing the right thing. I believe that this is our obligation to the people. If you find something that's valuable, you must continue, and I believe that we've found something that may be able to save lives." This credo would guide Burzynski for decades, through four grand jury investigations, 2,500 patients, a criminal trial and myriad disputes with insurance companies.

Meanwhile, Burzynski's operation was expanding. In 1979, he moved his clinic a few blocks west to new offices on nearby Corporate Drive, and he gave up working with Walker because his own practice now demanded his constant presence. Two years later he moved his chemical plant out of the Westline garage and into a modern industrial park just south of Houston's Southwest Freeway.

It was in the original garage laboratory that Burzynski had his initial personal contacts with the FDA. His lawyers first approached the agency in 1977, just as he was starting his clinic, and found that there was no federal objection to his making antineoplastons and using them in the state of Texas. "We asked them if we could do it, and they said 'Sure,'" Burzynski recalls. His lawyers next consulted the Texas attorney general's office, which gave Burzynski a formal written opinion agreeing with that initial FDA green light. One reason for both early approvals may have been that Texas law at the time did not incorporate FDA rules into state medical regulations. This changed in 1985, perhaps because of publicity about Burzynski's later disputes with federal authorities.

The FDA's first visit to Burzynski came in 1978, when inspector Alicia Abbott came to his laboratory to check things out. Her chief complaint: The mice on which antineoplastons were tested for sterility and toxicity lived in cages in the converted garage. Abbott told Burzynski this had to change, that the test animals could not be kept in the same space where urine was filtered and the peptides refined. Burzynski immediately moved the animals out of the garage and heard no more from the FDA until almost four years later.

During that period, he continued seeing about 30 new patients annually, which required the collection and refining of 1,500 liters of urine every day. "We had to buy a lot of freezers from Montgomery Ward because the urine would eventually eat through their inner walls and rust them out," he recalls with a wry smile.

Desperate to end his dependence on human urine, Burzynski could not begin synthesizing the antineoplastons until he had identified every molecule in them. That was impossible for him until the technique of mass spectrometry—now used to identify the chemicals in everything from earth rocks to the moons of Uranus—became available. Once he could combine mass spectrometry with his expertise in high-performance chromatography, it would at last be possible to identify the components of even the most unstable antineoplaston fragments. And in 1980, Burzynski learned that the major component of Antineoplaston A is a compound called 3-phenylacetylamino-2.6-piperidine-dione. To make this outside the human body, the crucial ingredient is the commercially available chemical L-glutamine. Burzynski also needed large quantities of phenylacetylchloride and smaller amounts of common chemicals such as sodium bicarbonate, sulfuric acid, sodium hydroxide and methyl alcohol. Once he knew exactly what to look for, he began buying chemicals by the vat and soon started synthesizing antineoplastons.

"I thank heaven for mass spectrometry," Burzynski says. "Without it, we would still be depending on urine. There was no doubt that we would artificially synthesize the medicine the moment we knew how. But first, we had to purify the antineoplastons from urine, and at the final steps of purification, the compounds always fragmented and disappeared so that we couldn't analyze them. We'd always wanted to synthesize these peptides. It is much easier, better and more pure that way. It wasn't that we had problems sterilizing the urine, but let's face it, that was an unpleasant type of preparation."

It was when he began to synthesize antineoplastons that Burzynski initially tested the substance phenylacetate—which would later become a key substance in his life—against cancers. This happened when he began making A10, a combination of phenylacetylglutamine and phenylacetylisoglutamine. When absorbed and processed by the body, both eventually become phenylacetate, itself a fairly common, well-known chemical.

Burzynski would eventually patent A10 and another antineoplaston he called AS2-1, but he opted not to patent phenylacetate, because it is so common and because when he tested it in cancer patients, its activity was limited. "We treated ten patients with phenylacetate, but we obtained a partial response in only one, a man with prostate cancer," he reports. "It gave us no major activity. We quickly learned from our use in treatment that it is completely inferior to our other preparations."

So Burzynski figured that there was no need to patent this chemical as a cancer drug, that once doctors saw how much more effectively other antineoplastons combat cancer, they would have no more interest in phenylacetate. He was wrong. Years later, both a large pharmaceutical house and the NCI would abandon the testing of antineoplastons and hang their hopes on phenylacetate as a major potential tool for curing cancer.

Meanwhile, after he accomplished the aim of chemically creating his own antineoplastons, Burzynski received no opposition from the FDA. It was as if the agency had forgotten about him. This changed quickly in 1982, when Canadian authorities began taking notice of his work. Their interest was piqued by a favorable story that appeared in the Canadian mass-circulation magazine *Maclean's* early that year. Soon, Burzynski was summoned to the nation's capital, Ottawa, where he met with officials of the Canadian drug-approval agency. "It was a pleasant meeting, but before they approved the drug for use in Canada, they wanted to send some experts to see our plant," Burzynski remembers. This visit would prove useful to Burzynski, who says the Canadian inspectors introduced him to the concept of "good manufacturing procedures," allowing his facility to earn high marks in future inspections by the FDA.

The *Maclean's* story spurred dozens of Canadian cancer victims to travel south to see Burzynski. It also caused oncologist David Walde of Sault Ste. Marie, Ontario, to visit Burzynski's clinic and plant. After his visit, Dr. Walde, in a privately circulated report later quoted in the Ralph Moss book *The Cancer Industry*, wrote: "I had no idea what to expect upon my arrival there and would not have been surprised to have found a backdoor operation directed to the exploitation of patients for financial gain, without the benefits of any therapeutic activity .... I also thought that the documentation of the clinical cases would be poor and incomplete, making evaluation difficult, if not impossible." But Walde soon changed his mind, saying that what he saw "was beyond my wildest expectations, and I had to rapidly backtrack on all my preconceived notions of the situa-tion...It was beyond my conception that an individual, with-out massive cash-flow funding from either commercial or government sources, would be able to single-handedly put together this sophisticated production capability. My impression was that the entire program, both research and production, was built on the financial backs of patients, supplemented by large personal bank loans by Dr. Burzynski."

This was correct and would later prove a major imped-iment as Burzynski sought government approval of his medication.

But after this favorable report, trouble soon arose when agencies such as the Ontario Health Insurance Plan began to question claims made by patients. That health plan stopped making payments to Burzynski shortly after his trip to Ottawa, and in October 1982, Ontario's deputy health minister asked the provincial medical association to send experts to review Burzynski's treatment. One month later, on Nov. 15, 1982, Dr. Martin Blackstein, chief of oncology at Toronto's Mount Sinai Hospital, and Dr. Daniel Bergsagel, chief of medicine at Princess Margaret Hospital in Toronto, arrived to delve into every aspect of Burzynski's operations.

"Because of the report written by Dr. Walde, I was not suspicious of those two," Burzynski remembers. Later, he would wish he'd been less hospitable. "I showed them X-rays that demonstrated how tumors went away, and they were unimpressed. Whatever they saw, their attitude was hostile." On their return to Canada, Blackstein and Bergsagel would write a scathing report, condemning the fact that Burzynski still made some antineoplastons from urine, claiming they had not seen evidence of significant antitumor activity by antineoplastons used in the test tube, and noting that Burzynski had not yet filed a New Drug Application with either the FDA or the Canadian NCI. Despite the non sequitur nature of these complaints, and the fact that the two Canadian doctors completely ignored all Burzynski's peer-reviewed journal articles, their report has been used against Burzynski in virtually every lawsuit he has fought since, with Blackstein and Bergsagel occasionally brought in to testify against him as expert witnesses.

Burzynski nevertheless followed one of the recommendations made by the sympathetic Dr. Walde and applied for an IND permit in Canada. For several months, it appeared that this would move forward smoothly, with use of antineoplastons to be sanctioned there on an experimental basis. But then Burzynski ran afoul of the steady cooperation between the Canadian and U.S. National Cancer Institutes, The Canadians sent samples of antineoplastons to the American NCI, which proceeded to put them through its usual array of tests in animals. Burzynski cooperated, shipping further supplies of A2, A5 and his new, synthesized A10 to Bethesda, Maryland, even though he was dubious that the drugs would accomplish much in animals.

The standard NCI practice at the time was to test any

purported new anticancer drug against the so-called P388 strain of mouse leukemia. Burzynski told both the Canadians and the American NCI scientists that he believed antineoplastons were species-specific—that each species produced its own versions of the peptides—and that his medications would therefore have little effect on the mouse leukemia. Further, he postulated that a specific antineoplaston exists for virtually every type of cancer.

As he predicted, the antineoplastons did little against the rodent disease. But NCI refused to act on Burzynski's suggestion that it also test antineoplastons on cell cultures of human tumors, particularly breast cancer. From then on, the failure of antineoplastons to affect mouse leukemia was used against Burzynski's medications whenever journalists or patients queried NCI about them.

It was not until after the Canadians enlisted the American NCI in their investigative efforts that the FDA appeared once again at Burzynski's door. This time, it was no short visit, with an inspector offering helpful hints on how to improve the operation. The agency's 1982 inspection of Burzynski's production plant lasted about one month. It was followed by another five-week inspection of his clinic.

But the first serious attack from the FDA did not come until Easter week 1983. Returning to Houston from a meeting in Philadelphia, Burzynski telephoned his office to pick up phone messages and return any urgent calls. "I was notified in transit that a lawsuit had been filed against me by the FDA," he says. "I learned later that they had actually gone to a magistrate judge and requested a temporary restraining order that would have forced me to stop manufacturing antineoplastons. But by coincidence, my lawyer John Johnson was in the courtroom at that moment on another matter and heard what was going on. He explained to the judge that if I were forced to stop making antineoplastons, people would die. And the magistrate did not issue the order. In fact, no such order has ever been issued."

But Burzynski would have to fight. It's a battle whose outcome remains in doubt.

Dr. Burzynski examines the MRI scan of a brain tumor in is Houston clinic. MRIs provide dramatic and graphic evidence that antineoplastons shrink many brain tumors that have been unaffected by conventional therapy.

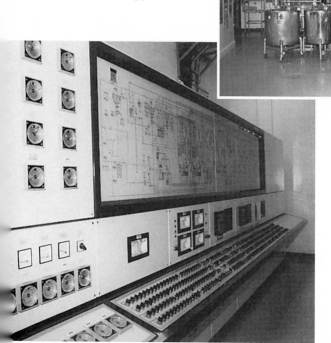

Pipes, vats and a complex control panel fill the suburban Houston plant where Dr. Burzynski synthesizes antineoplastons. Burzynski designed the complex machinery and supervises its operation, meeting every FDA standard for manufacture of pharmaceuticals.

Free of the lymphoma that afflicted her for years, Mary Jo Siegel joins cured brain tumor patient Neil Dublinksy and Dr. Burzynski, the man both credit with saving their lives.

Burzynski patients and their families demonstrate outside the White House, September 1996. Ironically, letters from patients to President Clinton complaining about the FDA's treatment of Dr. Burzynski before his criminal trials were routinely forwarded to the FDA.

Burzynski patients take their cause to Congress, meeting with Republican Rep. Richard Burr of North Carolina. FDA brass were called to testify in five separate oversight hearings after sessions like this.

Mary Jo Siegel leads Burzynski patients in a September 1996 protest in Washington, D.C. Patients raised more than $600,000 for Dr. Burzynski's defense.

Drs. Barbara and Stanislaw Burzynski receive a blessing from Pope John
Paul II at his Castel Gandolfo summer residence outside Rome in
October 1996 only months before the first criminal trial. The Pontiff personally summoned the Burzynskis to wish them luck in their battle with
the FDA

Dr. Stanislaw Burzynski addresses a crowd of his patients and supporters out-side the federal courthouse in Houston during a break in his first criminal trial. Prosecutor Michael Clark claimed daily demonstrations like this "certainly had an impact on the outcome" of both trials.

Patients and their relatives surround Dr. Barbara Burzynski during a break in her husband's first criminal trial. From left: Jared Wadman, Alice Cedillo and her friend Greg Bader, Mary Jo Siegel, Jared's grandfather, Barbara Burzynski, Jared's Father Ted Wadman, Randy Goss, Jared's mother Sandy Wadman.

Robert Spiller, the FDA's chief enforcement lawyer, focuses on testimony during Dr. Burzynski's first criminal trial. Spiller, one of the federal officials who declared "war" on Burzynski in 1983, has rebuffed all efforts to elicit an explanation of why the FDA sought to jail Burzynski.
(drawing by Eve Myles)

U.S. District Judge Simeon T. Lake 3rd knew even before the Burzynski trials began that "the patients are the real parties in interest here." Over prosecution protests, he allowed more than a dozen patients to testify.
(drawing by Eve Myles)

Brain tumor patient Robbie Graham (foreground) joins other Burzynski patients crowding the courtroom on opening day of their doctor's first criminal trial.
(drawing by Eve Myles)

With their lymphoma tumors gone, Burzynski patients (from left) Theresa Kennett and Mary Jo Siegel join cured brain tumor patient Neil Dublinsky at a fundraising dinner for the Burzynski legal defense.

Burzynski patient Randy Goss, cured of renal cell cancer, with sons Kyle and Jason.

Back in his beloved bass boat, Burzynski brain tumor patient Thomas
Wellborn displays a catch. Antineoplastons dissipated his brain tumor after
conventional treatments failed.

Dr. Burzynski holds patient Dustin Kunnari, whose conventional doctors
failed to cure his brain tumor, during a rally outside the federal courthouse
in Houston in early 1997. Dustin's parents testified in Congressional
hearings that antineoplaston treatment saved his life.

The Randy Goss Story

He Didn't Let Cancer Ruin His Life

Randy Goss didn't want a confrontation. A restaurateur and an equipment operator and recycling technician for Chautauqua County in western New York state, Randy had seen quite enough confrontations during his battle with cancer. He'd fought the disease for almost two years before his final visit to the world-famous Roswell Park Cancer Center in Buffalo, and he was not eager for an argument with his oncologist.

Randy wanted Roswell Park to continue making periodic CT scans of his body, but he was no longer eager to meet with any of its oncology staff. They insisted. "You keep skipping your appointments with the doctor," a secretary complained over the telephone before his CT scan appointment in June 1995. "So we can't let you have any more scans here." Randy, an experienced local politician who served two years on the city council in his hometown of Dunkirk, New York, responded with an offer. He would see his oncologist one more time, if Roswell Park would conduct the scan. But there was no real confrontation when Dr. Satish R.C. Velagapudi walked into the examining room where Randy waited. "You went to Houston, didn't you?" Velagapudi asked accusingly.

"I had no choice," Randy replied.

"Well, you have no cancer anymore. I'm glad you found something that worked for you," the doctor replied. Then he turned abruptly on his heel and walked from the examining room, not waiting to hear any details.

So ended Randy Goss' struggle against renal-cell cancer, one of the deadliest forms of the disease. In Stage 4 renal-cell cases, according to the American Cancer Society's Textbook on Clinical Oncology, the five-year survival rate is less than 1 percent.

When it was first diagnosed, cancer took Randy completely by surprise. An active sportsman who likes to ski both on snow and water, play football, golf, basketball and tennis and regularly attends Buffalo Bills football games, Randy Goss never let his cancer ruin his life. Just a week before it was diagnosed in 1992, he had bought a burned-out building, intending to renovate it and turn it into a fast-food restaurant. Throughout his cancer treatment, he continued working on the building, nailing down shingles and sprucing up the paint between surgery appointments and his regular civil service job. "I worked your basic 90-hour week for quite a while," he smiles. And by mid-1995, he not only was clear of cancer, but had a thriving eatery called Lenny's in Dunkirk, serving pizzas, chicken wings, hot dogs, hamburgers and tacos. Later, Randy would try to sell his restaurant so he could spend more time with his family.

Randy triumphed because he refused to believe that he would die and because he became so desperate to avoid death that he was finally willing to try almost anything that offered a significant chance for survival. But there were also plenty of times when he thought he might soon die. Then 41 and the holder of a degree in nursing, he tried never to miss the yearly physical exam county officials encouraged their employees to take. "I had skipped a year or two before 1992, so I wanted to be sure to take it that year, even though I felt no special need, no pain or anything." The exam revealed a microscopic trace of blood in his urine, but the doctors conducting the physical in Jamestown, New York, thought this likely didn't mean much. Traces of blood in urine are common, sometimes caused by things as simple as heavy lifting. "So I wasn't worried," Randy remembers. "But I still thought I should go to a urologist for follow-up tests."

Those tests included an ultrasound exam and a CT scan conducted for urologist Dr. Peter Sciarrino. The ultrasound showed something in the area of Randy's right kidney. "I thought I might just have a kidney stone, until one day just after the CT scan, Sciarrino called me into his office, sat me down and told me I had a large growth in my kidney. He said it was metastatic cancer."

Randy was shocked. "Cancer was the farthest thing from my mind. I didn't know how to tell my wife, Cheryl. All I could do was go home and wait for her to get home, and when she got there, we both cried. I don't break down easy. I tend to hold most of my feelings inside, but my younger son, Kyle, was just 9 months old then and the thought of not being around while he grew up was just killing me."

Within days, Sciarrino told Randy that his tumor had been identified as renal-cell carcinoma. "But no one told me how bad renal-cell really is," Randy would complain afterward. "I found out later by studying up on it that renal-cell is about the second most fatal type of cancer." Sciarrino scheduled surgery immediately in Dunkirk, planning to remove Randy's right kidney.

"But I wasn't about to rush into anything like surgery that quickly," Randy says. "I wanted at least one other opinion." So he sought out childhood acquaintance Dr. Justine Marutt Reilly Schober, now a urologist with offices in Erie, Pennsylvania, about 45 miles southwest of Dunkirk. "I called her at home one evening and she returned the call as I was sitting on my back porch looking at the sunset over

Lake Erie. She really didn't know me very well; she knew my brothers much better. But she told me to come down to Erie for some more ultrasounds and another CT scan."

Schober confirmed that there was a large growth in Randy's right kidney and agreed he would need to have that kidney removed. She also told him there was no way to be sure until after the surgery whether his cancer had spread outside the kidney. Schober and her associate, Dr. Victor Souaid, removed the kidney on July 31, 1992, and reported that it was one of the largest they had ever seen—about twelve inches in circumference, the size of a softball. But the good news was that the tumor appeared to be "encapsulated," confined just to the right kidney. "After the surgery, the doctors said they were amazed I had been in no pain with a tumor that size, but they told me everything looked good and there was a 99 percent chance I would be fine," Randy explains. "I believed that because I had never really had any pain. Even the day before surgery, I was in no pain and I went Jet-Skiing on Lake Erie."

Neither Schober nor Souaid recommended any kind of radiation or chemotherapy as a follow-up, Randy reports. Nor should they have. Oncology textbooks agree that those treatments can accomplish little or nothing against renal-cell carcinoma, even though many oncologists persist in trying them. "So I went home six days after the surgery and I felt relieved," Randy remembers. "I thought this was all over. I didn't yet know how serious and persistent renal-cell carcinoma can be."

After 10 weeks, Randy was back at work. He hadn't even lost any pay because his co-workers donated enough of their sick days to make sure he received full wages while he was recovering. He also continued working on the renovation of the building he'd bought. And he continued going to Erie for ultrasound checkups every few weeks.

It was on a particular visit that Randy received one of the biggest and least-necessary scares of his entire cancer story. "I went down there by myself and as I waited in the lobby after the sonogram was taken, Dr. Souaid walked in. I stood up to greet him and he said, 'Sit down. It looks like there's a large mass in the bed of the kidney we removed.' He said it was growing fast. Now I had to drive home again and tell my wife, which was no easy thing. A few days later, I went back to Erie for a biopsy. There I was, lying on a gurney in the operating room while they prepped me and lined up the X-ray machine to guide the biopsy needle on its way in. Suddenly the X-ray operator came running out of his little cubicle and shouted, 'There's nothing there. There's nothing there.' What had appeared on the ultrasound as a fast-growing mass most likely was a brief pileup of clotted blood. Yes, the ending of that one was a relief. But I thought there was no reason why they should have put me through an emotional roller coaster like that."

Until January 1993, Randy believed he had probably beaten his cancer. Then, while taking a shower, he felt a small bump under the skin near the right side of his ribs. "It was a hard spot about the size of a BB pellet," he remembers. "I'm amazed I even noticed it." But during his next checkup late that month he showed the bump to his doctors and "they told me not to worry." So Randy went home and for five months watched as the small bump grew until it was about the size of a large marble. Still, he says, his doctors in Erie told him not to worry, although they suggested he have the bump removed. Those doctors did not respond to attempts to query them about Randy's treatment for this book.

Dissatisfied with their reaction, in June 1993 Randy

visited another doctor in Westfield, New York, who felt the lump and immediately set an appointment for outpatient surgery to remove it the following week. "When he slit it open, he said right away that he didn't like the way it looked and he refused to cut it out," Randy recalls. "Instead, he biopsied a little bit of it, and the analysis came back as renal-cell carcinoma."

Now Randy knew the cancer had never been completely cut out of his body. He relayed the biopsy result to his doctors in Erie. "They seemed a bit more concerned than before. But still, no one told me or my wife the true severity of renal-cell cancer," he complains. Schober and Souaid now scheduled Randy for inpatient surgery at Erie's Hamot Medical Center, where his marble-size lump was to be excised by that hospital's chief of surgery. "Cheryl and I wondered why they needed a top doctor like that for something so little," Randy remembers. "But we didn't ask. I guess we just didn't want to know at that point."

After surgery, Schober and Souaid sent Randy to the Erie Cancer Clinic for follow-up therapy. There he was put on a regimen of daily injections of interferon, a drug that sometimes shows anticancer properties. This time it didn't. After five months of regular interferon treatments, Randy discovered another lump in the same area.

"I decided not to monkey around, and I went to Roswell Park," Randy remembers. "I thought at the time that it was the best place in the country for this kind of thing. By the time I got there, I had little hard bumps on my hips and arms, a total of seven or eight." At Roswell Park, Velagapudi and another specialist examined him and concluded that his cancer was spreading throughout his body.

"To me, emotionally it felt just like the first time I had been diagnosed," Randy says. "It was terribly depressing, especially after I'd been told that there was a 99 percent chance I'd be perfectly OK."

Velagapudi immediately scheduled Randy for surgery to remove all his lumps, which Velagapudi called cancer spots. In January 1994, Randy had surgery on his hip, forearm and chest as eight lumps were removed. A week later, biopsy results revealed that only one of the lesions had been malignant.

"To me, this meant that the cancer was back in one spot, but it might not have spread throughout my body, the way Velagapudi said it had," Randy notes. "He told me to come back every two months for CT scans, and I did." After the first of those scans, in March, Velagapudi told him that his body was now clear of cancer. Yet, on his next visit, in May 1994, Velagapudi reported that "they're getting bigger."

"'What's getting bigger?' we asked. We'd thought he was clear the previous time," Cheryl says. She recalls Velagapudi answering that the March scan had actually showed some spots, but he had not mentioned them because "it was in the normal range."

This time, the oncologist told Randy that he had small tumors in both lungs and in a lymph node under his right arm. Like the doctors in Erie, Velagapudi told Randy and Cheryl that chemotherapy and radiation would do him no good. "Go home, enjoy yourself and get things in order," Randy remembers the doctor saying. "We can do nothing for you."

By now Randy's cancer was designated Stage 4 renal-cell carcinoma. "Velegapudi told us I might live six months more, not much longer than that," Randy says. "When I heard that, I could physically feel my heart hit the floor. I remember as we drove home—about 40 miles—Cheryl and I didn't say a word. We were completely devastated."

(Neither Velagapudi nor any other Roswell Park doctor responded to repeated telephone attempts to query them about their treatment of Randy.)

But he didn't stay down long. A short time later, officials from Roswell Park telephoned to say that he might qualify for an experiment on the drug interleukin-2 at the National Institutes of Health (NIH) in Bethesda, Maryland. "I was considered a good candidate because I had had no radiation or chemotherapy, and anything that happened could therefore be attributed to the interleukin," Randy says. "NIH would pay for all my expenses if I went to Bethesda. They said I would have to be in an intensive care unit for 20 days each month I took the treatment, and that I had about a 15 percent chance of surviving the inteleukin itself. That didn't sound good, but we had no other options, so we pretty much decided to do it." Before making the final arrangements to join the NIH experiment, Randy headed to the Chautauqua County seat in Mayville, New York, planning to bargain with the county's insurance administrator. "Because they weren't going to have to pay NIH for my care, I wanted to see if they'd give me extra vacation time or sick days while I was on the treatment. But in the meantime, the last few months, I had also been researching Dr. Stanislaw Burzynski."

Randy heard about Burzynski shortly after the first operation to remove his right kidney, when he tuned into a CBS News Street Stories feature about the doctor. Eventually, he contacted the young mother of one of the patients featured in that story. "When I told her I had renal-cell cancer, she told me about her mother-in-law, who also had renal-cell, with the cancer metastasized to her liver and elsewhere. CT scans at the time showed Burzynski's medicine was working on her, but she later went off the medication because she didn't want to spend so much money on herself, and then she died."

He had also contacted Burzynski's office and spoken with the doctor. "He told me he had treated only a half dozen people with renal-cell," Randy reports. "I was favorably impressed that he didn't make any big claims." But he was still unsure about the doctor. So he checked with the AMA and discovered that Burzynski was a member in good standing. And he paid the Houston Chronicle $5 for a compendium of newspaper clippings about Burzynski and his antineoplaston medication. Randy also asked the Texas attorney general's office for a list of all lawsuits filed against Burzynski and discovered that the only one on record had been filed by the Texas Medical Association. "I was struck by the fact that no suits had ever been filed by patients, when everyone knows how common malpractice suits are," Randy remembers. "And from reading the Houston Chronicle clippings, I saw quotes from patients who said he had helped them, as well as quotes from doctors saying he was a quack. I soon saw the direction things were going." Randy thought about all this as he sat in his meeting with the county insurance administrator. Just as the session was about to break up and he was almost resigned to going to Bethesda, he spoke up, saying to the administrator, "I'm going to ask you something. Have you ever heard of a doctor named Burzynski?"

He vividly remembers the response from the administrator and his secretary, who took notes on the session. "They both said they knew about Burzynski and had sent one patient to him before. I was kind of shocked. And I couldn't wait to tell my wife that the insurance would cover this. So I went right home and called the NIH and told them I wasn't coming. Then I called and asked Velagapudi about

Burzynski. He said he had never heard of him, and that going there was probably a waste of time and money."

Now Randy believed that some kind of treatment was possible. What made it more attractive was that he would have to pay only for airfare and hotel bills in Houston. "So we went down there on May 24, 1994, less than a month after the doctors at Roswell Park told me I was terminal and should get my affairs in order," he relates. "I felt good that Burzynski is a Polish doctor. I'm Polish, too. My parents changed the family name from Gostomski because they wanted to make life in this country a little easier for their kids.

"But I still expected to find a storefront clinic with plywood on the windows and the doctor working in a little office behind it. So I was favorably impressed to see that his place is in a modern building and looks the way a medical office should."

Cheryl remained a bit skeptical. "This seemed like an off-the-wall thing," she says. "And there we were, with our two-year-old in tow. But we still went ahead."

Once in Burzynski's waiting room, Randy began chatting with other patients, asking about their case histories. The more he heard, the better he felt. "I had checked him out, but I still wanted more information, and everyone there cooperated. It didn't feel like any cancer clinic we'd seen so far," he remembers. "There were smiles. People were talking to each other. You actually felt hope in the air. And you did not sense the smell of death like we had everywhere else we'd tried."

Randy felt a sense of unreality as he and Cheryl waited in a small examining room for Burzynski. "I mean, I was waiting for this guy I'd seen on TV," he explains. "But when he came in, he acted like a doctor, all business in his white coat, with all kinds of medical papers in his arms. He told me he had had only seven renal-cell patients and the outcome with them was 50-50. But all the others had been weaker than me because they'd had chemotherapy, even though it does no good for this kind of cancer. And 50-50 were better odds than Roswell Park and the NIH had given me."

But Randy was still not completely satisfied or trusting. "So there in that little room, I looked him square in the eye and I said, 'Doc, tell me the truth. What are my chances?' He was very matter-of-fact and said, 'You should feel some tumor breakdown soon and be cancer-free in six months.' Then he just walked out. So I figured he was either a quack, or curing cancer was routine around there. I looked over at my wife, who had our two-year-old son on her lap and tears running down her cheek. I figured I was over the hump. And six months later, to the month, I was cancer-free."

"We got back in the cab after that visit and went to a vascular surgeon to have a Hickman catheter installed in Randy's chest," Cheryl continues. "The next morning we were at the clinic to start treatment."

Again, Randy spent the morning quizzing and chatting up other patients. "The more I talked to them, the better I felt. These people were getting results."

Randy and Cheryl stayed in Houston for 11 days, learning to calculate his dosage and sterilize his new catheter regularly. Eventually, they came to feel almost as if they were on vacation. Burzynski required Randy to infuse antineoplastons three hours out of each eight hours. When he wasn't attached to his pump, he'd lie by the hotel swimming pool or play basketball at the park.

But after just two days on the medication, Randy began to feel mildly ill. "It felt like a bit of the flu," he says. "I upchucked a little. And I had a mild fever. Burzynski seemed pleased to hear that. He said it was the body's initial reaction to tumor breakdown, and it would not last long. It was over in less than a day—about three hours."

The Gosses carted home nine crates of antineoplastons from that trip, enough to last six weeks. They returned to Houston every three months after that, with Randy undergoing CT scans in Buffalo before each visit. "In the first scan, it was clear that my tumors were decreasing," he recalls. "The next one was even better, and in the last week of November 1994, my scan finally showed no cancer. I was simply overjoyed. Something had worked, after I'd been told that nothing worked on renal-cell cancer. I've been clear ever since, and I can't help wondering why this guy can be helping people, but places like Roswell Park don't know about him and don't seem to want to."

Randy began speaking publicly in the Buffalo area about Burzynski and his experience soon after his scans became clear. During one 1995 appearance before a prostate cancer support group, he noticed Dr. Robert Huben, Roswell Park's chief of urology, come in and take a seat in the rear to listen. After Randy spoke for 45 minutes about his cancer experience, a listener inquired about Roswell Park's reaction to his history. "I paused about five seconds or so before answering, and while I paused, Huben stood up and said, 'Let me answer that. I have heard Mr. Goss and what he has said is true. He did have renal-cell carcinoma and he did go to Houston. But can we say the medicine cured him? No. We have seen a lot of spontaneous remissions in renal-cell carcinoma.'"

Yet the American Cancer Society reports that there are almost no such cases. Which leaves Randy shaking his head. "Regular medicine wants to ignore Burzynski and his antineoplastons if it possibly can," he believes. "It makes me wonder if our government and the medical profession really want to see a cancer cure."

Postscript

DUNKIRK, N.Y., midyear 2000—For Randy Goss, his trip to a 1999 PGA senior golf tournament in Pittsburgh, Pa. was a highlight of his life. "I got to meet [professional golfers] Bruce Devlin and Gary Player and they were really friendly to me."

Meeting those hall-of-famers gave was a tremendous thrill for Randy, a short but strong man whose new favorite pastime is golfing every chance he gets. "Hey, I had back-to-back eagles in one round," he says. "My longest drive last year was 360 yards. Not bad for a guy who's supposed to be dead."

Randy is far from dead. In remission since November 1994, he's now an official five-year cure that can be ascribed to nothing other than antineoplastons. "I'm in perfect health, better health than I've ever been in my life. Even my kidney function from the one kidney I have left is OK."

Randy's full life still includes his demanding, very physical job at the county's recycling plant. He's even taken up weight-lifting. But he's closed the restaurant he once owned and is trying to sell the building. "I realized life is too short to be all wrapped up in a business that takes as much time as a restaurant. I want to enjoy life.

"I know I can do that only because of Dr. Burzynski and his treatment," Randy says. "That's why I still write people about the treatment on behalf of the Burzynski Patient Group and why I still write to politicians about this. I've probably talked to over 2,000 people about this. I've given up on local politics, given up on being an officer in clubs. Dr. Burzynski is the only cause I still work on. I can't give up on him and his medicine because they're the reason I'm still here."

CHAPTER 5

The FDA Declares War

It was as if the United States had declared war on Switzerland and planned to make it one of attrition. When the FDA sued Dr. Stanislaw Burzynski in the spring of 1983, it brought to bear all the federal government's resources, lawyers and money against a tiny operation that was in essence a one-man, one-idea, one-product business. But the FDA could not know that it was in for some attrition of its own. For, like little Switzerland, whose scenic mountains hide a staggering array of military hardware, the surface appearance of Burzynski's clinic and his chemical-processing plant provided few clues about the depth and durability of the resistance he would mount and the support he would eventually inspire.

At first, the FDA sought simply to close Burzynski down. The government lawsuit against the doctor and his research institute aimed "to force the permanent cessation of all their scientific and medical work on the development, manufacture, and administration of antineoplastons." But the government did not reckon with the most potent force Burzynski could marshal: his patients. When Burzynski fought back against the lawsuit, his patients were on his side, filing *amicus curiae* (friend of the court) briefs and making sure U.S. District Judge Gabrielle McDonald knew there was much more at stake than the life of Burzynski's business. They made certain she knew they believed their very lives were also on the line.

The 1983 lawsuit would become the opening battle of a war that stretched into the late 1990s, a conflict that even two criminal trials may not have ended. For Burzynski had done the unthinkable: It wasn't so much his finding a cure for some cancers that offended the federal agency—the FDA never really disputed that—it was that Burzynski had not played its game. He had neither filed an application for an IND permit nor submitted antineoplastons to Phase 2 clinical trials in which the FDA could determine the extent of their efficacy. The bureaucrats became furious because he had all but ignored the FDA after getting its preliminary verbal approval to administer his drug within the state of Texas. Their anger would eventually find its outlet in four grand jury investigations, myriad court proceedings and questionable clinical trials conducted by the NCI.

But when Burzynski got word of the first lawsuit as he made his way home from an Easter week meeting in Philadelphia, he had no way of knowing that his life was about to be plagued by a welter of court appearances and legal technicalities. "When the suit was first filed, it affected me horribly," he recalls. "No one had ever sued me. Not a single patient had ever sued for malpractice or anything else. No employee ever sued me over anything. Now I suddenly had to spend a lot of time in court. It affected my work, and it was terribly disappointing."

The problem was not just the FDA lawsuit. The fallout from that action included a landslide of other legal moves. "All our creditors thought we would be put out of business, so everyone suddenly wanted their money instantly," Burzynski says. At least 18 lawsuits materialized in the next few months, including one from a businessman who earlier had tried to help Burzynski by lending him money, with his laboratory equipment as collateral. "He suddenly demanded that we assemble all the equipment in front of City Hall, literally, and turn it over to him," Burzynski would laugh later. At the same time, insurance companies that had been paying patient claims began to turn them down. "So from a situation where everything was in balance, suddenly our revenue was down 50 percent. But the patients kept coming," Burzynski says. In fact, his clinic's doors never closed for a single day because of any legal action.

If the first lawsuit accomplished anything positive for Burzynski, it was to spur him to seek his first-ever IND. One point in the government complaint was that Burzynski had never even applied for government approval for his medication. Normally, when pharmaceutical companies apply for INDs for promising new medications, the approval process takes only a matter of weeks. On the advice of his attorneys, Burzynski immediately set to work on an IND application and filed it before the FDA lawsuit was heard by Judge McDonald in early May 1983. But there would be no routine rubber-stamp approval for Burzynski, as there usually is for established drugmakers.

The FDA turned down the IND application, claiming that there was no proof antineoplastons worked. The agency's rejection letter claimed Burzynski had failed "to furnish information indicating that Antineoplaston A10...has activity against malignant cells of animal or human origin or against animal tumors."

That statement ignored hundreds of pages of published papers, most in peer-reviewed journals, about the effectiveness of antineoplastons against test-tube cancer-cell cultures. It ignored the patient files submitted with the application. Instead, the FDA demanded statements from "the Quality Assurance Unit" specifying when inspections (of the synthesizing plant) were made. It asked for information verifying that Burzynski had permission of an institutional review board to use the drug on human patients. And it demanded detailed information on animal tests.

Of course, Burzynski had no formal quality assurance unit, as most pharmaceutical companies do. And he had gone into business for himself in part because the institutional review boards at Baylor and Park Plaza Hospital refused him the very permission the FDA now demanded he get. As he had noted in 1977, it was impossible to obtain an IND without permission from an institutional review board, but the boards refused permission because he had no IND. This sort of circular illogic would plague Burzynski's IND application for the next six years. He would not receive approval for his first IND until 1989, when Congress began pressing the FDA to open its approval process to more alternative medications. Burzynski, of course, always maintained that antineoplastons were not classic "alternative medicine." They are based on scientific evidence and empirical scientific reality, not a placebo effect or anything fanciful, he contends. Still, he was happy to benefit from changes in the FDA's legislative-oversight climate.

But before Burzynski could pursue his first IND beyond simply applying for it, he had to make sure that his clinic and manufacturing facility would not be closed down by the FDA's sudden action. And federal authorities were open and definite about their determination to shut him down completely. If Judge McDonald would not issue an injunction that put Burzynski out of business permanently, they declared, they would nevertheless persist in their campaign.

The prosecutors appealed to the judge for a quick and definitive anti-Burzynski ruling. Said their motion for a summary judgment against Burzynski: "If this court declines to grant the injunctive relief sought by the government, thus permitting continued manufacturing and distribution of antineoplastons by [Burzynski] in violation of the Food, Drug and Cosmetic Act, the government would then be obliged to pursue other, less efficient remedies, such as actions for seizure and condemnation of the drugs or criminal prosecution of individuals who violated the act with respect to the drugs. This court would then be faced with ordering the government not to undertake such enforcement actions, if the court truly desired to allow the continued manufacture and distribution of the drugs." In short, the FDA was declaring that unless the judge specifically ordered its campaign to stop, the agency would never give up its effort to destroy Burzynski, his clinic and his drug-manufacturing plant.

That statement was signed by two Department of Justice lawyers and by Robert Spiller Jr., the FDA's associate chief counsel for enforcement. It turned out to be a road map for the struggle that took place over the next 14 years, as the government would repeatedly try to shut down Burzynski by pursuing those "other, less efficient remedies." For, after hearing all the evidence the government could bring to bear, Judge McDonald issued a ruling that straddled the fence between Burzynski and his tormentors.

During McDonald's two-day hearing on the motion for an immediate injunction, the FDA claimed that Burzynski was violating federal law by distributing his antineoplastons in interstate commerce. It also argued that the medication was "adulterated" because Burzynski's manufacturing methods and controls did not comply with the FDA's good manufacturing practice regulations. More than a dozen Burzynski patients were allowed to intervene and testify during the hearing, one reason for the judge's apparent compromise ruling.

On the surface, the order Judge McDonald issued when the intense hearing ended appeared to give the government almost everything it wanted. Burzynski was ordered to stop shipping and selling antineoplastons across state lines until such time as they might be approved by the FDA. He was told to bring his making of synthetic antineoplastons into compliance with good manufacturing practice.

But the order stopped far short of forcing him out of business. In fact, the judge made it plain that she didn't want Burzynski's clinic shut down. Her ruling: "Nothing contained herein shall be construed as restraining, enjoining, or in any way prohibiting the defendant's manufacture, processing, packing, holding, promotion, labeling, sale, or distribution of the antineoplaston A10 or of any similar article however designated [provided articles are not falsely labeled or marked] when that manufacture, processing, packing, holding, promotion, labeling, sale, or distribution is undertaken strictly and wholly intrastate."

So the judge was not even counting on lawyers for both Burzynski and the FDA to apply what law students call the first rule of injunctions—that which is not specifically forbidden in an injunction is permitted. This injunction not only spelled out what Burzynski could not do but also stressed that he would be able to continue operating as before, so long as he kept his sales within Texas state lines. Burzynski's lawyers would later argue that the first rule of injunctions did apply to his treatment of out-of-state patients who later carried antineoplastons home with them. "Judge McDonald's decision does not contain the specific, concrete words that presumably she was capable of uttering, namely that 'Dr. Burzynski is prohibited from treating out-of-state patients;'" Michael Ramsey and Richard Jaffe would argue in a brief filed in early 1996. This point was the basis for Burzynski's business practices through the late 1980s and early 1990s.

But the motion signed by Spiller before Judge McDonald's hearing had made it clear that the FDA would never be satisfied with a ruling like hers. And the agency was not.

After that injunction, the FDA would spend almost two years gathering more information to use in a criminal action against Burzynski. Agency investigator Kenneth Ewing interviewed dozens of Burzynski employees and patients, trying to prove that Burzynski cheated his patients, that he continued to ship antineoplastons over state lines despite the injunction, and that he profiteered. The affidavits signed by several former employees formed the basis for a search warrant Ewing and more than a dozen federal agents executed on July 17, 1985. They seized 11 file cabinets filled with more than 200,000 medical documents, most of them the records of Burzynski's patient treatments. One patient who was being examined when the raid took place said the agents ransacked Burzynski's clinic, looking through "every drawer, every trash can, every filing cabinet, every treatment room." They riffled through his personal correspondence and searched through his briefcase. Burzynski never did get the confiscated records back. Under an order from Judge McDonald, though, he was later permitted to set up a copying machine (at his expense) in the FDA building, almost 20 miles from his office, where he or his staff could copy medical records as needed. "This forced us to spend many hours driving and searching for patients' records when they would come to see us," Burzynski says. "It was obviously intended as harassment."

And what did the affidavits obtained by Ewing reveal? Copies in which the names of the witnesses are blacked out show that the FDA found one Burzynski patient in Ohio who died after trying the antineoplaston treatment for a few weeks and then giving up on it. His widow complained that Burzynski did not return the full initial deposit she and her husband made, even after their insurance company had paid the doctor in full. Responds Burzynski, "Sometimes these repayments were delayed in those difficult early days because we had a lot of financial problems. But eventually, patients were always repaid whatever they were entitled to. No patient has ever sued me for overcharging."

Another affidavit intended to show that Burzynski was profiteering appears to demonstrate just the opposite. This document, provided by a former Burzynski bookkeeper whose name was blacked out, contended that in 1983, Burzynski's clinic grossed an average of $220,000 to $230,000 per month. Burzynski's salary during that year was pegged at $91,812, while that of his wife—who was also an M.D.—was $42,000. His brother Tadeus, in charge of production, received $70,000. Burzynski's and his wife's salaries were both well below the average income of physicians in Houston that year, which was just less than $120,000.

Other affidavits contended that packages were frequently sent out of state via Purolator courier service, but the witnesses who provided those documents never charged that Burzynski was personally involved in either packing or shipping antineoplastons, which would have violated Judge McDonald's edict—or that they ever heard him order an out-of-state shipment. Most witnesses who spoke to Ewing also could not be certain that the interstate packages they saw contained antineoplastons.

Shortly after the raid, prosecutors called Burzynski before a federal grand jury for the first time. He would appear before three other panels before one eventually indicted him in November 1995. Such proceedings are secret, with all participants except the witnesses themselves forbidden by law from revealing their content. Following is Burzynski's version of what transpired behind the grand jury's closed doors: "In 1985, the session was all about our production records. They subpoenaed practically all our production records from the very beginning. These documents filled a small room. Then the prosecutors asked for details of who signed which document. They acted surprised when I sometimes didn't recognize someone's signature. Maybe they didn't understand that we had dozens of employees."

The 1985 grand jury returned no indictment, perhaps because of the flimsy nature of the affidavits Ewing had obtained.

But Burzynski was not to get off the hook so easily. The 1983 statement by Spiller and the Department of Justice had made this clear. So in 1986, he was again called to appear before the grand jury in downtown Houston. This time, Burzynski says, "They wanted us to give them even more data. They wanted patient records. They wanted to know everything about production of antineoplastons. They took a very broad approach. At the time, we were also involved in a lawsuit against the Aetna insurance company over payments for treatment, and they wanted the same information. We brought all the data, but the meeting before the grand jury never happened." Burzynski says he suspected that there was collusion between the FDA and the insurance companies that were resisting some of his patients' claims for payment. This idea is supported by a statement from Ewing, whose July 16, 1985, affidavit in support of the search warrant states that he acted after consulting officials of the Metropolitan Insurance Companies of Schenectady, New York, which administered the group health insurance plan for General Electric employees.

Burzynski now had several years of respite from possible criminal prosecution. But in 1991, he was again called before the grand jury. He spent a full day testifying. "They asked about treatment and production," he remembers. "There were a lot of questions about one of the members of our board of directors, Mike Driscoll." Driscoll, the elected Harris County (Houston) attorney and a Democrat, was the husband of a former Burzynski patient. "It seemed to me that they might have actually been after Driscoll, not me," Burzynski says. "He was a Democrat, and these were Republicans, and he was about to run for reelection in 1992. But they asked me questions about all aspects of my business. I wanted to speak directly to the grand jury and not merely answer the prosecutors' questions. Finally, I was allowed just two minutes to talk to them. I was not indicted."

Again, Burzynski had a few years off between grand jury appearances. Then his clinic was raided in March 1995; thousands of documents were confiscated. Later, he was summoned for repeated testimony in the spring and summer of 1995. "They asked about clinical trials, about treating patients, about bank accounts. It seemed like nothing extraordinary. But now they had three assistant U.S. attorneys, including Mike Clark, so maybe it meant they were more serious than before."

This time, Burzynski was indicted on 75 counts of contempt of court, interstate shipment of an unapproved drug and insurance fraud. Clark, chief of the criminal division in the Houston U.S. attorney's office, would later become his chief prosecutor.

The long breaks between his grand jury appearances were never simply relaxed time, free of legal or scientific entanglements. Even as the FDA was hounding Burzynski, forcing him before one grand jury after another in its effort to shut down his operation, the doctor-scientist never gave up on the possibility of obtaining government approval for use of antineoplastons in human patients. One-time Burzynski lawyer John Johnson recalls accompanying him to a meeting at the FDA's Rockville, Maryland, headquarters in late 1984. "The purpose was to try to resolve some of our problems with them," Johnson says. "They brought in about 10 of their doctors, and Burzynski had Tom Muldoon come up from Georgia." Muldoon had performed some laboratory tests on antineoplastons at the Medical College of Georgia. "Muldoon showed them slides and laboratory analysis of how well the medicine worked in the test tube and in mice," Johnson recalls. "It was clear that the antineoplastons worked to stop progression of cancers. Burzynski showed them some patient case histories. All these doctors were amazed and after a while there was dead silence. Then one doctor spoke up and said, 'Dr. Burzynski, do you know of any other drug that can stop lung cancer?' He said he didn't. Then I asked her, 'Do you know of any?' She said, 'I don't know.' And then after the meeting, they just started acting like bureaucrats again. It had no real impact on them."

There were also repeated lawsuits against insurance companies and a tangled case before the Texas board of medical examiners, in which an attempt to lift or limit Burzynski's medical license dragged on for more than a decade.

"We had followed his case since about 1978," claimed Dennis Baker, chief of the Texas Health Department's

Bureau of Food and Drug Safety. "We were the ones who complained to the medical board that he was using unapproved drugs on patients. Our basic complaint was that the drugs had neither Investigational New Drug permits nor any new drug approval. Hence, they were in violation of both state and federal law. We have no evidence that his drug works. He has not subjected it to independent scientific testing. Our foremost effort is to protect a susceptible population, those with terminal illnesses. This drug might interfere with conventional therapy, or it might simply be a waste of their money. What matters to us is that he must basically comply with what is required to put a new drug on the market."

Neither the state of Texas nor the FDA makes any special provisions for small companies that lack the $400 million or more it normally takes to bring a new drug through the approval process. This fact of life essentially gives control of all new drugs to a few big companies that can afford to take them through the process, often generating truckloads of reports along the way.

The Texas authorities also ignored the fact that at the very time they were trying to limit his license, Burzynski was negotiating terms of a major Phase 2 clinical trial in which the NCI planned to test the efficacy of antineoplastons. And they disregarded information presented to them about ongoing and successful tests of antineoplastons at the University of Kurume in Japan, where the drug has been used for years to treat liver and kidney cancers, including an apparent cure of the liver cancer suffered by that university's president.

Texas officials brought their first licensing case against Burzynski in 1988 after he appeared on the nationally syndicated Sally Jessy Raphael television talk show, the same appearance that moved terminal brain tumor patient Pamela Winningham to try antineoplastons. "We had many calls after that appearance and we had to explain that antineoplastons were not approved in Texas," says Baker. "We had to spend a lot of time explaining this." The state health officer first wrote Burzynski a warning letter, advising him to stop using antineoplastons. Then he took the case to the state board of medical examiners, which held hearings in Austin in the summer of 1993. The Health Department demanded that Burzynski destroy all his antineoplastons, stop making them and pay a fine of $25,000 a day for each day he had manufactured each of his two synthetic antineoplastons.

Burzynski patients promptly deluged the medical board with letters, more than 250 writing in detail about their recoveries. Some family members of former patients wrote to say Burzynski's treatment had eased the last months or years of their relatives' lives. But those stories could be dismissed by scientists as mere "anecdotes." The most persuasive testimony in the licensing case came from Dr. Nicholas Patronas, chief of the neuroradiology section at the NIH. Patronas, a specialist in reading scans and X-rays of cranial tumors, had been part of a panel sent from the NCI to evaluate some of Burzynski's patient case histories in 1991. Of the cases he examined, Patronas testified that "it's amazing, the fact that they are living and doing so well.... These particular individuals not only survived, but they didn't have major side effects. I think it is impressive and unbelievable." Patronas said he had never seen any treatment work so well against brain cancers. He evaluated a series of Burzynski's brain tumor patients, including Winningham, he said, and testified that for those patients he evaluated who were still on antineoplastons, taking them off the drug would mean certain death.

But the medical board was more persuaded by the Health Department's objections to Burzynski's supposed violations of the letter of the law than by the lives it now knew he had saved. The board voted to place his license on probation, insisting that he stop publicizing antineoplastons as an anticancer therapy. Burzynski appealed in a state trial court and won. He hoped the license matter was over. But the battle of dueling appeals continued as the medical board appealed that ruling and an appellate court reinstated probation, leaving Burzynski uncertain how long or in what manner he could practice medicine, even if he were acquitted in the federal criminal trial.

Almost as vexing were the numerous insurance lawsuits he was forced to fight. The first major action came in 1985, shortly after his first grand jury appearance. This suit originated when a breast cancer patient who had responded to antineoplastons early in treatment stopped taking the drug and sued the Aetna Life Insurance Co., trying to force it to repay the $70,000 she had spent. Burzynski's lawyers convinced him to join the patient suit, and Aetna responded with a civil action against Burzynski under the federal Racketeer Influenced and Corrupt Organizations (RICO) Act. Aetna charged that Burzynski used antineoplastons solely to file insurance claims. "Aetna was trying to put us out of business," Burzynski says. "So after a judge dismissed their entire suit against us, we then sued them for $190 million. We have evidence they contacted other insurance companies and advised them not to pay our claims."

Simeon T. Lake 3rd, the same federal judge who would preside over Burzynski's criminal trials, twice dismissed his lawsuit against Aetna and twice was reversed by higher courts. He declared in pre-trial interviews that this history had no influence on any of his rulings—and his decision to throw out all insurance fraud charges after the jury hung in the first trial bears him out.

In the long run, the most damaging of the insurance company lawsuits was filed in 1989 by the trustees of the Northwest Laundry and Dry Cleaners Health & Welfare Trust Fund. In this case, Burzynski submitted claim forms to the fund and received more than $90,000 for treating Huey Roberts, an Oregon resident and patient who later died of esophageal cancer. A trial court ruled that Burzynski's treating Roberts violated both Judge McDonald's 1983 injunction and a more recent Texas law prohibiting doctors from administering drugs that lack FDA approval. The 5th U.S. Circuit Court of Appeals upheld that ruling, saying health insurance should cover only treatments that "in accordance with accepted medical standards...could not have been omitted without adversely affecting the patient's condition." This left little room for anything new, inventive or unusual, and clearly excluded antineoplastons. The court also ruled that Burzynski defrauded Northwest Laundry by failing to disclose that using antineoplastons on Roberts was illegal. The judges added that the plight of terminally ill patients like Roberts "commands sympathy, but also attracts opportunists...while we do not impute evil motives to Dr. Burzynski, neither can we conclude that he is beyond the laws written to protect his patients." In short, the court said Burzynski had no right to treat Roberts—no matter what Roberts wanted—because the FDA had not yet given him permission to treat patients who carry his medication across state lines.

For years after, whenever FDA officials were asked for information about Burzynski, they responded by quickly sending out copies of that Northwest Laundry decision.

"This court says he's a fraud," the FDA's spokesman once told a reporter, stopping short of applying the same pejorative to antineoplastons.

Burzynski, however, dismisses all his legal troubles. "They are the result of my challenging a scientific paradigm," he says. "Anytime someone challenges the accepted way of thinking, he has trouble. Look at Galileo. Look at Copernicus. I know I will win in the long run because I have something very good."

The Zachary McConnell Story

"Why Won't the FDA Let Me Have My Medicine?"

Dear President Clinton, Why wont you stop the FDA from taking my antineoplastons from me? You could fire the man who won't let me have my medicine. I really want my medicine! I don't want to have cancer anymore.

—Exact text of a handwritten letter sent to the White House
by Zachary McConnell in July 1996

Dear Doctor, Why are you cuting me off this medicine? It's not doing anything bad to me. It's fighting off the tiny cancer cells and that's good, isn't it? I don't want to have cancer anymore .... Antineoplastons make me feel better. Radition gives me headaches and makes me throw up. Please change your mind.

—From a handwritten letter sent by Zachary McConnell to
an official of the Food and Drug Administration in July 1996

Romping on the playground of McDowell Mountain Elementary School in the Phoenix suburb of Fountain Hills, Arizona, on a sunny, warm September day in 1996, Zachary McConnell gave few clues of the ordeal he'd undergone in the past year, an ordeal that was not over yet. The towheaded boy rode the slides and climbed the monkey bars as if there were no differences between him and his second-grade classmates. But there was a huge difference.

For Zac was the only child on the playground with a brain tumor. Because of it, he missed all but the first week of his first-grade year. During that time, he underwent brain surgery, followed by a five-month course of intensive chemotherapy. Later, he became one of the focal points of the political struggle over antineoplastons. And Zac, an uncommonly perceptive boy, understood virtually everything going on around him.

"I wrote those letters because I thought they might respond better to a kid than to grown-ups," he said, pausing in his play and speaking eloquently about a concept few other seven-year-olds could grasp.

"It's been impossible to put anything over on Zac," smiled his father, Shawn. "You can't fool him for long. He figures it out. So we told him very early what his cancer was, which was basically that there was something in his head that didn't belong there, and that we were going to get it out. He picked up a lot more from just overhearing adult conversations. And he did ask me once if he was going to die. I told him no."

Coping with their precocious son was never completely easy for Shawn and Desiree McConnell. Both young parents were reared in the Phoenix area after being born elsewhere, Shawn in Southern California and Desiree in Ohio. He was 22 and she 17 when they met in the apartment complex where both lived. Desiree dated Shawn's one-time roommate for a while, but Shawn was the one who became deeply interested in her. Desiree gave birth to Zac about a year after the couple met.

"I've never seen a father and son as close as Shawn and Zac were those first couple of years," remembered Desiree. "But we had some really hard times. Zac is probably the reason we're still together. If he hadn't been there, I'm not at all sure we'd have had the motivation to stay together."

Because they needed to support Zac and because the couple decided that Desiree should stay home to care for him, Shawn dropped out of school after two years at Mesa Community College and opened a window-washing business. Desiree's schooling ended with her high school graduation. Even after Zac's sister, Samantha, arrived in 1992, he remained a primary focus of the couple's attention. They filled their rented home with Dr. Seuss books and Legos for both kids. They constantly read to him. They noted with pride Zac's surging reading skills. By the time he reached second grade, he was reading on the ninth-grade level. And since neither child ever went to day care before starting elementary school, both parents knew their every idiosyncrasy.

So when Zac began suffering headaches and vomiting during the summer of 1995, Desiree and Shawn quickly knew something was wrong. "He would have both the headaches and the vomiting at the same time, like clockwork at about 10 a.m.," Desiree remembered. "After he'd vomit, though, the headache would leave, and then he'd instantly go to sleep. While he had the headaches, he would cuss and swear and hit me—very different from the way he was before. I couldn't believe this was my son. Then he'd wake up from these sleeps and he'd run around and play like nothing had happened."

But the headaches didn't come every day, so Zac's parents were often lulled into thinking they were of no significance. "He could go a week and a half with nothing happening, then he'd suddenly get a headache and vomit," Shawn said. After his second attack, they took Zac to their family doctor, a naturopath. "Don't worry," they were counseled. "It's probably just a food allergy." So the McConnells suffered through another four weeks of intermittent attacks while the naturopath tried to find the cause. When Shawn asked if Zac might have a brain tumor, the doctor assured him that could not be. "A brain tumor would cause constant pain and headaches," he told him. The parents eventually became disillusioned with their naturopath, who often couldn't be reached when Zac suffered a severe headache—he was off taping a radio show.

"So we made an appointment with a neurologist," Shawn recalls. It was the first week of Zac's first-grade year, the last week of August 1995. "She didn't think it was a brain tumor, either, because Zac had no classic symptoms except occasional lethargy, headaches and vomiting. But she ordered an MRI just in case. 'We'll do it just so we can check off a brain tumor as even a possibility,' she said."

The imaging session was on a Saturday morning. "We waited and waited and waited," Shawn recalled. "After a while, I began to suspect that something was wrong. Finally, a nurse came out and asked us to come to a phone to talk to the neurologist. That's when we knew."

The neurologist told them Zac had a brain tumor, but she didn't know what kind or how large it was. She immediately sent the family to the emergency room at Good Samaritan Regional Medical Center, where two floors assume a separate identity as the Phoenix Children's Hospital. For Shawn, this was the worst day of Zac's entire cancer odyssey.

"They put us in a little room, and the emergency room doctors left the MRI films hanging on a screen outside the room," Shawn said. "Now, I'm not trained to read X-rays—I was a music major in college—but I saw a giant white mass in those pictures." The tumor itself was the size of a golf ball. With the edema, or swollen tissue around it, it took up about one-third of the space in Zac's skull, and any layman could see something was wrong. "You could actually see how it was squashing his brain over to one side,"

Shawn added.

Soon the family was moved to the intensive care floor of the children's hospital, where they met neurosurgeon Dr. David Moss, who was to guide them though much of the next few months. "It was a strange feeling in the hospital," Shawn said. "The nurses and the residents all looked at us with a sense of dread. You could tell by their attitude and their unwillingness to make eye contact that they were sure our son was going to die."

For Shawn and Desiree, that first day in the hospital was like being thrown weaponless into a raging battle. "We thought we were just going for a test that would check off a brain tumor as any kind of possibility," Shawn said. "But now we were thrown into a war zone. We never anticipated anything like it that morning. But of course, if we'd waited another three weeks, Zac would have been in a coma."

And there was never any doubt that Zac would have brain surgery to remove as much of the tumor as possible.

Neurosurgeon Moss was of little comfort that first day. His educated guess on reading the MRI was that the mass was a primitive neuroectodermal tumor, usually called a PNET (or medulloblastoma). He also guessed that it would have "fingers" extending into nooks and crannies of Zac's brain. "We were standing with him and two residents in a narrow hallway, with the scans hanging on light boxes on the wall," remembers Shawn. "He started using the term five-year survival rate. Zac was then six, so I asked what the odds were of Zac living until he was 11. He said it was just one in three that Zac would survive the operation without major handicaps. There also could be breathing difficulties, a stroke, coma or even paralysis of his left side. It was clear they really expected the surgery to harm Zac in some way."

The couple was given two days to enjoy their son the way they had always known him. Moss didn't want to operate that Saturday. He wanted Zac to be treated with an antiinflammatory steroid for two days before the surgery in order to reduce the swelling in his brain. And he wanted to wait until he could have his usual surgical team at hand the following Monday.

"We didn't know how Zac would be when this surgery was over," Shawn admitted. "It was the worst feeling of my life." During those two days of terror, the parents' firm religious faith began to play a major role. "I had a vivid image, maybe a vision, that Sunday as I drove home from the hospital in a daze to get a change of clothes," Shawn remembered. "I saw this image of Jesus, bearded and looking like he does in the pictures you see, standing over Zac in the operating room with the doctors. He wasn't all gowned and scrubbed the way they were. A very bright light was coming from his hands, and he turned to me and said, 'Everything is going to be OK.'"

Moss had guessed that the operation would last four to six hours. Shawn accompanied his son into the operating room, staying by his side until the anesthesia put Zac to sleep. At the nurses' insistence, he removed Zac's socks before the operation began. "So then we sat in the waiting room together," Desiree said, "each of us holding one of Zac's little socks. We'd wind them around our fingers and play with them as if they were worry beads."

Two hours after the operation began, Moss emerged from surgery wearing a big smile. "We got it all," he grinned. Later he told the McConnells that "there was something strange about this tumor. It was encapsulated and it almost looked as if it wanted to come out. It had very distinct borders, when most PNETs have a lot of fingers running in many directions." Shawn wasn't sure, but he wondered immediately if what he saw during his dazed drive the day before surgery had anything to do with this outcome.

There was, in any case, little divine about what followed. During the week after surgery, while Zac still languished in the hospital, radio-oncologist Michael Sapozink delivered the pathologist's report. The tumor was definitely a PNET, the report said: "malignant small blue cell tumor (PNET)." Unless Zac underwent a months-long course of chemotherapy and radiation, the tumor would surely grow back and Zac would die, Sapozink told the McConnells. He recommended that they enroll Zac in an ongoing Phase 2 clinical trial to assess the efficacy of aggressive chemotherapy, followed by radiation of the entire brain and spine. The couple would sign a consent form subjecting their son to a regimen of chemotherapy using vincristine, cisplatin, cyclophosphamide, carboplatin and vincristine again. The chemicals would kill cancer cells that remained in Zac's body, Sapozink assured, but they could also wreak havoc on healthy tissue.

Among the possible side effects listed on the consent form the parents and Sapozink signed were muscle weakness, constipation, hoarseness, lowered red and white blood-cell counts, easy bleeding or bruising, decreased ability to fight infection, sterility, vomiting and nausea, kidney damage, hearing loss, diarrhea, headaches, drowsiness, hair loss, liver damage and an increased risk of developing leukemia at a later date. The consent form also noted that "an increase in life expectancy cannot be guaranteed by participation in this study."

Despite this lack of any guarantee of success, the McConnells agreed. They would do almost anything to save their son. Of course, the parents had a hard time believing he needed the sort of suffering outlined in the consent form. When Zac came home from the hospital six days after surgery, "he was energetic, bouncing off the walls," recalled Desiree. "There was no more irritability. He was a sweetheart. And he hadn't lost a thing mentally. He even made a musical instrument like a washboard out of the staples in the side of his head. There were 38 above his right ear." Zac had a vigorous, joyful three weeks at home before starting chemotherapy. "We wanted to say 'Forget it,'" his mother said. "He seemed perfectly OK."

This made the act of starting him on chemotherapy difficult for his parents. "It was just so hard to take this healthy, happy boy and see the first batch of cisplatin in an IV bag dripping into his arm," said Shawn. But Zac would undergo five three-week regimes, three of which would require a week's hospitalization as they began. He wound up spending 10 days in the hospital after each chemotherapy course, too, and he soon had neither white blood cells nor an operative immune system, laying him open to every conceivable illness. "Yet we had to fight sometimes to get him into a private room in the hospital," Shawn continued. "They would bring in a kid with bronchitis and put him in the next bed and say, 'It's OK, all you have to do is close the curtain.' It amazed us how stupid they sometimes were."
Zac lost all his hair about a week into his use of vincristine, even though that was the easiest of the chemotherapies he underwent. "We hadn't told him he'd lose his hair, but when he found it lying in clumps on his pillow, we had to come clean," said Shawn. To soften his son's blow, Shawn agreed to shave his own head.

As he suffered through chemotherapy, Zac dropped from 45 to 32 pounds. He had several gastrointestinal infections, along with almost constant stomach cramps, diarrhea and pain. Twice he was hospitalized for the intestinal infections. He permanently lost his ability to hear high tones. Most embarrassing, he briefly lost all control of his bowels.

His parents never left his side. Every night Zac was in the hospital, Shawn slept on a cot in his room. Every day, while Shawn went off to wash windows, Desiree sat by Zac's bedside. "His pain was for real," said Shawn. "You can tell when your child is just whining or when the pain is serious. But the doctors would just say, 'Oh, he's having slight discomfort,' and not take it seriously."

When all that was over, Sapozink stepped in to begin radiation. Zac was to get just a five-week break in between. Then he caught a cold, so the treatment was put off for two weeks. Sapozink constantly assured the parents Zac would be "just fine" during radiation.

Meanwhile, Shawn and Desiree had begun to educate themselves about radiation and other anticancer therapies. "One day I sat down and asked Sapozink about potential IQ loss," Shawn says. "I had read studies that show kids can lose as much as 30 or 40 IQ points as a result of radiation. His answer? 'Zac will probably lose a few IQ points, but he'll be a functioning adult. Don't worry, we'll take good care of him,'" Shawn remembered the doctor saying.

Sapozink rebuffed several attempts to reach him and confirm or deny his statement for this book. But notes he incorporated into Zac's official hospital record show that he grew increasingly annoyed with the McConnells' reluctance to subject Zac to radiation. "His attitude was that radiation is not worth doing if you don't do a lot of it, and that if we didn't allow it, our son would die," said Desiree.

But Zac's parents remained hesitant about radiation. As Shawn studied scientific journals during and after the course of chemotherapy, he found several references to Dr. Stanislaw Burzynski and his antineoplastons. But neither that nor Sapozink's attitude was enough to dissuade him and Desiree from going the conventional-therapy route.

Finally, the day of Zac's first radiation treatment arrived early in March 1996. He was to get two doses, five days a week for seven weeks, a total of about 7,000 rads. After the first dose, Zac began to complain almost as soon as Desiree took him home. He had a headache. He was nauseated. A neighbor wrote in a sworn affidavit, "When I arrived at the McConnell home, Zachary was sitting on the couch vomiting violently and continuously. He had absolutely no energy and was unable to move, his mother had to hold a bowl under his head .... I had never seen him so ill, weak or devoid of color after being treated with chemotherapy .... After throwing up for an hour, Zachary complained of a severe headache and began crying from the pain. The McConnells called Zachary's doctor and informed him of the situation. The doctor instructed the McConnells to give Zachary Tylenol for the pain."

Doctors at Good Samaritan couldn't understand Zac's reaction to cranial radiation. "Two nurses and a doctor told me this was impossible," remembered Desiree. "They said, 'No one has this type of reaction until they've had two weeks of treatment.' They said this couldn't possibly be reaction to radiation. And they told me not to be concerned unless he vomited and became lethargic. Of course, he was already vomiting." Desiree accepted this and took Zac back to the hospital later that day for his second radiation dose. "He fell asleep in the car en route home. He clutched my hand, and when we got home he banged his head on the wall to try to relieve some of the pain."

Shawn immediately called the hospital, frantically trying to reach Sapozink. "I told them their criteria had now been met—both the vomiting and the lethargy. I never reached Sapozink that day, but the other doctors I spoke with said there was absolutely no way this could be a result of the radiation. Then they changed their tune and said it was a normal reaction. So they were changing their story and wanted him to have more radiation."

This was the last straw. Shawn felt he could no longer trust the doctors treating his son with radiation; maybe it was time to look for something else. "As this was happening, we had been reading more about Burzynski," he notes. "The weekend before the radiation, we prayed for some kind of guidance, some kind of sign to tell us whether we should go to him. I was washing a woman's windows and I heard her talking on the telephone about Burzynski. It turned out she was talking to a friend who was a Burzynski patient."

Within a few days, the McConnells were tuned in to a network of Burzynski patients. Most important to them was the conversation Desiree had with Mariann Kunnari, the mother of a four-year-old Minnesota boy whose aggressive medulloblastoma was undergoing apparently successful treatment with antineoplastons. "She told me that her son Dustin had not done any chemotherapy or surgery, and his tumor had shrunk," Desiree remembered. "So on what would have been the fourth day of radiation for Zac, I called the Burzynski Clinic in Houston. During those four days, we had not taken him for radiation; we were praying for a sign. I think talking to the patients was a sign."

Days later, just a month after a postchemotherapy MRI showed Zac with one possible speck of tumor in his brain, the McConnells drove to Houston. Before going, they had a vascular surgeon insert a new catheter into Zac's chest, in the same spot where he had received much of his chemotherapy. Radiologists say the speck on Zac's February 1996 MRI might or might not have been a small piece of tumor. They said it might also be scar tissue.

Zac started Burzynski's treatment on March 19, 1996. On the fourth day, he complained of a leg cramp, and he vomited. Burzynski interpreted these symptoms as a sign of the swelling that sometimes accompanies tumor break-down. He gave Zac one dose of an anti-inflammatory steroid to ease the swelling. "Zac never needed more," Desiree said.

Zac's life on antineoplastons went smoothly for the next two months. An April MRI scan showed that the speck was gone. "Now we knew the speck the last time definitely was not scar tissue. [Scar tissue] could not disappear in two months, or ever, for that matter," Shawn explained. Zac and his dad returned to Houston in May 1996 for what they expected to be a routine office visit during which they'd pick up a new supply of antineoplastons to take home. Enter the FDA.

Under indictment since November 1995 for selling antineoplastons to out-of-state patients without FDA approval, Burzynski was forced to abide by a condition of bail demanding that he treat no one with antineoplastons unless the FDA agreed they fit the criteria to enter the IND protocols the agency was allowing him to pursue. In Zac's case, the FDA objected.

"He looks very good, but unfortunately, I cannot give you the medicine," Burzynski bluntly informed father and son.

"Why did he let us go all the way down there if he couldn't give us the medicine?" complained Shawn. "I get the sense there's no game plan in the clinic. You can sit in the waiting room for three hours and then Burzynski is very quick, just taking a look."

Burzynski's sad announcement to the McConnells resulted from his interpretation of an April 26 letter from Dr. Robert DeLap, then acting director of the FDA's Division of Oncology Drug Products, Office of Drug Evaluation. "We are concerned about the large number of new patients that you have now revealed were started on antineoplastons between February 24, 1996, and April 15, 1996, outside your [IND permits] and outside of the many new protocols you had filed to your INDs," wrote DeLap. "Regarding Zachary McConnell... antineoplastons may be continued in this patient provided you submit the following information within 15 days of this notification: the age of the patient, a copy of CT scan and/or MRI report providing evidence that the patient has a residual brain tumor, and a copy of a report from the patient's radiation oncologist indicating the tumor is not potentially curable with radiation therapy."

In short, Zac was to stay off antineoplastons unless an MRI scan of his brain showed measurable tumor. But his April scan had shown no trace of tumor. So Burzynski believed he had to stop providing his medication or go to jail immediately.

The McConnells, however, did not stop. They still had some antineoplastons at home. They also sent heart-rending appeals to all their acquaintances and to every Burzynski patient they could locate. They asked anyone who read their appeals to contact either President Clinton or members of Congress. "God knows that cancer victims and their families have exhausting burdens laid upon them, and to ask more of them than to just concentrate on healing and on the daily tasks of life seems absurd," wrote Shawn and Desiree in June 1996. "Yet, as you know, if a certain governmental agency had their sick fantasies fulfilled, none of us would have antineoplastons as a weapon against our nightmares."

The response was overwhelming. Zac's plight became the focus of newspaper, TV and wire-service stories. His father testified in a Senate hearing on the so-called Access to Medical Treatment Act. Boxes of antineoplastons began arriving on the family's doorstep, sent by concerned fellow patients who had extra supplies.

So Zac stayed on the medication, even though his dosage often changed, depending on how much antineoplaston was on hand at his home. He went off the medication for a few days when the family traveled to Washington for the Senate hearing. Several times in June and July, his catheter ruptured, forcing him to stop taking the medicine for a day or two at a time. And his parents never knew whether the antineoplastons coming from fellow patients were fresh enough to be effective. Normally, the medication must be used within three to four months of manufacture.

The overall campaign succeeded. Almost two months after DeLap effectively ordered Zac off antineoplastons, the FDA bureaucrat reversed himself. In a July 12, 1996, letter, he told Burzynski that because the April MRI scan showed "no evidence of tumor recurrence," Zac could once again be given fresh antineoplastons. "We are now able to conclude that Zachary may have a very good prognosis and it is not clear that administration of radiation therapy at this time would substantially improve his chances for cure .... We have determined that administration of antineoplastons to Zachary may continue."

In short, the same official who in April ordered Burzynski to stop treating Zac because his MRI showed no measurable tumor now said a lack of tumor was grounds for resuming the treatment. This left the McConnells shaking their heads in disbelief over the complete contradiction, but nevertheless relieved.

"They learned nothing new between those two letters," said Shawn. "The only things that happened were political and media pressure. Now we know these decisions aren't based on science or the welfare of the patient. They're based on power and politics."

Soon after that reprieve, the family scheduled another MRI for Zac, exactly a year and a day after the scan that first revealed his tumor. "We wanted to make that date meaningless in our lives," says Desiree. "We wanted to make it so that date was not something we would dread every year." It was not to be. The new MRI showed a small tumor the size of a marble.

Moss told the parents they must act within three or four weeks. New surgery was probably a must, he said. Burzynski counseled waiting and increasing the dosage of antineoplastons. The McConnells and Moss acceded.

Within days of starting the new dosage of antineoplastons, Zac once again suffered leg cramps and vomiting, just as he did during his first week on antineoplastons. For once, the symptoms made Zac's parents optimistic. But they faced a new period of uncertainty.

"This is a real test for us," said Shawn. "The easiest thing would be to do the surgery right away and then use antineoplastons to prevent regrowth. Again, we will pray and rely on faith. But we know that Dustin Kunnari's tumor also recurred and then responded to increased antineoplaston dosage. We know that Dr. Burzynski and all of us are still learning about this.

"The bottom line is that we weren't able to give him the

usual dosage all the time. I'll never know if the FDA's action caused this recurrence, but I do know they forced us to break the law for a while so our son could survive. I guess the FDA doesn't expect patients to fight back when their medication is stopped. But we did. I sure would love to feel it is safe to run to the big daddy in the white coat, the medical establishment, whenever we have a problem, but I can't. And neither should anyone else."

For six months after Shawn McConnell made those observations, he and his family lived in a state of uncertainty over Zachary's fate. By the beginning of October 1996, despite renewed application of antineoplastons, Zac's tumor had regrown to a diameter of about three centimeters and the McConnells could see that it had to be removed. When surgeon Moss removed this tumor, it was encapsulated, just as Zac's first one had been. And an MRI scan of his spine revealed no growths there.

But once the tumor was removed, the McConnells opted not to put Zac back on antineoplastons."We had tried a heavy dose for 30 days during September 1996, and there was no visible impact," Shawn recalled. "So we decided after the second surgery to try to get localized, focused radiation of the area of the tumor. The doctors in Phoenix all pressured us to go for full-brain radiation, because that was the only way they could be sure to get all stray cancer cells that might be in his brain. But we knew how that affected Zac, and we couldn't allow it. We went to the University of Arizona in Tucson and they said the same thing. Finally, we were referred to Dr. William Wara at the University of California at San Francisco, who agreed to what we wanted."

After giving Zac a month's rest, the McConnells drove to Northern California. Once they arrived, they stayed on the dusty suburban ranch of Ric and Paula Schiff, whose daughter Crystin, ironically, had once undergone full-brain radiation under Wara's supervision. This time, the doctor agreed to perform a targeted process known as three-dimensional conformal radiation, aiming his beams only at the specific area where Zac's tumor twice had grown. "We did this for five weeks, five days a week," Shawn reports. "Zac ended up with a total dose of about 3,000 rads, only about half of what they wanted to give him. The doctors there were shocked when we told them we were leaving at that point. One resident told me, 'You can't leave after only half the treatment.' But we did. And even so, we can see some of the side effects of the radiation. Zac gets moody and irritable at times in ways that closely mimic how he was when he had the tumor." But one month after he returned home, in January 1997, an MRI scan showed Zac—by now back in school in Arizona—free from cancer.

The McConnells don't know what might have happened if Zac had been permitted by the FDA to stay on antineo-plastons while they initially appeared to be preventing the regrowth. "He went a whole year without a tumor, so I believe Burzynski's stuff was probably working at that time," insisted Shawn. "After the first FDA order came down, we used some medicine that I can only call smuggled, sent to us by other patients. Some of it was received after the expiration dates on the packages. So we certainly weren't always sure we were doing it the way Burzynski wanted."

Burzynski believes Zac's recurrence might never have happened if he hadn't been forced to interrupt his direct supervision of the boy's treatment. "We don't know what medicine Zac was getting, and we don't know how much, either," he says. "Perhaps, if he had come to Texas and I had examined him when his tumor recurred, we could have altered the dose. Often, when tumors recur, they are more aggressive, but we can nevertheless fight them effectively with increased dosage. But his treatment was interfered with."

Postscript

FOUNTAIN HILLS, Ariz., midyear 2000—Zac McConnell is dead. He died at 10:27 p.m. on Dec. 31, 1998. New Year's Eve. As Arizona Republic columnist Laurie Roberts reported a few days later, "Zac was a boy who for three years and four months fought and fought and fought against the cancer that invaded his brain."

For much of that time, he was forced to fight with one hand behind his back because the FDA took away the medication that had apparently kept his tumor from regrowing for many months after its removal in early 1996. Yes, under political pressure, the FDA eventually allowed him to go back on the medication. His tumor reappeared when he was compelled to stop infusing antineoplastons in the dose and manner Burzynski ordered. But the new tumor didn't respond to the Burzynski-directed doses Zac took when he went back on the treatment. So no one will ever know if the FDA was just as responsible as cancer for the death of this precocious nine-year-old.

"I still don't understand why Dr. Burzynski hasn't just gone to some other country where they'd let him operate in peace, even welcome him," Shawn McConnell said in early 2000, still heartbroken more than 18 months after losing his only son. "I'd have taken Zac to Europe, Mexico, anywhere. And then there would have been no problems with the FDA. Then we'd have been able to see if staying on the medicine would keep the tumor down. It just seems to me the doctor could do more for his patients by going to a friendlier country."

But Shawn never took Zac back to Houston after the FDA allowed him to resume antineoplastons. So Burzynski could not examine Zac personally after his tumor reappeared. Shawn and Zac's mom Desiree report they gave Zac exactly the doses Burzynski called for after he was allowed back on the treatment, and they kept him on for more than five weeks, which they say Burzynski told them might be sufficient time to determine whether the new tumor would respond. It did not respond, and it was surgically removed again—one of seven times Zac underwent brain surgery in his short life. Of course, many other brain tumors also don't respond quickly to antineoplastons, but do begin to diminish after several months.

"The problem here was that we never saw Zac again," says Burzynski. "He was taken care of in an unsupervised manner."

Said Shawn, "I did not and still don't see why it was necessary to take Zac back to Texas. We were sending scans to Burzynski and giving Zac whatever dose we were told to."

But Burzynski says things are not so simple. "Zac's dosage was probably too low when he was allowed back onto antineoplastons," he said. "He could have taken far more. Our records indicate our doctors told Mr. McConnell to increase the dose, but we don't know if he did it to the extent recommended. But that's not all one needs to do. To have good results with a recurrent tumor, his dosage probably should have been three times higher than it was. But this would have required frequent blood tests and observation—every two or three days—to check on possible excessive salinity levels. But he had only one in four months

after he went back on the medication, and this is completely unacceptable. Zac probably needed to be in Houston for
three weeks as his dosage was gradually increased. You
can't triple it all at once without danger and you have to
monitor the patient every day."

Burzynski said that under ideal circumstances, he
would have placed Zac on a new and higher dosage and
continued treatment at that level for two months. "Only
then should we stop—if the tumor increases," he said. "If
the tumor were not growing at that time, we should continue treatment." But months-long treatment with the vastly
increased dosage never occurred.

The bottom line: No one will ever know whether Zac
would have lived had there been no FDA interference. No
one can know, either, whether his second tumor was one of
the minority of its type that don't respond to antineoplastons or anything else.

CHAPTER 6

The War Moves to the Laboratory

Ingrid Schultz never intended to make her body a battleground. But from the moment she decided in 1994 to become part of a clinical trial at the National Institutes of Health, her brain stem was destined to become a key element in the long-running legal and scientific war between Dr. Stanislaw Burzynski and the federal cancer research establishment.

All Ingrid wanted was to survive, comfortably if possible. Fifty when she was diagnosed with a malignant Grade 4 glioblastoma multiforme brain tumor just after Labor Day 1993, she and her husband, Lon, lived in Fort Smith, Arkansas, and operated an audiovisual business. They had met in 1969 while working at the same Panasonic electronic-products service center in Chicago. Married in 1973, the couple moved to Arkansas to get away from the frenzied pace of big-city life. They bought a homestead and soon had two children. Until Ingrid, a native of Germany, began suffering from paralysis in her left side, their life was placid.

With the diagnosis of a glioblastoma, everything changed. Ingrid immediately had brain surgery at St. Edward's Hospital in Fort Smith to remove the major part of her tumor. But its tentacles were so intertwined with her brain stem that removal of all the cancerous tissue was impossible. Still, her alarming symptoms were temporarily eliminated. This gave her and her husband time to decide whether she should undergo the recommended radiation therapy.

"We eventually declined it," remembers Lon Schultz.

"My mother had died of breast cancer, and we both had experience with what I call 'slash-and-burn' radiation technologies. We thought it would be prudent to examine the side effects, and after reading two textbooks on radiation oncology, we opted out."

Yet they were far from giving up on Ingrid's life and future. Soon after her surgery, they visited an immunotherapy clinic in San Diego but found the treatment offered there accomplished nothing for Ingrid. And by January 1994, Ingrid's tumor had grown back in full force. She had a second surgery, but again it proved impossible to remove the entire tumor. Once more, her surgeon urged her to try radiation, but as Lon recalls, "Even the radiologist said there was only a slim chance it would help."

Meanwhile, the couple had read book after book on alternative cancer therapies. "Of everything we read about, we felt Burzynski's seemed the most effective," says Lon. "And after Ingrid's tumor grew back, we looked seriously into antineoplastons; we learned that the NIH was going to do a trial on them. We contacted both the NIH and Burzynski's clinical trials director, Dean Mouscher."

Because Burzynski's therapy would have cost them more than $3,000 per month, the couple opted to try to get Ingrid into the NIH trial. Similar trials at Minnesota's Mayo Clinic and the Memorial Sloan-Kettering Cancer Center in New York had not yet begun, the couple learned. But all three trials sponsored by the NCI required that entrants had undergone every available form of conventional treatment—and failed. Ingrid had not undergone radiation, so she was initially rebuffed.

"We sought an exemption," Lon says. "We kept talking to them, and after a series of difficulties, just as we were about to give up on NIH and go to Burzynski in spite of the cost, they called and told me I was welcome to bring Ingrid to their hospital in Bethesda, Maryland."

Once there, Ingrid was forced to wait 10 days while doctors verified that she really had a glioblastoma. Her surgical records didn't satisfy the NIH scientists, who insisted on taking an MRI of their own. "Eventually, they decided to let her into the trial," Lon recalls. "She was the second patient accepted, and she underwent treatment for six weeks."

Supervising her care was Dr. Alain Thibault, who would later become the principal investigator in an NCI-approved trial of the chemical phenylacetate against pancreatic cancer. But her husband says Ingrid soon grew wary of Thibault's motives. "She had only been back there for a week when she called me one day and said Dr. Thibault had come into her examining room excited and happy, and couldn't stop talking about another patient named Didi. Ingrid's feeling was that he was delighted that Didi had not responded to antineoplastons," Lon Schultz reports. "That was Ingrid's first hint that something was not right."

Lon says another came when one technician who helped administer the medicine mentioned to Ingrid that the antineoplastons used in the NIH—most of them sent to Bethesda by Burzyski—were being diluted before they were administered to patients out of a concern that they were so acidic they might burn through the IV bags used in administering them. "There is almost no way to verify this or rule it out," said Dr. Mario Sznol, head of the NCI's Biologics Evaluation Section. "All sorts of things are said to patients. It may have just been an explanation of the standard way of administering the drug."

Thibault, who was more closely involved in administering the drug, failed to return several telephone calls intended to give him an opportunity to respond to this claim.

When her treatment at NIH ended, Ingrid Schultz was convinced that most NIH doctors wanted the antineoplastons to fail. "After several weeks, it was determined that the treatment was not working on her," Lon Schultz says. "Ingrid felt Dr. Thibault was tremendously excited and pleased that they were not working. And after they pulled her off the drug, Ingrid met with four or six other doctors there who said she needed to go home and die. They emphasized that she needed to die, that it was the proper thing to do."

But Ingrid would not pass away on schedule. She once again contacted Burzynski, who agreed to treat her at no charge after he learned of her travails at NIH. And his treatment appeared to affect her tumor. "Her tumor growth slowed and eventually stopped," recalls Lon. "It started growing again months later. It took about six months to grow as much as it earlier had in six days. I wondered why, if she was in fact getting full-strength antineoplastons at NIH, she didn't respond there, when she did respond later at Burzynski's clinic."

Thibault also declined to return telephone calls intended to give him an opportunity to explain his reported attitude. This left open a serious question: Would NIH doctors want the antineoplaston trial to fail? And if they did, why?

For answers to these questions, it's necessary to turn the calendar back to the late 1980s and early 1990s. All through the late 1980s, Burzynski never stopped treating patients and got positive responses from many. He also began approaching major pharmaceutical companies; he supplied antineoplastons to other researchers who inquired from institutions in several parts of America, Europe and Japan.

Most drug companies responded with letters like one from Abbott Laboratories, which simply thanked Burzynski for his interest and said antineoplastons "don't fit into our plans at this time." Their motives were unclear, but Burzynski's troubles with the FDA represented a serious pitfall for any company that might be interested. Abbott's letter carried an undertone of fear—fear that getting involved with Burzynski could sour all its other dealings with the FDA. But one major company bit. The Irish firm of Elan Corporation PLC, a major pharmaceutical maker with American headquarters just outside Atlanta, entered into a letter of intent with Burzynski on June 20, 1990. The agreement appeared to give Burzynski everything he had wanted for years: Elan would see antineoplastons through the regulatory process and eventually bring them to market. Burzynski would be paid handsomely for providing the medication—a minimum of $2,500 per kilogram of antineoplastons, with Elan estimating that it would use at least 2,500 kilograms in the year after it obtained its first IND permit for the medication. Elan also was to give Burzynski a nonrefundable advance of $500,000.

Once antineoplastons completed the FDA's approval process, the agreement called for Burzynski to get 10 percent of gross sales and 40 percent of any gross royalties Elan might receive if it licensed antineoplastons to any other company, anywhere in the world.

Upon signing this agreement, Burzynski believed that his troubles were over. He was delighted to cooperate when Elan sent its scientists to inspect his facilities and review the documentation of his work. After all, the agreement contained a pledge that both parties would "share information regarding the products and research." This was a mistake, one of the most serious Burzynski would ever make.

For the Elan agreement, signed by corporate chairman and CEO Donald Panoz, contained a 60-day "review period" during which Burzynski was to cooperate with Elan's representatives, but all other parts of the agreement would be placed on hold. Either party could back out during the review period.

"During this time," Burzynski recalls ruefully, "they discovered that we had never patented Antineoplaston AS5, which is the same as plain phenylacetate." Burzynski had stopped using AS5, one of the original fractions he had made from the broad-spectrum Antineoplaston A, as early as 1981, concluding that its anticancer activity was much less than the more complex A10 and AS2-1. His lawyers at the time advised him that phenylacetate was such a common industrial chemical that it could not be patented.

The sequence of events indicates that Elan's scientists quickly saw that phenylacetate was the prime chemical in at least one antineoplaston. They clearly realized they could manufacture plain phenylacetate themselves far more cheaply than Burzynski could make antineoplastons. Their apparent reasoning: If antineoplastons are made up largely of phenylacetate and other products that the body metabolizes into phenylacetate, why not just use it by itself? Who needed Burzynski, even if he did discover the fact that peptides made up largely of phenylacetate could reverse the growth of many cancers? Why bother even giving him credit for any part of the discovery?

Burzynski's answer has always been that the other ingredients in antineoplastons, including phenylacetylglutamine and phenylacetylisoglutamine, combine to make the phenylacetate stay in the body longer before it is excreted in the urine in the form of its eventual metabolite, phenylacetylglutamine. The other ingredients, Burzynski says, also render phenylacetate less toxic, doing less harm to the liver and causing less disorientation, thus allowing use of much larger doses.

The net result, however, was that Elan canceled its agreement with Burzynski before the two-month review period ended, hooking up instead with researcher Dvorit Samid, then working at the Uniformed Services Medical School in the Maryland suburbs of Washington, D.C. Samid had become interested in antineoplastons in the late 1980s, when she became acquainted with a Burzynski patient who was responding to treatment. "She approached us and wanted to work with us," Burzynski remembers. "We gave her samples and some money to do some work for us."

Samid says she began working on phenylacetate independently of Burzynski. "All these studies came from natural compounds that were developed in my laboratory," she insists. But she offers no argument about the timetable of her involvement with Elan: The company began supporting her work in 1991, just after it canceled its agreement with Burzynski. The Samid-Elan connection was no accident, Burzynski maintains. "We introduced them."

At the same time it began funding Samid's work with a grant whose amount both she and Elan refuse to divulge— the company obtained licenses for the use of phenylacetate and a related compound, phenylbuterate, as anticancer drugs. "We do have the right to study both phenylacetate and phenylbutyrate as cancer therapeutics," said Michael Sember, chief of the firm's market development division. "As part of our agreement, we provide support to the government in their trials of these substances. They provide us the results." In the Elan use patent, Samid is listed as the inventor of phenylacetate as a cancer treatment. "We got involved through Dr. Samid," said Dr. David Tierney, another Elan executive. Elan refused to discuss why it canceled its agreement with Burzynski.

But the sequence of events makes it plain that sometime after it discovered Burzynski had not patented his all-phenylacetate AS5 as a cancer cure, Elan resolved to try to develop that drug rather than antineoplastons and found Samid's laboratory a convenient venue for such work. The company paid little heed to Burzynski's assertion that he had stopped using AS5 because it has far less impact on cancer than the other related drugs he had discovered. And despite years of exposure to Burzynski's work, Samid still says, "It has been hard to sort out the details of exactly what Dr. Burzynski gives his patients."

The impact on Burzynski of the Samid-Elan connection would not end with this simple effort to develop a drug like his without involving him. Because Samid is a well-established researcher, she displayed results of the Elan-funded work she did on phenylacetate at a variety of cancer research meetings. Walking through the poster area at the 1991 meeting of the American Association for Cancer Research, where Samid displayed poster presentations on two research projects, was the NCI's Sznol, head of its Biologics Evaluation Section and a top official of the institute's Cancer Therapy Evaluation Program, usually known as CTEP. He took one look at the Samid posters and concluded that the substance was worth a deeper look. "We thought the data were very interesting—namely that phenylacetate differentiated [caused the death of] cancer cells," said Sznol. Never mind that Burzynski had been saying and publishing the same thing for almost 15 years about antineoplastons, and had made no secret of the fact that they were composed chiefly of that same chemical compound.

"We are in the business of bringing new potential anti-cancer agents into our clinics," Sznol added. One result of Sznol's interest was a full-fledged trial of phenylacetate against various types of cancer, from brain tumors to pancreatic lesions. Samid's career also took off, first to the research labs of NCI and later to the University of Virginia's medical school, where she said administrators made a "major commitment" to phenylacetate research. Along with her went her close associate, Dr. Alain Thibault.

As all this was happening, Burzynski's patients and the publicity he had won continued to generate a stream of visitors to his laboratory. None would be more important to the future of antineoplastons than a team of six scientists who arrived from the NCI for a day in mid-1991. Their visit was spurred by an earlier guest observer, Dr. Charles Vogel of the University of Miami Comprehensive Cancer Center. Oncologist Vogel had seen several of his patients, who had gone to Burzynski out of desperation, respond to antineoplaston treatment. In one case, a woman's otherwise untreatable brain tumor dissipated within two months. After Vogel visited, Burzynski recalls, he recommended that NCI conduct a site visit of its own, dispatching a team of scientists to verify Burzynski's results.

In the years leading up to Vogel's visit, Burzynski neither had nor wanted much contact with the NCI. He remembered his run-ins of the early 1980s, in which antineoplaston samples were relayed by Canadian scientists to the NCI, where they were tested against P388 mouse leukemia. "I told them what to expect, that we do not anticipate much activity of antineoplastons in animals because antineoplastons are species-specific," Burzynski says. "But they tested them in this manner anyway. After that, they could make a blanket statement that antineoplastons do not work on animals. Yet we never stopped curing patients. It just goes to show the wickedness of some of these people."

At about the time of Vogel's visit, NCI had established a new program to evaluate the best-response cases involved in various alternative cancer therapies. "I began asking in 1981 for the NCI and the American Cancer Society to review our patient records, but for years, neither would do it," Burzynski says. This time, however, there was a response. "Vogel had worked at the NCI, and he also had brought with him when he came to Houston a brain tumor expert from Washington, D.C., to review my work. It was only after he contacted the NCI that I heard from them again."

The result was the NCI site visit, with a team of six doctors evaluating Burzynski's work. But not all of it. For years after, the NCI would point out that its team had examined only a "best-case series" of seven case histories.

Says Burzynski, "I have no idea why, but they spent only one day here. We had prepared 20 brain tumor cases for them, but they had time to examine only seven. They reviewed all the medical records in each case, including MRI and CT scan films and pathology slides. They also inspected our chemical plant. When I asked them to stay longer and look at more cases, they told me that seven would be more than enough to prove the point."

And for some purposes, it was. The report of the NCI scientists seemed conclusive. "The site-visit team determined that antitumor activity was documented in this best-case series," read one of their reports. "The conduct of Phase 2 trials was indicated to determine the response rate." On specific cases, the team confirmed "possible complete responses," or total disappearance of otherwise-incurable brain tumors, in four of the seven cases, and partial response, defined as more than 50 percent tumor reduction, in the others.

So compelling were the results that Dr. Michael Friedman, then NCI associate director for the CTEP program and later an acting FDA commissioner, wrote in an internal memo to the director of NCI's Division of Cancer Treatment that "antineoplastons deserve a closer look. It turns out that the agents are well defined, pure chemical entities .... The human brain tumor responses are real. We will keep you informed."

Those reports, Burzynski thought, might end his many years as a scientific pariah working on the periphery of the health care system and the cancer research community. But what followed was yet another nightmare, leading him to believe that the NCI wanted antineoplastons to fail—the same conclusion reached by patient Ingrid Schultz and her husband, Lon.

For two years, NCI officials delayed putting antineoplastons into a large-scale clinical trial against various types of cancer. Later, they would explain that "there were difficulties with the labeling of the antineoplastons Burzynski sent." Finally, in mid-1993, a three-site trial of antineoplastons was authorized, with patients to be accepted at NIH, the Mayo Clinic and Memorial Sloan-Kettering. No patients, however, were signed up until early 1994. In a letter signed by Friedman, the NCI agreed that the trials would take patients with anaplastic astrocytomas and glioblastoma multiforme, two of the fastest-growing and deadliest brain cancers. Thirty-five patients would be treated; none would have tumors that exceeded five centimeters in diameter and none would have multiple tumors or cancer that had spread elsewhere in the body.

Satisfied with these parameters and having received a

written assurance that he would be kept informed of patient progress via regular reports from the NCI's Theradex information service, Burzynski returned to his routine. But he was in fact not informed of everything that happened in the trial. This is confirmed in an internal memo written while the trial was still open, in May 1995, by CTEP official Joan Mauer: "The clinical trials monitoring service, Theradex, has been instructed not to send any antineoplastins [sic] clinical trial data to Dr. Burzynski, the Burzynski Research Institute Inc., or anyone inquiring about the antineoplastins trials. Any inquiries of Theradex about the antineoplastins clinical trials or any information they [sic] may be related to the trials or Dr. Burzynski are to be referred to the Associate Director, CTEP." Copies of this memo went to Friedman and Sznol, among others.

Why would the NCI want to deprive Burzynski of such information? One clue is provided in a 1992 internal memo from Sznol to Friedman and several other colleagues: "There is reason to believe from preclinical data provided by Dr. Samid...that the active component of the antineoplastons is phenylacetic acid, the final breakdown product of the antineoplaston preparations. It would be preferable to study phenylacetic acid [since it is easier to produce and obtain, and since a pharmaceutical company has been identified that is more likely to reliably provide drug supplies] rather than the more complex mixtures of antineoplastons."

Sznol also inquired in his memo whether drugs supplied by Burzynski for any upcoming trial might come from urine, even though he knew Burzynski had stopped using urine derivatives 10 years earlier. And Sznol questioned whether Burzynski was sincere about wanting an honest test of antineoplastons.

"If Dr. Burzynski acted in bad faith, he could use the

results of the NCI trial [and the fact of NCI involvement] to advertise his institute and to continue to treat patients of all disease types without medical evidence that the treatment is in fact beneficial to those patients," he wrote to Friedman. Later, Sznol would say that he believes "there is some low level of [anticancer] activity there, but I don't know how much. The problem is that he covers everything with a smokescreen, a laying on of lies." In short, the NCI wanted to test antineoplastons or something like them, but would have preferred to test them without involving Burzynski. And Sznol, having seen Samid's presentation and made arrangements to begin testing phenylacetate with help from Elan, was making it clear that he believed antineoplastons were no better than this single ingredient.

"We felt we could develop both antineoplastons and plain phenylacetate," Sznol would say later. "There was no reason why we shouldn't. A drug company can give you whatever quantities of a medication you want. And interactions with drug companies are more straightforward than with Dr. Burzynski."

There were no objections from Burzynski, however, as the three-site 1994-95 antineoplaston trial went forward using medication he supplied. In fact, Burzynski knew little about what was transpiring. Only much later would he get reports. So Burzynski didn't know about the patient identified in an internal NCI report as "SM," whose tumor was stopped in its tracks by antineoplastons for months but died within three months of leaving the trial. "It is expected that his life would be saved if he had continued the treatment under the protocol," the report said, without explaining why "SM" left the trial. Reports on other patients were neither dramatic nor conclusive. One official note expressed doubt that Ingrid Schultz, identified in the report as "patient IS," really had a glioblastoma multiforme, speculating she might have a different kind of tumor. This may explain the 10-day wait she endured after arriving at NIH.

Burzynski was told none of this. Instead, he received a March 24, 1994, letter from Sznol, informing him that the NCI proposed major changes in its clinical trial of antineoplastons. The restriction on tumor size was to increase from five centimeters to eight, and multitumors or metastatic cancers would no longer be excluded. The explanation: Not enough patients had been recruited who met the admission criteria for inclusion in the trial. "Because of this, there is strong interest on our part and that of the investigators to broaden the eligibility criteria, Sznol wrote.

Burzynski's immediate response was that the entry criteria should not be expanded without also increasing the dosages given to patients. Antineoplastons, he explained, are dosed according to a combination of body size and size of tumor. The larger and more persistent the tumor, the higher the dosage of antineoplastons Burzynski generally administers. Ordinary chemotherapy drugs, by contrast, are dosed exclusively by body size. This is largely because they are so toxic that patients' tolerance for them is limited. The lower toxicity of antineoplastons makes it possible to give them in a greater variety of doses. But the NCI researchers who proposed expanding the antineoplaston trial did not take this into account. Burzynski instantly realized that treating larger and more widespread tumors without increasing dosage would bias the trial against antineoplastons and guarantee they would appear useless or at least no more effective than plain phenylacetate.

In a March 29, 1994, letter to Sznol, he said he "would expect that there will be a significant difference in response between the patients admitted under the current acceptance criteria and the expanded eligibility criteria proposed in your letter of March 23." Instead of lumping all the patients into one trial, Burzynski suggested a separate trial for patients with large and multifocal tumors "to be treated and evaluated according to a modified protocol."

This wasn't good enough for Friedman and Sznol, who responded, "At the investigators' request, the amendments... have been approved." His wording appears to have put the onus for changing the protocol squarely on the leading investigators in the trial, Dr. Jan Buckner of the Mayo Clinic and Dr. Mark Malkin of Memorial Sloan-Kettering. But a Jan. 31, 1995, letter from Malkin to the chairman of his hospital's Institutional Review Board states that "amendments, as described below, have been made at the request of the NCI."

Sznol later said the decision to alter the protocol and to ignore Burzynski's suggestion of an expanded trial for larger tumors was jointly made. "The investigators and I recognized accrual to the trial was going slowly, and we were concerned," he claimed. "I went to the investigators and asked what they could do to increase accrual." But this was in February or March 1994, just two months after Ingrid Schultz had been steered to NIH and barely a month after the first patients were accepted. Wasn't it a bit quick to conclude that the original entry criteria were too restrictive?

Sznol tried to clarify. "The investigators thought the problem was the eligibility requirements. So we tried to change the eligibility criteria, and Burzynski said no. I then checked to see if what they wanted to do was consistent with other brain tumor studies, and it was. I went to Mike Friedman and told him I thought this was fair and would jump-start the study. And we said, 'OK, let's move forward regardless of what Burzynski says.'

"Next, we went back to the best-case series he presented to the NCI site-visit team and saw how patients were treated. It was essentially identical to the way we wanted to treat them. There may have been small differences, but we basically said, 'Why not do what Burzynski is actually doing?'"

Except it wasn't what Burzynski was actually doing. "If they really looked at the best-case series, they would see that the patients who had the least or slowest response in that group were those with the largest tumors," Burzynski says. "We usually give patients with larger tumors higher doses. I told Sznol in the beginning that if he wanted to treat more advanced tumors, he would need more antineoplastons. Instead of giving them one gram of A10 per day per kilogram of body weight, they might need five grams per kilogram." This, he notes, is consistent with the finding of the 1991 site-visit team, which reported that "no significant [anti-tumor] activity was seen in tissue culture studies when low concentrations were used."

The ultimate result was that in the summer of 1995, the NCI trial of antineoplastons was canceled. Meanwhile, the parallel trial of phenylacetate went on unaffected. But the NCI was not finished with Burzynski. Shortly after canceling the antineoplaston trial, it released a "fact sheet" via its Cancernet newsletter and World Wide Web page, reporting that in the site-visit review, "Dr. Burzynski selected from his entire clinical experience seven brain tumor patients whom he felt had a beneficial effect from antineoplastons." The Cancernet statement added that the material reviewed "did not include all available patient information." And Cancernet said the NCI trial was closed "because a consensus could not be reached with Dr. Burzynski on the proposed changes in the protocol."

Burzynski objected in a letter to NCI director Richard Klausner, noting that he was not responsible for the 1991 site-visit team's refusal to stay and look at more than seven cases. He added that the documents and scans the team examined did include all available patient records, and he pointed out that the NCI never made an effort to reach a consensus on changes in the trial-entrance criteria. In fact, the NCI never responded to Burzynski's suggestion of a separate clinical trial for larger tumors.

Even after this "fact sheet" appeared, the NCI and its researchers were still not finished attacking Burzynski. The Mayo Clinic's Buckner and Memorial Sloan-Kettering's Malkin, together with several of their associates, prepared a 31-page paper for publication in scientific journals, summing up their experiences with antineoplastons. Besides noting that they didn't care for the odor of the medication, they said in their abstract that "none of the seven evaluable patients demonstrated tumor regression. All patients developed tumor progression and have died." This, of course, ignored the earlier unsigned NCI report in which the agency noted that at least one patient would likely have survived if he had stayed on the treatment. Neither Buckner nor Malkin would answer questions for this book about whether they diluted the antineoplastons they used in the trial, and Thibault did not respond to repeated efforts to obtain his comments on this claim.

Altogether, the NCI's actions left the impression that it did not want the antineoplaston trial to succeed and was relieved when it issued the Cancernet summation implying that antineoplastons were still completely unproven. But the NCI exhibited an entirely different attitude toward the phenylacetate trial. "The scientific question of whether antineoplaston or phenylacetate is more active is a very difficult one to assess," said Sznol. When he made that remark, he was in possession of a copy of the Buckner-Malkin paper, in which the authors reluctantly conceded the major biochemical point Burzynski had been making for more than a decade. Burzynski maintains that phenylacetylglutamine, one of the two other major components of antineoplastons, causes the activity of phenylacetate to intensify and be sustained over a longer period of time. Similarly, Buckner and Malkin conceded on page 19 of their manuscript (later published in Volume 74 of the Mayo Clinic Proceedings, February 1, 1999, Pages 137-145) that studies of blood drawn from their patients showed that those who received antineoplastons had a higher blood content of phenylacetylglutamine than those who received plain phenylacetate. This meant patients on antineoplastons did not excrete phenylacetylglutamine in their urine as quickly as patients who got plain phenylacetate—precisely the reason Burzynski gave up using plain phenylacetate more than a decade earlier. In addition, upon analyzing the results of blood tests of patients published in the Buckner/Malkin paper, Burzynski submitted a response to the Mayo Clinic Proceedings. This was published on Pages 641-642 of the journal's June 1999 issue, pointing out that the blood tests proved patients in the NCI-sponsored trial were receiving doses 53 times smaller than Burzynski's own patients. "It is a dosage-sensitive medication," Burzynski said. "These dosages guaranteed the results would be poor."

Through all this, there were no major glitches in the anticancer trials of phenylacetate, one of them headed by Dr. Michael Prados of the University of California's San Francisco medical center. This was the same Prados who sat in meetings in which Pamela Winningham's brain cancer was discussed in 1987. Winningham says there is no question that Prados had been aware for years of her survival and treatment with antineoplastons. This is also the same Prados who told Ric Schiff in 1993 that he knew of no alternative to chemotherapy and radiation for young Crystin Schiff's malignant rhabdoid brain tumor.

Yes, it was true that the rare rhabdoid tumors were not included in the protocol for the phenylacetate trial. But no, it was not true that Prados knew of nothing else that might work on brain tumors.

Prados gave the first formal report on the phenylacetate brain tumor trial at the 1995 meeting of the American Society for Clinical Oncology. Of the first 19 patients who could be evaluated, he reported some tumor reduction in five. One saw tumor shrinkage of 66 percent, one was reduced by 48 percent and three others were in the 20 to 30 percent range. It was a finding that heartened Burzynski, whose reaction seemed a bit naive. "It can only help us if they get good results. If they get good results using plain phenylacetate, when our medicine is so much better, that has to help us."

As the war on Burzynski moved to the laboratory, the series of events made a few things reasonably clear. The events establish that the NCI never gave antineoplastons a fair trial because some of its officials found it difficult to deal with Burzynski and because Burzynski refused to agree to a trial he felt was surely stacked against his medicine. They also establish that it is in the financial interest of Elan to make phenylacetate—and not antineoplastons—a featured anti-cancer drug, even if it is demonstrably less effective and even if the chemical reasons for the lesser performance are known. And these events also establish that from the earliest days of their relationship, the top clinical trial supervisors at the NCI wanted to be relieved of the need to deal with Burzynski.

Postscript, Spring 2000

Less than a year after Burzynski's criminal trial, action at the United States Patent Office made it clear that even if the NCI wanted to avoid dealing with Burzynski, scientists there still found as much promise in his medication as their memos from the early 1990s indicated they saw then. In late 1997, the Department of Health and Human Services, parent agency for NCI, acquired five patents for use of phenylacetate and phenylacetylglutamate as anti-cancer therapies. Applications for all five were signed by Dvorit Samid, who was listed on the cover sheets as the inventor. The applications were made over a three-year period between 1992 and 1994, but did not become public records until patents were issued in 1997. Thus their existence was not publicly known or acknowledged at the time of the first printing of The Burzynski Breakthrough. The timing and the steady stream of patent applications make it plain that even as the FDA was investigating Burzynski, preparing to indict him, and taking him to trial, the NCI was aping his work. In fact, all five of Samid's patent applications, vetted by NCI officials before they could be filed, are strikingly similar to Burzynski's pre-existing patents, featuring chemical drawings portraying the same molecules central to his formulation.

Here's what Samid's patent applications declared about infusing phenylacetate and phenylacetylglutamine—the prime ingredients of antineoplaston AS2-1—into the cerebrospinal fluid of patients with metastatic prostate cancer: "Stabilization of PSA [prostate specific antigen] for more than two months was noted in three...patients with prostate cancer. One patient with glioblastoma multiforme [a deadly brain tumor] has had improvement in performance status [and] intellectual function...of greater than five months duration." Samid reported this finding on page 122 of her application for a patent to use a "therapeutically effective amount of phenylacetate or pharmaceutically acceptable derivatives" against cancers.

Some statements in the NCI patents, in fact, read almost like advertisements for antineoplastons. "Phenylacetate can induce cytostatis [cell stability] and reversal of malignant properties of ... human glioblastoma cells when used at pharmacological concentrations that are well tolerated by children and adults...Phenylactetate would be expected to affect tumor growth...while sparing normal tissue," Samid wrote in describing one instance (labeled Example 7) of "growth arrest in malignant gliomas" in an application that became Patent No. 5,635,533. "Therapeutic benefit of sodium phenylacetate is stable in the absence of further treatment," she added while describing Example 27 in the same application. In short, the NCI unequivocally stated that ingredients of antineoplastons can reverse development of gliomas, a family of severe brain tumors, and the benefits remain after treatment stops.

Each of Samid's five patent applications also contained one flat statement that contradicts some Burzynski critics who contend that blood salinity increases sometimes associated with antineoplastons make the medication toxic. "Clinical experience indicates that acute or long-term treatment with high sodium phenylacetate doses is well tolerated, essentially free of adverse effects," the NCI documents declare.

Further, in her application for using phenylacetate or its derivatives to treat AIDS, anemia and cancer—an application that became Patent No. 5,635,532—Samid writes a passage that could have come from a Burzynski speech describing the benefits of his formulation. He frequently mentions that antineoplastons are cell-differentiating agents which prevent tumor growth by acting only on malignant cells and not on those that are normal. "Several differentiation agents are known," Samid wrote on the first page of her application. "But their clinical applications have been hindered by unacceptable toxicities and/or deleterious side effects. Accordingly, the present invention provides methods and composition for treating various pathologies with phenylacetic acid." Burzynski could not have said it better: One of the main reasons antineoplastons are preferable to other therapies is that they are non-toxic, while effectively differentiating between healthy and cancerous cells.

Samid adds in the same application that "In terms of cancer prevention, the beneficial effect of sodium phenylacetate may be even more dramatic than [we have] observed in experimental models...Even if chemo-prevention will require continuous treatment, such treatment would be acceptable considering the lack of toxicity." Further along in the same application, she mentions use of a combination of phenylacetate and phenylacetylglutamine, exactly what Burzynski has been doing with AS2-1 since 1976. Samid also writes that the chemicals she needed for her work were provided in large part by Elan Pharmaceuticals, although there is no indication of the extent of financial support the company provided. Meanwhile, Burzynski's own patents, acquired between 1982 and 1990, repeatedly describe using the same chemicals against the same maladies in the same manner Samid claims to have invented. Samid said one reason her patent applications do not mention the level of support Elan kicked in was that she had no idea how much money the company spent supporting her work or the clinical trials associated with it. "Elan had an agreement to support research with NCI and mine was the prime research involved," she said. "I never knew how much they spent."

Somehow the obvious duplication did occur, whether or not it was deliberate on Samid's part. Without admitting there was duplication, Samid passes the buck to government bureaucrats. "Both during my time at the Uniformed Services Medical School in Bethesda, Md., and while I was at NCI, it was routine for my work to be reviewed to see if it involved anything that was patentable," she said in an interview during the spring of 2000. At that time, she was on sabbatical leave from a post at the Medical College of Virginia in Charlottesville, where she had moved from NCI in 1996, shortly after signing the patent applications. "Before you can publish any paper while working at NCI, the office of patent review looks to see if there is any 'prior art,' any reason the work cannot be patented."

But when official spokesmen for NCI are asked whether the procedure she described is standard within the institute, they say it is not. "There is no requirement that papers be vetted by lawyers or patent experts," said Robert Kuska, an NCI spokesman. "Typically, scientists will hand in an invention report at the time they publish their work. This is at the initiation of the scientist." Researchers at several major universities also confirmed that virtually no institution requires scientists to submit their work for patent review before it is published.

Samid insists that other officials at NCI, and not she, made the decisions to apply for the patents whose applications bear her signature. "I did not do it," she said. "And they cannot be duplicative, anyway. They were evaluated by the United States Patent Office. There's no way to trick somebody there. They compare and decide if the work is original or not, and they took years to evaluate this work."

Although he learned of the NCI's patents in early 1998, more than two years later Burzynski still had not filed a patent infringement lawsuit against either the institute or its parent agency. "There is no doubt these patents are very close as far as the technology is concerned. The chemistry is very similar," Patricia Kammerer, Burzynski's Houston-based patent lawyer, said during the spring of 2000. "But Dr. Burzynski can't yet try to suppress these patents. If one holds a patent, one can enforce it against every active infringement. Active means the use, sale or manufacture of a product. So it's too early to sue because we don't know what the government is doing with the patents. All we have now is a heads-up because the patent applications have been published. If they are testing the drugs, we can sue. But we have no way to know what they are doing."

Inquiries to NCI, including a Freedom of Information Act application for information, yielded no clue about what is being done with the five patents stemming from Samid's work and her signatures. As of early 2000, the FDA's on-line listing of all clinical trials featured only trials of plain phenylacetate—which Burzynski had long before neglected to patent for use as a cancer drug—against some types of tumors.

But duplication did occur and still stands. The Patent Office refused to comment on this. Kammerer speculated that "You could have had a lazy examiner who did not do a search." She said such slipups are uncommon, but not unprecedented. "It is very suspect," she observed.

What is clear, however, is that by putting Samid's work

through the patent process, the National Cancer Institute has officially endorsed the potential of the chemical formulations Burzynski discovered during the 1960s and '70s. But the institute gives him no credit, beyond listing a few of his published papers in its patent applications as footnoted references. No one at NCI would discuss the institute's motives or its plans for using its patents. But if NCI should ever act on its patents by making a push for phenylacetate and phenylacetylglutamine as cancer-fighting agents, and Burzynski does not try to stop them, he could be prevented from benefiting from his discoveries in any way, either financially or through recognition as a pioneering scientist and inventor.

The Mary Jo Siegel Story

The Making of a Devoted Advocate

Dr. Burzynski saved my life. And while he did this, the quality of my life was completely normal. I need to continue having access to him and his treatment.

—Testimony of Mary Jo Siegel before the House Committee on Commerce, Subcommittee on Oversight and Investigations, Feb. 29, 1996

Mary Jo Siegel's epiphany came late one April night in 1992. It marked the end of more than a year of torture for the feisty 40-year-old mother of three who had been plagued by a repeated diagnosis of Stage 4 non-Hodgkin's lymphoma, a slow-growing but almost always fatal cancer.

True, she had believed right along in the efficacy of the antineoplastons she was buying from Dr. Stanislaw Burzynski and pumping into her chest 24 hours a day. But she couldn't be completely sure until that night.

"I woke up in the middle of the night and had a terribly sore neck, where I had had a large tumor for quite awhile," she remembers. She was convinced that her tumor was completely gone.

It never came back. Not surprisingly, Mary Jo Siegel and her husband, Steve, became two of Burzynski's leading patient advocates. They organized bus trips from Houston to Austin, Texas, for patients who wanted to attend court hearings when Burzynski's medical license was in jeopardy. They testified before the House Commerce Committee in Washington, D.C. They helped raise more than $700,000 to defend Burzynski against criminal charges.

Before any of this began, the Siegels were forced to endure years of medical mistakes, physical pain and mental torture. Their family life was disrupted by Mary Jo's illness. They mortgaged their house to the hilt because insurance companies refused to pay for her treatment, causing them to spend $90,000 of their own funds over more than four years.

Before Mary Jo Siegel ever heard of Burzynski and his treatment, she had already endured a torturous medical odyssey. More than a foot of her intestines was surgically removed because a large tumor had formed a blockage and made part of her colon gangrenous. She underwent several painful bone marrow biopsies. And she traveled the country in search of a cure, one that wouldn't leave her hairless and sterile with cataracts, little or no saliva, damaged kidneys and bladder and a shrunken heart—all common side effects of various "conventional" cancer treatments.

She traveled from her home in Pacific Palisades, California, to Houston to see Burzynski almost as soon as she learned about him. The decision was simple for Mary Jo and her business-consultant husband. "We were feeling desperate after what we had learned about bone marrow transplants," Mary Jo says. "I had joined a cancer support group, and one day I was walking on the beach with one of my friends from that group. She said she had tried to go to a doctor named Burzynski for her ovarian cancer, and he wrote her that he couldn't help her because he had not yet done research on how his drug affected ovarian cancer. I felt that if he was actually telling people not to come to him when he wasn't sure he could help them, he was probably an honest man. So Steve and I immediately got on a plane to Houston."

The treatment she received there was unlike anything

she had encountered at the prestigious cancer centers at the University of Southern California, Stanford University or the Dana Farber Cancer Institute in Boston. "He did not promise to cure me," Mary Jo remembers of her first visit with Burzynski. "He only said, 'I've had some good results with lymphoma.' Then, unlike the other doctors we had asked to do the same thing, he gave me the names and phone numbers of six people he had treated. I called them all, and they were all doing well. I told Steve, 'I want to do this right now.'"

Less than two days after her first visit to Burzynski's clinic, she began taking antineoplastons in capsule form. "It might work," Burzynski told her, warning her at the time that even though it would be easier, taking his medication orally might not prove as effective as direct intravenous infusions. In fact, the capsules did not help at all.

"I stayed on the capsules for about three months, and during that time I got a huge tumor in my neck," Mary Jo says. "It was about the size of half an orange; I wore turtle-necks to hide it. Then one day, Steve and I were in Las Vegas on vacation and I noticed it was growing fast. I immediately flew to Houston. Burzynski took one look and said he wanted to put me on higher doses of medication, but I would need a catheter."

Convinced from her talks with other patients that the higher dosage could help her, Mary Jo immediately went to a nearby vascular surgeon, who implanted a catheter in her chest in less than 20 minutes. The procedure went so smoothly that she and Steve were lunching in a restaurant less than an hour later. That same day, Mary Jo was back in Burzynski's clinic, ready to start infusing antineoplastons through the new tube, which fed directly into her inferior vena cava, a large vein bringing blood to her heart.

Nothing much happened for three weeks. Her neck tumor stopped growing, but it was still present. Then came her nighttime epiphany.

It was the moment for which Mary Jo had spent years waiting and hoping. Never before or since had she faced anything remotely like the pain, discomfort, fear and anxiety she felt during the years leading up to that April night.

Small, brunette, always alert and almost always smiling, Mary Jo began having symptoms in late 1989. "I suddenly started having bad stomach attacks; these were much more than aches."

She went to her personal physician. "She treated me for ulcers for about one year. I was on Zantac and Pepcid. In the beginning, my attacks were infrequent and lasted only about an hour. But I soon noticed that the medications did nothing for them." During that year, the Siegels made repeated trips to the emergency rooms at Santa Monica and St. John's hospitals in the Los Angeles area. On each visit, doctors would administer shots of Demerol to Mary Jo, relaxing her intestine and easing her suffering. "I was in so much pain when we'd go there, I wasn't even sure where we were going," she says. "I was also vomiting and having diarrhea. Eventually I told Steve, 'This can't go on. If we don't do something about this, I'm going to die.'"

The couple consulted a gastroenterologist. "He concluded that the first doctor was wrong and that I had no ulcer. He told me I needed merely to change my diet and get the stress out of my life. But I have always had a good diet and a happy life," Mary Jo says, shaking her head.

"We call this time 'doctor hell,'" she says, grimacing at the memory. "I was glad the tests showed nothing, but I was still having stomach attacks. Only now, after more than a year, they were coming every time I ate. When I was in a restaurant, I would just hope I could get home before the next attack would start. Later, I learned that the food was being blocked in my intestine."

Mary Jo began to discover the real problem in February 1991, after she had a severe attack of stomach pain and nausea and Steve rushed her to the emergency room at St. John's. "They were about to give me Demerol again when Steve told them it just didn't work. A young radiologist named Rusty Greenberg spoke up. 'Let's get a CT scan of her abdomen while she's in pain,' he said. So I had to drink a glass of barium solution while I was in pain. It was awful, trying to hold it down," she remembers.

Greenberg soon saw from the CT scan that there was a major obstruction in Mary Jo's bowels. He immediately called in surgeon Barry Mann, and less than a day later, Mann removed more than a foot of her intestine. "It was gangrenous," Mary Jo says now. "Without the surgery, I would not have lived much longer."

But Mann also had bad news. Three days later, he came to Mary Jo's hospital room and called her parents and Steve out into the hallway, telling them tests had found that her blockage was a cancer tumor. He asked Steve how he wanted to deal with it. When Steve was unsure, Mann suggested simply telling Mary Jo the truth.

The truth was that her tumor had been diagnosed as a low-grade non-Hodgkin's lymphoma. Doctors at first believed the growth was only in her intestine and that her cancer was therefore Stage 1, a growth that had not spread beyond its original site. Doctors immediately began offering Mary Jo their brand of comfort. "Don't worry," said one oncologist who evaluated her. "You have a slow-growing cancer." This not only was wrong, but it also gave Mary Jo false hope. "They didn't tell me that even with chemotherapy, I could expect to live only about five or 10 years. In fact, there were four other people in my cancer support group who were diagnosed with lymphoma about the same time I was. They all decided to go the conventional-therapy route. Three of them are dead now, and the other one is dying. (Author's note: the woman died less than one year after Mary Jo was interviewed in August 1996.) It was really hard for me to see what happened to them. And it was even harder for them to see me as they've gotten worse and I've just gone on."

Another cheery doctor breezed into her hospital room a short time later, on a break from his campaign for the presidency of the Los Angeles County Medical Association, the local branch of the AMA. "It's nothing to worry about, but you're probably going to have diarrhea the rest of your life," he told her. "But why worry? You can always take pills for it."

Mary Jo and Steve felt desperate. Both were ready to have her start chemotherapy immediately, while she was still hospitalized after surgery. But her hematologist advised against an immediate start. "He sat on the edge of my bed and started to talk about lymphoma," she recalls. "We had not only never heard of lymphoma, we didn't even know how to spell it."

The blood-disorder specialist assured them, "A little chemo, that's all it's going to take. Your cancer is indolent." His use of that word intrigued Steve. "The only time I'd ever heard that word was when my father called me an 'indolent, lazy slob,'" he explains. "And lazy is what the word meant in this context, too. It meant that the disease wasn't doing much, wasn't very active."

The hematologist soon referred Mary Jo to Dr. Peter Rosen, a lymphoma specialist at the USC Norris Cancer

Center in East Los Angeles. Rosen, he flippantly said, "is a 'lymphomaniac.' He knows more about this disease than anyone in the Western states."

So the Siegels went to Rosen. "I wanted to do something," Mary Jo states. "But I wanted to do something right. I was utterly fed up with the hell of mistaken diagnoses."

That form of hell was finally over the first time she met with Rosen. Not only did he confirm the lymphoma diagnosis, but after he'd heard Mary Jo's complete case history, he observed that it would be "very unusual" to find the disease in only one focal point. He conducted a manual exam and found a lump under Mary Jo's right arm. No other doctor had spotted it, but it immediately propelled her case from an "indolent" Stage 1 up to a far more pernicious Stage 3 lymphoma. She would soon climb to Stage 4 as more and more cancerous nodes turned up. Mary Jo still trembles at the memory of the moment. "It was terrible. I said to myself, 'Oh, God! This isn't indolent at all. It's not lazy. It's hard at work.'"

Rosen's first piece of advice was that radiation would do little against this cancer. Because the lump meant that the cancer had spread, it would be useless to target radiation at a single location. The immediate consequence was a series of painful needle biopsies on the underarm lump, all of which came back positive for malignancy several days later. Then came a bone marrow test. "That was a nightmare," Mary Jo grimaces.

"By now, all my kids were really upset. We had a big fight with our oldest daughter, Jamie [then 15], the morning of the test, the biggest fight we'd ever had. I can't even remember what it was about, but I know the tension was causing conflict." The argument still festering in her mind, Mary Jo was off to St. John's Hospital, where she was laid facedown on a table while a nurse deployed a needle that "looked like a pencil, it was that thick" over the rear of her pelvis. As the needle went through layers of fatty tissue and finally ground audibly against bone, Steve Siegel remembers that "blood was all over the place." That's all he remembers. He fainted just as the nurse pulled the needle out and told Mary Jo, "I didn't get enough. I have to do it again..."

That was the first of six bone marrow tests Mary Jo would undergo. "They hurt like hell, but they're the best test of how you're doing. When the disease leaves the bone marrow, you know you're clear," she says. "On my sixth test, I was clear, but I wanted a repeat just to make sure. I must be the first person ever to ask for a bone marrow test."

The results from that first test confirmed that her cancer was widespread. Now Rosen explained to the very worried Siegels that disease like Mary Jo's is incurable. "We can treat you for a period of time," she recalls him saying. "We might even be able to treat you for a long time. But we can't cure you."

Rosen knows her case in intimate detail. "She had low-grade, slow-growing lymphoma," he said in a 1996 interview. "She had [swollen] lymph nodes you could examine and feel." He laid out the options now facing the Siegels, listing various types of treatment, from doing nothing to pursuing aggressive chemotherapy and radiation.

"We didn't think we could wait," Steve says. "Once we knew for sure what she had, we studied up on the disease. We learned it always becomes aggressive, and you can't predict in any one case when that will happen. Sometimes it takes 10 years, other times three or less. And there was some thought in the literature that if you treat it in its early phases, that's more effective than waiting."

The most aggressive of standard lymphoma therapies is a combination of massive chemotherapy, radiation and bone marrow transplant, with chemical and radiation doses so high—equivalent to the exposure received by persons standing within one mile of the atomic bomb dropped on Hiroshima—they almost kill the patient.

The Siegels learned that the most sophisticated bone marrow transplants were available at the Dana Farber Cancer Institute. Most of the patient's bone marrow is removed, then cleansed of cancer cells and frozen before it is reinfused to the patient. "We went there and met Dr. Lee Nadler, who had treated [former Massachusetts senator] Paul Tsongas," says Steve. "He took one look at Mary Jo and I saw his eyes light up. I think he saw her as fresh meat. She had had no prior radiation or chemotherapy and he wanted to start her right away." But the Siegels wanted to wait. "I at least wanted to be feeling reasonably well for my son Mark's bar mitzvah. He was 12 1/2 at the time," Mary Jo says. "So Nadler suggested we come back in a few months. I was about 90 percent sure I should do it."

That trip to Boston was one of the saddest times of Mary Jo's life. "We went to the 'Cheers' bar and I looked around and said, 'My God, everyone here's having fun but me. Everyone is living and I'm dying.'" But she didn't feel physically ill or that she was about to expire. She hadn't had severe pain since her abdominal surgery. "Even when I had the surgery in the hospital, I had energy. I walked miles around the halls every day. I'd schlep my little IV pole everywhere. Then, when we walked around Boston, I was feeling fine, too, and here was Dr. Nadler saying we should do this thing, which would practically kill me and definitely sap every once of energy and vitality I ever had as soon as possible."

Nadler took care to warn her about some of the side effects of the therapy. Her eyes, mouth, kidneys, bladder and heart would all be harmed. "We bring you as close to death as we can, and then we rescue you," Nadler said. The Siegels learned survivors also have a strong chance of contracting leukemia after about 10 years because of aftereffects of the radiation.

"And with all this, they weren't even giving us much hope," Steve notes. "They said there was a 40 percent chance of surviving for two to five years. Of course, there was also a 3 to 6 percent chance Mary Jo would die during the procedure."

"I broke down crying when I went to see the autologous bone marrow isolation room," Mary Jo remembers. "The nurses tried to tell me it was wonderful, they'd give me whatever I wanted to eat, Haagen-Dazs ice cream and all. But I'm social, and for about six weeks there would be no contact with any person who wasn't completely gowned and sterile. Right then, I couldn't deal with being six or eight weeks away from my kids. I decided I probably had a little time left and I should continue my search for something better. I joined a cancer support group. And then I heard about Dr. Burzynski."

Mary Jo refused to become discouraged even when there was no immediate success with Burzynski's capsules. "I had talked to the other people and I believed the stuff works," she says. "You have to believe. You have to be a full participant in this therapy. It's an active thing."

Burzynski now supplies patients with antineoplastons in solution in plastic intravenous feeding bags they can easily attach to the pumps they carry. But when Mary Jo began treatment, the fluid was dispensed in bottles, and patients had to transfer it to the plastic bags every day. Every two days, she'd have to replace and sterilize the tubing in her catheter to avoid risking infection. But that didn't bother her; rather, it made her feel she was doing something constructive for herself.

Soon after starting the treatment, Mary Jo informed Rosen that she'd begun seeing Burzynski. Normally a cheerful, almost cuddly man, Rosen reacted like a jilted lover. "He told me Burzynski is a fraud and a charlatan. But I decided I was going to keep doing his antineoplastons anyway. It's completely nontoxic and I figured at the very least, it couldn't hurt me," Mary Jo says.

Then came the epiphany. "I had believed from the start that the antineoplastons worked and would help me, but now I knew," she maintains.

But the apparent overnight disappearance of her neck tumor was not the end of her therapy. "I stayed on the catheter for exactly one year after that, until April of '93. Then I was pronounced in remission." Throughout that year, Mary Jo underwent CT scans every three months. Each time, the films showed reductions in the multiple tumors that had infested her intestine, underarms, groin and neck. "Every two months, I would go to Houston, too, and bring back a new supply of antineoplastons."

Again, this was necessary because Burzynski was under a 1983 federal court injunction forbidding interstate shipment of his drugs until or unless they were approved by the FDA. During that time, the Siegels twice took out second mortgages on their house. Blue Shield of California refused to pay for the therapy because antineoplastons lacked FDA approval, and Steve couldn't get the insurance company to budge.

Still, Mary Jo reached her goal. She was in remission, as pronounced by Rosen, who by now had transferred from the USC Norris Cancer Center to a similar facility at UCLA. "Rosen was really happy when he told me I was in remission," Mary Jo says. "But he never conceded that the antineoplastons worked. I've heard him say I'm a spontaneous remission. He has told me the disease waxes and wanes. But it doesn't wax and wane from Stage 3 or Stage 4. It only waxes."

Nor would there be many spontaneous remissions among the 52,700 new victims diagnosed with non-Hodgkin's lymphoma in 1996 in the United States. Some 23,300 persons died of the disease that year, according to American Cancer Society statistics. No one knows exactly how many spontaneous remissions occur in any year, but some doctors list one out of every 100,000 cases as a rule of thumb.

"Spontaneous remissions are very, very rare," reported one top official of the cancer society. "There are so few that we can't keep any statistics on them."

Yet Rosen sticks to what Mary Jo heard him say when she entered remission. "It's unclear what caused her improvement," he says. "Yes, she is now perfectly well clinically. Her lymph nodes improved coincidentally. We don't know why she's improved. There's a scoundrel and a charlatan treating her. The best way to assess whether the medication works is to study it scientifically, in double-blind studies, which he has never done. This man is posing as a savior. But he's got a credit card machine. He charges exorbitant fees, and he shares no information."

In fact, Burzynski in the early 1990s offered to supply antineoplastons to Rosen if the Los Angeles-based physician wanted to conduct his own scientific trial on them. Rosen declined.

Despite this conflict, Mary Jo Siegel expects to continue seeing Rosen every six weeks or so for years to come. And the road has not been completely smooth since she was declared in remission in 1993. In October 1995, a CT scan showed two lymph nodes in her neck in a condition consistent with lymphoma. "It's back," she shuddered when she was informed. "I cried when they faxed me the results." A quick trip to Houston ensued, after which Mary Jo went back on antineoplaston capsules. On her next CT scan three months later, the nodes were gone; she was back in remission. But she nevertheless stayed on oral antineoplastons.

Her history is completely consistent with Burzynski's expectations. "To be absolutely sure a tumor will not return, we must eliminate every cancerous cell," he says. "But it is very hard to be certain when we have accomplished this." Patients who are pronounced in remission can have recurrences. Simply renewing the therapy, as Mary Jo did, almost always restores those patients to remission, Burzynski explains.

As her treatment progressed, Mary Jo and Steve became aware of Burzynski's ongoing disputes with federal food and drug authorities. They threw themselves into his defense with the same vigor and determination they had shown while seeking a nontoxic treatment for cancer.

"I became an advocate for Burzynski even before I was officially pronounced in remission," Mary Jo says. "I watched as my tumors shrunk. That's a big reason why some things judges have said about Burzynski's case simply appall me. These judges won't allow the needs of the patients to stand in the way of the FDA. But I have always felt that we as patients have to make ourselves heard. I've always been sure that some compassionate judge would eventually listen to us."

The Siegels testified in three congressional hearings

and two courtrooms between early 1994 and mid-1996. "If we can keep Dr. Burzynski in the limelight, it won't be possible for the government to do as much to him as they would like," stresses Mary Jo. "I need this man. He has saved my life. I am very sure that without him and his drug, I would be dead right now, like the people I knew who were diagnosed with the same disease at the very same time I was."

Postscript

PACIFIC PALISADES, Calif., midyear 2000— "There's nothing dramatic going on with my health," says Mary Jo Siegel. Nothing dramatic, that is, unless you consider that more nine years after she was diagnosed with cancer and told it would almost certainly be terminal, she's completely free of the non-Hodgkin's lymphoma that threatened to destroy her life.

The other good news for Mary Jo and her husband Steve, still active leaders of the Burzynski Patient Group, is that the Burzynski Clinic is active and has no serious pending legal threats. "I still work on the patient group every single day," says Mary Jo, whose dining room no longer resembles the command center it once was. "I maintain the patient group web-site (www.burzynskipatientgroup.org) and I get between 15 and 30 emails every day from all over the world from people who want to know more about Dr. B." She refers some to other patient activists like Ric Schiff (see The Crystin Schiff Story), and some to other patients and to parents of patients. "I even deal sometimes with parents who are terrified because doctors threaten them with arrest if they don't put their children on the standard chemotherapy and radiation treatments. But we're not raising money seriously right now. Our main political activity is to lobby for approval of the drug and for compassionate use exemptions so patients who don't qualify for Dr. B's clinical trials can get the treatment."

When she's not lobbying and helping other patients, Mary Jo is often walking. Near her home are a four-mile walk from the top of the canyon behind her house to a waterfall, a 10-mile walk into the Santa Monica Mountains National Recreation Area and several others.

Like almost all cancer patients in remission, Mary Jo gets CT or MRI scans every year—all have been clear for the last five years. She still sees Dr. Peter Rosen at UCLA every year and he still refuses to believe antineoplastons had anything to do with her recovery. And she visits Burzynski's clinic yearly.

After her years in "doctor hell," with every other woman in the cancer support group she once attended now dead—none sought antineoplaston treatment—Mary Jo's current life seems like heaven to her.

CHAPTER 7

Answering the Critics

Mention Dr. Stanislaw Burzynski to Dr. William Jarvis, president of the National Council Against Health Fraud, and one of the first words he utters is "quack." Then he quickly asks, "Have you heard of Saul Green?"

Saul Green. Retired biochemist from New York's Memorial Sloan-Kettering Cancer Center. Formerly a consultant to Washington lawyer Grace Monaco, an attorney assisting Aetna Life Insurance Co. in its actions against Dr. Stanislaw Burzynski. Author of "Antineoplastons: An Unproved Cancer Therapy," an article that appeared in the June 3, 1992, issue of the Journal of the American Medical Association. Still the most outspoken critic of Burzynski.

Green's article may have caused more harm to Burzynski's reputation than anything ever written about him. It was intended to. "Many physicians don't know how to rebut their patients' arguments when the patient says, 'Doc, I have so many months to live, so why don't I go see Dr. Burzynski or someone like him?' This gives the physician the ammunition to say, 'Here are the facts,' without sounding paternalistic," said Dr. David Cooper, then a contributing editor to *JAMA* and director of the division of endocrinology at Sinai Hospital in Baltimore. Cooper said five physicians peer-reviewed Green's article before it was accepted. His comment was published in the June 5, 1992, issue of *The Cancer Letter*, a nationally distributed newsletter.

Since then, Green's article has been the prime source cited by virtually every so-called quackbuster who has attacked Burzynski. One example is a 1996 commentary by

Dr. Barrie Casselith, carried in *Cancer*, an official publication of the American Cancer Society. She calls Green's analysis a "laboratory investigation by a respected scientist who concluded antineoplastons don't even exist." But she never mentions that Green frankly admits he performed a "literature review," never attempting any actual laboratory analysis. And she makes no mention of Green's links to Aetna's legal actions.

Then there's the *Readers Guide to Alternative Health Methods,* published in 1993 by the AMA, by coincidence the parent and owner of *JAMA*. This book cites Green as the major authority on Burzynski and concludes, with Green, that "none of the independent tests carried out with antineoplastons in experimental tumor systems have shown anticancer activity."

The problem is that Green's article doesn't always supply "the facts," as Cooper suggested it would. At times, it supplies a highly colored mixture of questionable quotations and half-truths. Green never visited Burzynski's clinic, never examined the records of even one patient or spoke with a single patient or employee of Burzynski. Instead, his "literature review" tries to use Burzynski's own written words and those of others who have worked or corresponded with him to discredit his theory that antineoplastons work by "normalizing" cancer cells and causing them to resume the usual healthy cycle of cell replication and death.

He begins by claiming that Burzynski has lied about his credentials. "Burzynski's bibliography does not identify a Ph.D. dissertation," Green asserts. In fact, it does list one, a 274-page tome. The title: "Investigations on Amino Acids and Peptides in Blood Serum of Healthy People and Patients With Chronic Renal Insufficiency." Burzynski keeps a copy on his office bookshelf, bound in a green jacket. In letters he wrote later, Green claims that Burzynski never received a Ph.D., but only a DMsc. degree. He says, "Polish authorities in Warsaw state that the DMsc. and Ph.D. degrees are not equivalent." Burzynski responds with a sworn affidavit from Zdislaw Kleinrok, written on stationery identifying him as rector and president of the Medical Academy of Lublin. It states that "after receiving an M.D. degree in June 1967, Dr. Stanislaw R. Burzynski also received a Ph.D. degree...for his studies in biochemistry on October 16, 1968."

Green goes on to attack Burzynski's manufacturing facility, saying that "the FDA will not confirm that it stated in writing that it considered the manufacturing plant at the Burzynski Research Institute to be operating in accordance with the FDA's good manufacturing guidelines." He reports that this information came to him via a telephone conversation with Sharon Miller, an official in the FDA's Houston office. But when Burzynski aide Dean Mouscher telephoned Miller to ask why she would have refused to confirm that Burzynski's plant had passed all FDA inspections, she responded that she never told Green the plant had flunked, only that she had no firsthand knowledge of whether the plant had passed inspections. In fact, it had repeatedly passed, but Green never mentions this fact.

Green also suggests that antineoplastons can't possibly work against cancer because they are "insoluble in aqueous solutions." He adds that this means Burzynski can't really be using antineoplastons in his intravenous treatments, but rather must be using something like a sodium salt of phenylacetylglutamine. This chemical, he says, "results from conjugation of glutamine in the liver with...phenylacetic acid." It is true that antineoplastons A10 and AS2-1 contain L-glutamine, phenylacetate and phenylacetylglutamine.

Burzynski responds that "the solubility of [antineoplastons] in water is within the range of solubility of amino acids—more soluble in fact than tyrosine and tryptophan. Many important biological substances, such as steroid hormones, have lower solubility." And in their paper summarizing the aborted NCI-sponsored antineoplaston clinical trial, Jan Buckner and Mark Malkin make no mention of any difficulties with the solubility of either A10 or AS2-1. They claim to have infused antineoplastons in exactly the method used by Burzynski, complete with portable programmable pumps that patients could take home after initial hospitalization. Could they have done any of this if the antineoplastons were insoluble, as Green suggests?

Green's next line of attack involved in vitro testing of antineoplastons in laboratories not operated by Burzynski. One site where such testing was done was the Medical College of Georgia in Augusta, where researchers tested A10 against cultures of cancer cells. In his *JAMA* article, Green says the Georgia researchers "have advised Burzynski that their work does not provide support for the use of A10 in human subjects." But in a letter to the editor of *JAMA*, written just one week after Green's article appeared, the former clinical director of the gas chromatography-mass spectrometry laboratory at the Medical College of Georgia took exception to what Green wrote. "The work at MCG has not involved human use, but it has demonstrated inhibition of the growth of MCF-7 breast cancer and Nb-2 rat lymphoma cells in vitro," wrote Dr. Edwin D. Bransome Jr., referring to two well-established lines of laboratory cancer cells. "Therefore [Green's] conclusion that 'none of the independent tests carried out with antineoplastons in experimental tumor systems have shown anticancer activity' is incorrect." *JAMA* never published

Bransome's letter.

Similarly, Green reports that he wrote to foreign researchers who have tested antineoplastons. One is Hideaki Tsuda of Japan's Kurume University School of Medicine, whom Green quotes as responding, "We have not published any results of our clinical investigation on antineoplastons .... We do not think that you are going to pick up any biological effect of Antineoplaston A10 in our study." But when Burzynski asked Tsuda what he actually wrote to Green, the Japanese scientist replied in a letter, "We also told him [Green] that we do not think he is going to pick up any biological effect of Antineoplaston A10 in our study. In this sentence we said very much that since Dr. Green is not an M.D., he will not pick up any biological effect of Antineoplaston A10 in our study even when there is effect there. That is what we said and what we meant in our letter."

Green had used a partial or questionable quote from Tsuda in a transparent attempt to discredit Burzynski. And none of the five physicians who peer-reviewed Green's article possessed either the information or the inclination to dispute him.

Tsuda, meanwhile, had corresponded for years with Burzynski, the sole supplier of the antineoplastons Tsuda uses in clinical trials against liver and colon cancers. Just after the Green diatribe appeared, Tsuda advised Burzynski, "We think you do not have to rebut this article because NCI will give the straight answer sooner or later from their clinical trial on brain cancers. Sometimes silence has more power than anything and it is not wise for you to give the impression to other scientists that you are fighting all the time. Nobody wants to get involved in such a fight .... We will publish some case reports indicating that antineoplastons have been beneficial for cancer patients."

In another letter, Tsuda reported in 1995 that "the interest in antineoplastons in Kurume University is now growing rapidly because we are treating multiple liver metastases from the colon of our president. He has been quite well during the last six months. We also have a good control case with hepatoma....Hepatoma is one of the biggest medical problems in Asia."

Some of this, of course, was private correspondence, so Green didn't know of it when he wrote to Dr. T. Sugimura, head of Japan's National Cancer Center, for information on antineoplaston research in that country. Green reprinted Sugimura's response: "I am afraid that Antineoplaston A10 has no popularity in our country."

Green next cites a letter from Dr. Carlo Trevisani, president of the Italian pharmaceutical company Sigma Tau, who reported in 1991 that his firm "did not intend to proceed with the development of antineoplastons." Trevisani, whose firm tested antineoplastons supplied by Burzynski, said that "on the basis of these results, the project has been discontinued and more extensive testing or clinical trials have not been planned. Dr. Burzynski was notified of these results."

Green, however, provides no details of the precise types of testing Sigma Tau conducted. And the company's correspondence with Burzynski indicates that Sigma Tau never understood the distinction he makes between the human immune system and the so-called biochemical defense system. So Sigma Tau tested antineoplastons to see whether they would stimulate immune responses. They did not. "They tested it the wrong way," Burzynski says. "The scientist in charge was an immune system therapist. Antineoplastons do not produce a response from the immune system. We never said they would."

Subsequently, Green resurrects the P388 mouse leukemia controversy. He reports, as if he were the first to find out, that in 1983 and 1985, the NCI conducted tests of Antineoplastons A2 and A5, two of the earliest fractions of the broad-action Antineoplaston A. "The results showed that those doses which were high enough to produce toxic effects in the mice were not effective in inhibiting the growth of the tumor or in killing it," he writes.

Burzynski, of course, had predicted precisely that result when supplying antineoplastons for testing by the NCI. Green says nothing about Burzynski's explanation that because antineoplastons are species specific—sometimes even tumor specific—it would be all but impossible for them to have any impact on P388 mouse leukemia. Nor does Green mention that the P388 strain is no longer used as a major benchmark for measuring new drug potential, precisely because it doesn't provide an accurate measure of the possible benefits of many new drugs.

Green moves on, noting that in 1990, the NCI tested Antineoplaston A10 against a panel of tumors from cell lines, including lung cancers, colon cancers, cancer of the central nervous system, melanoma, ovarian cancer and renal-cell cancer. He quotes the chief of NCI's drug synthesis and chemistry branch as reporting that "the drug exhibited neither growth inhibition nor cytotoxicity at the dose levels tested."

Those levels, Burzynski responded, were about 10,000 times smaller than what he says would have been needed to obtain a significant response. What Green doesn't report in his *JAMA* article is that on March 24, 1992, Burzynski received a report from that same drug synthesis and chemistry branch showing that when tested at higher doses, antineoplastons demonstrated anticancer activity against the very same tumor cultures. When Burzynski reported this glaring omission in a letter to the editor of *JAMA* published in January 1993, Green responded that he has received "communications from [NCI] stating that the tests done at NCI in 1991...did not give any positive results." But the NCI's report to Burzynski on those tests makes no judgments about the test results. Instead, it consists in large part of a series of graphs showing how much tumor-cell cultures grew after varying amounts of antineoplastons were introduced into them. Those graphs demonstrate clearly that the more A10 and AS2-1 were placed into tissue cultures, the less tumor-cell growth occurred. This was true for lung cancer, cancer of the central nervous system, colon cancers, ovarian cancer and renal cancer, with greater responses in most types from AS2-1 than from A10.

At the very least, this means the actual charts made in an NCI laboratory demonstrate some level of tumor-growth inhibition in the test tube, regardless of what some NCI scientists or technicians may have told Green earlier. What's more, the NCI report to Burzynski states that some of the antineoplastons tested were from lots received as early as 1984, eight years before the tests were done. The drug normally loses much of its potency after a few months, so any results achieved with aged samples simply reinforce the notion that the more antineoplaston administered and the newer it is, the more potent its effect.

All this thoroughly debunks Green's conclusion that "none of the independent tests carried out with antineoplastons in experimental tumor systems have shown anticancer activity." This raises a serious question about *JAMA's* peer-review process: How did Green's conclusions make it past the scrutiny of five physicians to be included in this prestigious journal of scientific record? Cooper's comments reported in *The Cancer Letter* offer a clue. He wanted Green's conclusion, or something like it. What's more, none of the five doctors on the peer-review panel had access to all the original documents Green cited. So they were essentially taking his word for it, precisely the problem Green claims to find with non-peer-reviewed journals where many of Burzynski's papers have appeared. What good is peer review if the supposed peers have no direct knowledge of what they are reviewing, or have a political agenda?

And what about Green's own agenda? He denies that he has ever worked for Aetna in any of its legal actions against Burzynski and his patients. His exact words, in a letter he wrote to the author on Nov. 19, 1996: "I was never employed by Aetna and can prove it. I was employed as a consultant to a lawyer assisting in the [Aetna] lawsuit. She wanted a scientist to explain the 'science' in [Burzynski's] papers. The report I prepared for her was based on what [Burzynski] himself said in his own papers. My report would have been precisely the same had I been paid to do it by [Burzynski] himself." Making a distinction between working for Aetna and working for its lawyer in an effort to create an aura of impartiality is typical of the reasoning throughout Green's writing on Burzynski. It is sophistry, a half-truth, at best.

That's essentially the conclusion reached by researcher Dr. Lichuan Chen, who in late 1996 completed an independent in-house analysis of Green's *JAMA* article for the Office of Alternative Medicine at the NIH. Chen calls many of Green's statements "misrepresentations and misinterpretations."

His evaluation of Burzynski: "I find his work credible and it warrants further investigation. By no means is he a charlatan or his treatment a sham…. What are the quack-busters afraid of?"

Green is not Burzynski's only critic, merely the most prominent, public and persistent. Some of the other criticisms include an alleged failure to publish results in peer-reviewed journals; failure to keep reliable statistics on response rates of his patients; the cost of antineoplaston therapy (Green maintains that antineoplastons are no better than plain phenylacetate, which costs a fraction of what Burzynski charges for antineoplaston therapy); and a failure to perform true double-blind studies to determine whether antineoplastons really work.

What transpired around the Green article provides an example of why Burzynski feels a lack of trust for the entire peer-review journal process, despite its acceptance as the single way for information to achieve general recognition among most modern scientists. Nevertheless, anyone who charges that Burzynski hasn't published in peer-reviewed journals simply hasn't read his bibliography. He lists papers carried in journals such as *Experimental Clinical Chemotherapy*, the *International Journal of Tissue Reaction, Future Trends in Chemotherapy*, and the *Journal of Cancer, Chemistry and Biophysics*. He also lists articles in more than a dozen books published between 1980 and 1995.

It is true that Burzynski offered few statistics about his patients during much of the 1980s. But this began to change in late 1988, when he published results of a study of 20 brain tumor victims in the journal *Advances in Experimental and Clinical Chemotherapy*. In that paper, Burzynski reported a 55 percent objective response rate in patients with metastatic lung cancer and astrocytoma and glioblastoma multiforme brain tumors. He defined objective response as reduction in tumor size and reported that only 25 percent of the group had increased disease, while 20 percent demonstrated stable disease with eased symptoms.

Since then, Burzynski has continued compiling statistics more carefully than he did in the earlier years of his private practice, a time when he was plagued by lawsuits and grand jury appearances. Even after his indictment in November 1995, he continued those efforts, sending scans and case files of scores of his patients to outside experts, who verified his frequent successes.

In late 1996, he submitted 28 current brain tumor cases for review by independent radiologists at the Southwest Neuro-Imaging center in Phoenix. The results reported by independent radiologists: Thirteen patients saw their tumors shrink by more than 50 percent, while three more had significant improvement but less than a 50 percent reduction. Then he submitted 17 cases for evaluation by Dr. Robert Burdick of the University of Washington. Results: Almost half were complete remissions. These results were achieved for brain cancers that are almost always fast-growing and deadly. They establish that while antineoplastons are promising and appear to dissipate many cancers, they are still not a "silver bullet" that can instantly destroy all tumors. Burzynski has never made such a claim, even though it is often implied by critics who call him a quack.

The FDA also frequently has criticized the costs of what it calls unproven cancer therapies, decrying the "financial hardship that results from spending money for unproven... remedies that raise false hopes." It is certainly true that antineoplaston therapy is one of the more expensive alternative therapies, costing about $3,000 to $9,000 per month. But in the frequent instances when it works, it's a bargain.

Ordinary chemotherapy can often cost more than $10,000 per month, a sum willingly paid by the same insurance companies that often resist paying the claims of Burzynski's patients. Meanwhile, the clot-dissolving agent TPA, made by the California firm Genentech, runs more than $2,000 per injection. When insurance companies refuse to pay for antineoplastons, the financial burden rests solely on the shoulders of Burzynski's patients and their families, some of whom raise the needed funds through appeals to friends, relatives, colleagues and neighbors. Although Burzynski has sometimes treated needy patients without charge, most of his patients must pay. It's the only way to support a modern clinic with dozens of employees, a chemical manufacturing plant with more than 50 employees, and a work force that includes more than two dozen people who have doctoral degrees.

Then there's the matter of double-blind studies. "They are the only way to prove that a drug works," says Dr. Jarvis of the National Council Against Health Fraud. Yet even Burzynski's harshest critics admit that no researcher performs double-blind studies on terminally ill cancer patients, which involves half the group randomized onto a placebo of some kind. "I simply won't do it," Burzynski says. "If I did, I would be sentencing half the people who come to me to certain death."

Rather than using double-blind studies, cancer researchers often test new cancer drugs in patients who have already failed every other established form of treatment. But this can bias a trial against a new drug like antineoplastons in two ways. First, patients who have failed other therapies are often so debilitated that nothing can save them. The side effects of highly toxic chemotherapy and radiation can devastate an already weakened body. When patients die after having sought antineoplastons as a last resort, skeptics are quick to chalk it up as failure of the drug. Second, there's the occasional residual effect of radiation. Patients who don't appear to respond to radiation therapy at the time it is administered can respond significantly weeks or months later. So it has been easy for some oncologists to say that patients who failed radiation and benefited after they sought out Burzynski have actually been helped not by antineoplastons but by delayed effects of radiation.

The bottom line is that Burzynski has persuasive answers to virtually every scientific and medical criticism leveled at him. Whether or not an observer chooses to respect them often depends on preconceived notions.

Postscript, Spring 2000

For many years, Saul Green's article in *JAMA* was the key piece of propaganda the FDA and many oncologists used to discourage patients from seeking treatment from Dr. Burzynski. While most of what Green states was long ago refuted in the first printing of this book, the actions of one scientist whose letter he quotes establish the claims in Green's article as even more untenable than they seem on the surface. That scientist is Dr. Hideaki Tsuda, the Japanese cancer researcher from whose letter Green took a partial quote which distorted Tsuda's meaning to such an extent that Green gives the impression Tsuda was saying the exact opposite of what he meant to say.

Subsequent to this book's thorough debunking of the Green article, Tsuda took a step on his own that established even more firmly his conviction that antineoplastons throw many cancers into remission: He translated the first edition of this book and assisted in having it published in Japanese by the Tokyo publishing house Aoki Shoten. Japanese publication came in September 1999. "If this doesn't demonstrate how completely my impressions of antineoplastons were misinterpreted, I don't know what could," said Tsuda.

With the Green article completely discredited, FDA publicists and established cancer doctors needed a new, credible-looking critique with which to dissuade those who inquire about Burzynski. In September of 1998, *The Cancer Letter* provided it to them. The newsletter published a special issue devoted entirely to a supposedly impartial report on Burzynski's work. The issue contained an analysis of the annual report on his clinical trials, filed by Burzynski with the FDA. *Cancer Letter* editor Paul Goldberg, in a sincere effort at fairness, conducted an extensive interview with Burzynski before submitting the annual report to three prominent oncologists: Dr. Howard Ozer, director of the Allegheny University Cancer Center in Philadelphia; Dr. Henry Friedman, professor of pediatrics at Duke University Medical School, and Dr. Peter Eisenberg, an oncologist in private practice in Marin County, California. The problem: Goldberg was apparently unaware of the anti-Burzynski bias that pervades most of the conventional-medicine anti-cancer world.

The threesome chosen by Goldberg arrived unanimously at several conclusions, all commonly trumpeted afterward by the FDA to prospective patients who contacted the agency for information about Burzynski and antineoplastons. Their main contentions: Burzynski's protocols are "poorly designed and data are not interpretable," antineoplastons have "significant toxicity," and a claim that Burzynski should not use the "stable disease" category as a indicator of positive responses to his medication. *The Cancer Letter* also reported that "The reviewers did not audit the data in the annual report. [They] first assessed protocol design and the quality of data. [They] concluded that the studies were so flawed that auditing them was meaningless."

Burzynski immediately answered all their criticisms, in a response also published by *The Cancer Letter*. But the FDA has never sent those responses to a single patient. Burzynski in his initial response said that, "It may come as a surprise to the reviewers that the protocols they are criticizing were designed by doctors from Memorial Sloan-Kettering Cancer Center and used in Phase II studies of antineoplastons by the National Cancer Institute." In short, Burzynski explained, he used the protocols fashioned for the abortive NCI-sponsored clinical trials because he knew almost everything he does is immediately blasted by his critics. So the critics, in effect, this time were lambasting several eminent colleagues without knowing it. Said Burzynski, "If our protocols are flawed, so were those used by the NCI and its chosen investigators. We have always attempted to live by the standards set by the NCI."

Burzynski's response to *The Cancer Letter* reviewers' claim that antineoplastons are toxic was an equally effective rebuttal. Ozer, Friedman and Eisenberg all complained that many Burzynski patients suffer from hypernatremia, an excess of sodium in the bloodstream. Wrote Friedman: "Hypernatremia in patients with cancers outside the brain is a problem, but when you have somebody with a mass in the brain…you are really asking for a much more pronounced problem because of the fluid shifts that go along with that. When you correct hypernatremia, you can produce a significant intracranial swelling of the tumor and—ultimately—kill somebody. When we get a patient who is hypernatremic, he or she is handled incredibly gingerly.

Hypernatremia places brain tumor patients in double jeopardy. First, there is the danger from hypernatremia itself. Second, after you correct hypernatremia, a patient can develop cerebral edema [swelling]. When you have a brain tumor and you get cerebral edema, it's frequently a lethal event."

Burzynski responded that "serious hypernatremia" occurred in fewer than 1 percent of his patients. "In the other patients, hypernatremia was only a laboratory result without any clinical change in the patient's condition, and was reversed by simple measures such as hydration," he said. Burzynski speculated that the three reviewers may have focused on hypernatremia because, at the FDA's request, he reports even the slightest increase in blood sodium to the agency. "The standard practice [among oncologists] is that such small change which occurs in clinical trials using chemotherapy is usually not reported because it is of no clinical significance," Burzynski added. "Studies with antineoplastons reveal that the entire sodium load due to antineoplastons is [almost always] rapidly eliminated through the kidneys." Burzynski said serious hypernatremia was not reversed in just two of the 967 patients listed in the 1997 annual report—the vast majority of whom had no such problem. One of the two died of an unrelated stroke before the hypernatremia could be treated and the other, Burzynski said, refused treatment for the condition.

Burzynski added that it is standard practice for him to stop treatment of patients whose blood sodium counts rise by one point. "In practically all of these patients, the next day sodium is back to normal," he said. "Usually we don't have to introduce any treatment for this, and simply ask the patients to drink more fluids."

The danger of hypernatremia, in fact, is the main reason

Burzynski insists that new patients remain near his clinic at least 10 days, and usually two weeks, after starting treatment. Besides receiving instructions in how to load and prime their infusion pumps, patients get multiple blood tests daily monitoring the salinity of their blood. The tests come as frequently as every seven minutes with very new patients. Doses are adjusted until any problems are eliminated. When patients return home, they also undergo frequent blood tests, with results faxed immediately to Burzynski, who makes changes in dosage wherever it's needed.

And contrary to Friedman's fear, Burzynski reports that "cerebral edema is usually reduced during the treatment because of the osmotic effects of the formulation. Patients when they are under treatment usually have less chance of cerebral edema. When we stop the treatments, then they may develop signs of cerebral edema. Some may have a rebound effect. So sometimes with such patients we have to resort to other medications to decrease edema. But about 98 percent of our patients have a tendency to eliminate more than the usual amount of fluid and about 1.5 percent have a tendency to retain fluids. This situation seems to be beneficial, because many cancer patients have problems with fluid retention." In fact, many Burzynski patients list frequent urination as one of the inconveniences they put up with during treatment.

The Cancer Letter's panel also objected to Burzynski's frequent mention of stable disease as a positive response to antineoplastons. By FDA standards, stable disease is defined as either no increase in the size of a tumor or a reduction of 49 percent or less during the first six months on a treatment. Of course, most patients with rapidly-growing tumors that suddenly stop growing and even reverse themselves somewhat after a treatment begins react with relief and consider their improved condition a response to the treatment. This, however, is insufficient for the FDA and for *The Cancer Letter's* threesome. Said Ozer, "I am surprised by Dr. Burzynski's statement that stable disease is a positive outcome. That runs contrary to established criteria for trial design."

Burzynski responded immediately by citing reports of clinical trials published in three different peer-reviewed journals (*Clinical Cancer Research*, 1996; *the Journal of Neurosurgery*, 1995, and *Cancer*, 1991) in which stable disease was considered an "objective response." Those studies were conducted by doctors at leading cancer centers including Memorial Sloan-Kettering in New York; M.D. Anderson in Houston; the Mayo Clinic in Rochester, Minn.; Johns Hopkins in Baltimore; the University of California at San Francisco, and Duke University. Noting that he could have cited many more such reports, Burzynski said the three demonstrate that "it is customary to include stable disease as objective response in peer reviewed articles describing clinical trials in brain tumors."

Having dealt with the main complaints from *The Cancer Letter* and its panel, Burzynski also demolished numerous smaller issues raised in the newsletter's voluminous report. Here are some examples:

The Cancer Letter reports that co-investigators who follow Burzynski patients after they return home "have no knowledge of Burzynski's protocol." Said Burzynski, "All co-investigators are given copies of the protocols that affect their patients."

The Cancer Letter quotes an FDA statement saying "[Burzynski] has administered antineoplastons to several thousand patients without, for the most part, gathering enough information to determine whether the product is safe or actually works." Responded Burzynski, "All information gathered in the treatment of all patients is compiled to be submitted to the FDA in support of safety and efficacy of antineoplastons. Because the FDA delayed for years giving us INDs, we have only recently been able to gather the sort of detailed information the agency says it wants." The FDA also refuses to say precisely what evidence it would require from Burzynski before approving his medication.

The Cancer Letter quotes Dr. Mark Malkin, chief investigator on one of the aborted NCI trials of antineoplastons as saying, "In two...patients we observed somnolence and seizures that resolved by stopping antineoplastons. In two patients, edema appeared to have been attributable to the therapy." Burzynski's rebuttal: "The somnolence and seizures in these patients were typical symptoms of brain tumors, not the results of treatment with antineoplastons. The patients with edema suffered from this before the treatment with antineoplastons. In our experience, based on thousands of patients, less than 2 percent of the patients have a tendency to retain fluid."

The Cancer Letter quotes Malkin as saying of hypernatremia, the only condition singled out by Ozer, Friedman and Eisenberg as a toxic effect of antineoplastons, "You can monitor it, you can detect when it starts, and you can treat it if necessary." Said Burzynski, "The statement of Dr. Malkin, who was an NCI-approved investigator of antineoplastons at Sloan-Kettering, indicates that hypernatremia is usually negligible and an easy-to-treat complication."

The Cancer Letter reported that its reviewers "did not audit the data in the annual report." Said Burzynski, "This statement confirms again the bias of the reviewers who criticized the protocol designed by Memorial Sloan-Kettering Cancer Center and approved by NCI and FDA. They did not even care enough to review the data in the annual report, yet they expressed negative opinions. Since they did not review the data on the treatment, their review is scientifically invalid."

Dr. Ozer writes that "Dr. Burzynski is studying a heterogeneous, ill-defined patient population. He treats patients who come through the door and only patients who come through the door. He organizes data by the disease site, whatever the patient's stage, and whatever treatment they received prior to walking through the door of his clinic." Without even mentioning the obvious problems in Ozer's statement—the fact that he comments on data he has said he didn't bother to review, and the physical reality that Burzynski cannot treat anyone who doesn't enter his clinic —Burzynski responds: "The reviewer ignores the fact that each protocol is designed for the treatment of a specific type of cancer. The protocols define exactly what stage of the disease is accepted for the treatment and define what previous treatment patients are allowed to have received. Only some patients who come through the door are accepted to clinical trials. Most are not accepted for trials. We can prove this."

Dr. Ozer complains that "I see problems of adherence to protocols. While protocols call for evaluation of response every 90 days, in some instances I see Dr. Burzynski making these evaluations monthly." In short, his complaint in effect was that Burzynski was too thorough and prompt in filing reports. Said Burzynski, "Most of our protocols call for clinical evaluation monthly, but some only every 90 days."

Dr. Ozer writes that "I do see patients with responses who subsequently withdraw from the study. That means to me that the patient's perception of their benefit is less than what Dr. Burzynski is interpreting." Answered Burzynski, "Some of the patients felt so well that they decided to discontinue treatment sooner than I advised. Their tumors disappeared and they did not feel it was necessary for them to continue the maintenance treatment. We can provide names, telephone numbers and home physicians for these patients."

These are only some of the specifics to which Burzynski responded, but they demonstrate that the complaints of *The Cancer Letter* panel were consistently both specious and inconsistent. All three panelists said they did not evaluate Burzynski's data, but then all attempted to rip it apart. Perhaps more important than anything this panel said was the statement of Dr. Dieter Schellinger, chief of neuroradiology at Georgetown University Hospital in Washington, D.C., who frequently reviews MRI scans of patients Burzynski classifies as responders. Schellinger insisted to *The Cancer Letter* that "I know very little about the drug. I look only at images." Those images, which cannot be influenced by politics of any kind, demonstrated that "The majority of the cases I have reviewed were in concert with [Burzynski's] assessments. In some cases I rated them higher than he did," Schellinger said.

Patients who requested information from the FDA during the last years of the 20th Century and the opening of the 21st saw neither the Schellinger statements nor the published Burzynski refutations of virtually every criticism leveled against him in *The Cancer Letter*. One conclusion easily drawn from this behavior: The FDA fears letting prospective patients know everything it knows about Burzynski. This may be because anyone who is fully informed would perforce question many FDA actions over a period of almost 20 years.

The Thomas Wellborn Story

Back in His Beloved Bass Boat

I don't care if Burzynski robbed Fort Knox and shot the pope. His stuff works.

—Virginia Wellborn in September 1996, after two
MRI scans showed that her husband's brain tumor
had completely disappeared

Thomas Wellborn's health was absolutely perfect before he retired in 1989 to the green, tree-lined shores of Pickwick Lake near Florence, Alabama. "The lake is full of small-mouth bass, and I wanted to spend my time fishing," said Wellborn, who devoted most of his working life to curing the diseases of catfish while serving as a fisheries biologist at Mississippi State University in Starkville and at the University of Florida.

Thomas, then 62, was fishing with a former student on the scenic man-made lake, created by the Tennessee Valley Authority, early on the morning of June 17, 1994, when his brain tumor first made its presence known. Yes, Tom said later, there was one earlier clue that something might have been amiss. He'd spent much of 1990 and 1991 traveling in Africa and Egypt and suffered a high fever on his first night home. "We imagined all the different parasites I might have picked up in those places," he says. "Our imaginations ran rampant." But the 24-hour emergency clinic he consulted could find nothing wrong, so Tom and Virginia Wellborn went home to sleep it off. His fever never left. It would occasionally ease, but Tom ran a low-grade fever for the next two years, never above 102 degrees and never below 99. "I felt rotten every afternoon, and I had muscle aches all the time," he said. It was only later that he and Virginia, a registered nurse, realized the fever was probably a symptom of something far more pernicious.

But the fever couldn't keep Tom Wellborn out of his 18-foot Astro bass boat for long. He was standing in the bow running a trolling loader when the first seizure struck him that June, and the next thing Tom knew, he was sitting on the deck, unable to move his left arm or the left side of his face, which twitched uncontrollably. Saliva drooled from his mouth, and he was unable to talk. "I could not control myself beyond just sitting there," he recalls. "I thought immediately that I'd either had a stroke or I had a brain tumor."

That was also what fishing companion Terry Bates, a fisheries biologist for the U.S. Department of Agriculture, believed. "We'd already caught quite a few fish that morning. I was sitting in the back of the boat and Tom was in the front. He suddenly turned around and I looked at him, and he was squatting and holding his head with both hands. Saliva just came running out of his mouth. Pretty soon he started asking, 'What happened?' I was spooked and uncomfortable and wanted to put in to shore right away, but he wanted to fish some more, so we stayed out there another hour. Personally, I thought he'd had some kind of stroke."

Tom never lost consciousness and recovered quickly, feeling normal again within five minutes. "I really wanted to fish a bit longer," he said. "Maybe there was some part of me that sensed I wouldn't be back in the boat for quite a while."

It was to be his last fishing trip for more than two years. "He made light of what had happened," remembered his wife. "I thought he might have had a very transient stroke, and I told him he ought to go to the doctor." She didn't say so at the time, but Virginia Wellborn also knew that seizures are common among victims of brain tumors. Two days later, Tom still had not seen a doctor. In fact, he was planning to go fishing again. Rising at 4 a.m. for the excursion, Tom suddenly had another seizure. "He turned around in our bedroom and turned on the light and just pointed to his face, which was twitching out of control," says Virginia. "I knew immediately it was a seizure. And again, after five minutes, he was fine."

But this time he was going to a doctor, not on a fishing trip. At first, the physicians in the Wellborns' outpatient clinic didn't even want to see him. "They didn't take my description seriously," complains Virginia, a former operating room nurse at the renowned Emory University Hospital in Atlanta. "They kept telling me to bring him in when he was having a seizure; they wouldn't listen when I told them these things were not that predictable and they didn't last long enough to make the trip to the clinic while one was going on." Finally, she prevailed on an emergency room doctor to refer Tom to a neurologist.

When that doctor could find no obvious problems, he suggested an MRI scan of Tom's head. The results showed a tumor the diameter of a quarter perched on the right motor strip in Tom's brain. That area controls the motion of the left side.

"I hoped beyond hope when I went in for that scan that it would be negative and that I'd only had a stroke," recalled Tom two years later. "But I figured it was most likely a tumor. I just hoped it would be benign and wouldn't really matter in any big way. But I also thought it might be my death knell. And without Dr. Stanislaw Burzynski, as it turned out, it would have been just that."

"I felt just the same as Tom did," remembered his wife. "I had some experience as a neurology scrub nurse in Jackson, Mississippi, and I worked on the neurosurgery postoperative ward at Emory. I also had worked in a nursing home where brain tumor patients would come to die. So I felt the prognosis was not good."

The Wellborns resolved to do whatever they could, spend whatever they had, if there was any chance it might help preserve Tom's life. Their next stop was Baptist Memorial Hospital in Memphis, Tennessee, about 140 miles northwest of their retirement home. Their Alabama neurologist had suggested this was the closest center where a reliable biopsy could be performed. The Wellborns were forced to wait, nervously pacing the floor of their home for almost a month before there could even be exploratory surgery. "There were a lot of vacations just then, so it was hard to get scheduled," Tom says. "We had to wait four weeks, until July 31, 1994, to get anything done." When the biopsy was completed via a needle inserted through a hole drilled in his skull, the news for Tom was far from good. "The diagnosis came back as a Stage 2 astrocytoma," he says.

Immediately Dr. Clarence Wattridge, who performed the exploratory operation, prescribed a course of radiation and chemotherapy, even though chemotherapy is rarely effective against brain tumors. Surgery was out of the question, Wattridge said, because of the tumor's location. Any serious cutting on it would probably leave Tom completely paralyzed, he said, a likelihood confirmed later when the family consulted with a Nashville oncologist specializing in precisely aimed gamma ray surgery. Wattridge gave the Wellborns no false illusions. Tom's tumor, he said, would be hard to treat. "All brain tumors are hard to treat," he emphasized. And he advised Tom that it was time to "get your affairs in order."

"I thought I was going to be a widow," Virginia admits. "All four of our children were upset. Two of them were actually there in the hospital during the biopsy."

Tom wasn't quite so upset. "The thought of dying didn't bother me except for my feelings about my family," he says. "I hated the idea of not seeing the grandkids, all three of them, grow up."

Tom insisted on getting some estimate of his prognosis; it was not good. "The doctors in Memphis told us I would live two months to a year longer if the treatment they recommended didn't work, and that I could probably expect to live about two to five years more if it did." If he died from the tumor, Tom would most likely first experience paralysis, then an inability to swallow and talk, followed by an inability to breathe.

Burdened by this news, the Wellborns returned to the Florence MRI Diagnostic Center to start treatment, supervised by local oncologist Dr. J. Patrick Daugherty. He promptly sent Tom to a center in Decatur, Alabama, about 35 miles away, for seven weeks of daily radiation doses. In all, Tom received 5,970 rads while undergoing simultaneous intensive chemotherapy, consisting partly of large doses of the drugs vincristine and procarbazine. "I felt really bad on that stuff," Tom remembered. "My feet and arms tingled while I was on it and they kept right on tingling a little afterward, too. Still do. I would burn terribly when they'd put the vincristine in by the IV in my hand." Nerve damage is an occasional side effect of chemotherapy, and Tom believes that's the source of his tingling.

He had gotten through the full radiation regimen and

five of six scheduled weekly chemotherapy sessions when Daugherty called a halt to the process after a second MRI scan was taken in March 1995. "I had another seizure while we were doing all this, so Daugherty figured something was wrong and wanted to take a good look," explained Tom. "This time, the tumor had grown to about the size of an apricot and now it was a Stage 3." The conventional therapy obviously wasn't working, so Daugherty stopped all treatment.

"Nobody suggested anything else right away," Tom said. "I was being written off. Daugherty said he would try to find some kind of new experimental protocol to put me on, but he never did come up with one."

About this time, Virginia Wellborn caught a glimpse of a brief feature about Burzynski and his antineoplaston therapy for cancer on the CBS Evening News. "The patients they interviewed looked like intelligent people," she noted. "I could tell they were speaking from their hearts, too, telling the truth as they knew it. Of course, I also thought this man might be a quack, and we might go to Houston and spend every cent we have and Tom might not get any better."

The couple sought advice from Daugherty. They asked the oncologist to telephone Burzynski, and he did. The call soon brought a packet of Burzynski's scientific papers to Daugherty, who read them and concluded that "it sounds possible to me." His major concern: that Burzynski might be conducting a money-making scam. Daugherty advised the Wellborns,"You have nothing to lose but some money, so you might as well try it."

The Wellborns arrived at Burzynski's clinic on May 4, 1995. "My first impression was very, very favorable," Virginia Wellborn recalled. "The waiting room was almost like a family atmosphere, with everyone talking and comparing notes. It was also professional. But it was much friendlier than most doctors' offices."

Burzynski himself was matter-of-fact. "I think I can correct your condition," he told Wellborn, stopping short of an outright promise. "I've had some very good results on this kind of tumor." The Wellborns' major question: Would Tom be randomized to some kind of placebo or would he actually get antineoplastons? "Everybody gets the medicine," Burzynski replied. He suggested that Tom try the treatment for two months, then take another MRI. "If there are any positive results, we can continue; if not, we will stop the treatment."

The Wellborns next visited a vascular surgeon who installed a Hickman catheter into Tom's chest, one end of its tube inserted directly into his subclavian vein and the other end free so that medication could be administered directly into his bloodstream. The following morning, the couple returned to Burzynski's clinic, bought a pump and immediately began training on how to use it. The price: $5,000 for a new pump and $13,000 in advance for instruction, training and the first two months of treatment. None of these costs would be reimbursed by insurance. Altogether, the couple spent 10 days in Houston, living in a motel while Burzynski's staff monitored Tom's response to the antineoplastons. Then the Wellborns went home, where they kept Tom connected to the pump 24 hours a day.

"For the most part, the treatment was not at all uncomfortable," reported Tom. "Yes, carrying the pump around was a pain in the rear end, and it was uncomfortable to sleep with it. Not that it was painful; it was just cumbersome because I couldn't even roll over in bed."

After two months, he had another MRI taken in

Florence. The tumor was still present, but the scan indicated that it might not be as thick as it had been previously. It had not grown since antineoplaston treatment began. "There is no evidence of acute hypoperfused segments or new masses," the formal MRI report stated.

"I felt some relief and was cautiously optimistic when I heard that," recalled Tom. "Nothing else had worked, but at least I was no worse off now than before." Oncologist Daugherty, who reviewed the MRI scan and report, repeated his earlier observation that "you've got nothing to lose" by continuing. So Tom stayed on the treatment, making the two-day drive to Houston every two months for an office visit and a resupply of antineoplastons. Along the way, he and Virginia would stop overnight at the Mississippi home of one of their daughters.

"I would try once in a while to fish while I was still attached to the pump," Tom said. "But it was difficult carrying the thing around. I had great difficulty getting my boat back on the trailer. Once I tried and I was just too weak. My knees buckled and I ended up rolling in the sand."

While on radiation and chemotherapy, Tom had lost 55 pounds from his 195-pound frame. "I was down to 140, the same as I weighed about 40 years ago when I met Virginia," he said. "I was fatigued both during the conventional therapy and while on Burzynski's treatment intravenously. That didn't surprise me; he had told me that the antineoplastons would make me tired and thirsty, but that it would not be permanent." Tom also suffered a potassium deficiency while on the treatment, something Burzynski had also warned was possible. But he corrected that with nonprescription dietary supplements.

Tom stayed on the treatment for one more month before

undergoing another MRI scan. This one, taken in August 1995, showed that the tumor had shrunk. "I felt euphoric," he remembered. "It was as if someone had lifted a death sentence off my shoulders. I had guessed the treatment must be working because I wasn't having any more seizures once the tumor stabilized. But this was solid proof. And Dr. Daugherty was also pleased. His skepticism was beginning to wear off. Burzynski just said, 'Let's keep you on the treatment and I believe you'll continue to do well.'"

So the Wellborns continued driving across the South every two months until early 1996, forced to make the trek by federal regulations that prohibited Burzynski from shipping antineoplastons across state lines. Tom also had his head scanned every eight or nine weeks. And on Dec. 20, 1995, MRI pictures revealed that Tom's tumor had disappeared completely. Said the formal MRI report, "Comparison with the October 2, 1995 study shows even further contraction of the small right cerebral lesions, with only a small fluid filled area remaining in the right periventricular white matter."

Said Tom, "By now, there was no doubt this treatment was doing me good."

Even oncologist Daugherty became a believer. "Although I am in no position to judge Dr. Burzynski's work, I am in a position to make a judgmental decision on Dr. Wellborn," Daugherty wrote in a February 1996 letter."There is no doubt in my mind that he has certainly benefited from the infusions he has received under the direction of Dr. Burzynski. X-ray data also confirmed this as is described in [my] progress notes."

Months later, he would say, "There is no doubt that every analysis showed Tom's tumor was progressing. But the scans since he went to Dr. Burzynski are clear. The people who believe in this will say he responded to the treatment. Others will say it was residual effects of the radiation treatment he got. I personally think that is very unlikely. It's hard to argue with these results—and I for one am very pleased. And I've sent another patient, one with lymphoma, to Dr. Burzynski since Dr. Wellborn went. I know this will be considered just an anecdote, but spontaneous remissions are very rare, less than 5 percent, probably less than 1 percent."

But a new fear arose while Tom was in the final phases of his intravenous antineoplaston treatment. Burzynski was indicted in November 1995 for selling an unapproved drug across state lines in cases just like Tom's, and on dozens of charges of insurance fraud. Federal prosecutors in Houston asked U.S. District Judge Simeon T. Lake 3rd to close Burzynski's clinic as a condition of bail. The judge eventually refused to take this step but did impose many conditions on Burzynski's continuing medical practice. Among them: a requirement that the FDA be advised of the progress of every patient under Burzynski's care. "We were terribly afraid Tom wouldn't be able to finish the treatment because of what the FDA was doing," recalled Virginia. "And we were sure that if he didn't finish it out, his tumor would grow back. We didn't think every single cancer cell had been killed off yet, and neither did Burzynski."

Virginia immediately dashed off letters of protest to Senators Phil Gramm of Texas, Trent Lott of Mississippi and Howell Heflin of Alabama, hand-delivering Heflin's to his district office nearby in northern Alabama. "Everyone except Trent Lott ignored our letters," Virginia reported. "Lott said he sympathized but could not interfere in a judicial action." Desperately afraid Tom would be cut off from antineoplastons and his tumor would quickly regrow,

Virginia finally wrote to first lady Hillary Rodham Clinton. Again, no response.

As it turned out, the FDA never stopped Tom's treatment. While awaiting trial, Burzynski was allowed to continue caring for patients who had been on his therapy previously, even gaining permission now to ship his medication to them across state lines under terms of his newly granted IND permits. So Tom stayed on the antineoplaston infusions six months after his December scan showed him cancer-free. The only change in his treatment regimen was that the FDA now required him to undergo weekly blood tests. "That just seemed like silly harassment to me," Tom said. "Earlier in the treatment, Burzynski had me take blood tests every week to check on my electrolyte balance; the results were faxed to him right away. He was very thorough and responded promptly when there was even a slight problem, so I don't know why the FDA should be interfering."

Another MRI in April 1996 and yet another follow-up scan in July 1996 both showed no tumor in his head. And after the July scan, Tom was finally about to shed the pump he had carried around for more than a year.

"Burzynski gave me a choice of staying on the IV for three more months or switching to capsules and staying on the medication until January 1997," Tom remembers. "I chose the pills so I could have more freedom of movement."

After all the treatments he underwent, Tom reported in the fall of 1996 that "I'm almost back to enjoying life. I'm as healthy now as I was before all this started, just a little lighter and a little weaker. But I'll build up the muscles again. I'm already lifting a few weights. I started that as soon as I got rid of my pump. And now, as soon as I get my catheter removed, I'll be back on my boat. While it's in, I don't want to take any chances of doing anything that might rupture it by accident."

Tom looked on with amazement and indignation as the FDA prosecuted Burzynski in 1995 and 1996. "If it hadn't been for him, I have no doubt that I'd be dead right now. Every dealing I've had with him, he's been a gentleman. I think he's a pioneer. And I think the FDA is criminal not to be making antineoplastons available to people who have no other hope, people in the situation I was in. What they're doing reminds me of someone who sees a drowning person and pushes their head further underwater. I can see giving people the conventional therapy first, but I can't see denying this to anyone who has failed it. At the very least, antineoplastons can give people some hope. I know they gave me new life."

Postscript

HOUSTON, Miss., midyear 2000—Tom Wellborn has been dead almost two years now—but the brain tumor that once afflicted him apparently had nothing to do with his passing.

"Tom had a MRI scan just about a month before he died in September 1998 and it showed nothing but a little scar tissue," recalled his wife Virginia. A report on the scan, signed by radiation oncologist B.L. Sullivan of Columbus, Miss., and dated August 25, 1998, confirms her memory. The death came suddenly and without much warning on Sept. 22, less than one month after the scan. "We had gone out to dinner and he had laid down to rest afterward while I went to town to do some early Christmas shopping," Virginia remembered. "When I returned, I found him lying on the kitchen floor. I still regret I wasn't there for him in his last moments."

There were no indications Tom's astrocytoma had returned, and no autopsy was performed.

The Wellborns had moved from their retirement home in Alabama to the small town of Houston, Miss., about 120 miles southeast of Memphis, Tenn., to be near their daughter Susan and her family after Tom suffered a seizure or a stroke—no one was quite sure—in December 1997. He never fully recovered, so his daily fishing trips had to end.

Officials listed Tom's formal cause of death as aspirational pneumonia. No one will ever know for sure whether the massive radiation treatments he endured before taking antineoplastons caused this. But those familiar with The Crystin Schiff Story strongly suspect it may have.

Said Burzynski, "The circumstances make me believe Mr. Wellborn might have died from a stroke, rather than from pneumonia, as the death certificate says. Mr. Wellborn received a lot of radiation before he came to us, and that could have affected his blood vessels and made him more susceptible to a stroke."

CHAPTER 8

The Future: Making Antineoplastons a Conventional Therapy

It doesn't matter if I win at trial or not. We will still win. Within a few years, antineoplastons will be accepted everywhere.

—Dr. Stanislaw R. Burzynski, February 1997 (during jury deliberations in his criminal trial)

All through his first criminal trial in early 1997, there was no doubt about the optimism of Dr. Stanislaw R. Burzynski. He knew what was at stake: As much as 300 years in mandatory prison terms if he were found guilty on all counts—along with a possible death sentence for all his patients. The certainty that if he were imprisoned, someone else would not only steal his life's work, but deprive him of any credit for it. Yet he remained the cheeriest person in the courtroom of Judge Simeon T. Lake 3rd, greeting his patients and others with wide smiles, wry jokes and hearty handshakes every day. "I have no doubts," he said time and again during breaks in the proceedings. "I will win. They can try me as often as they like, but they will never defeat me."

After both his trials were over, Burzynski approached his next major task with the same positive spirit. Vilified in the pages of everything from the *Journal of the American Medical Association* to the *New York Times*, he never wavered in his determination that antineoplastons would not only come to market one day soon, but would in time become the standard therapy against many cancers.

"This is the next thing we will do, go for a new drug

application," he declared. Any such New Drug Application (NDA), of course, would have to be processed by the very same FDA that had dogged Burzynski since 1983 and steadfastly tried to carry out the "declaration of war" it filed against him during the first of its many legal actions against him. Just how difficult and fraught with contradictions the FDA could make Burzynski's quest for widespread acceptance of his drug became clear in September 1996, while he was still awaiting trial.

Between his indictment in 1995 and his trial in 1997, Burzynski had been permitted to keep his clinic open. As a condition of bail, he was required to fit every one of his pre-existing patients and all new patients into the protocols for FDA-controlled IND permits. The irony of the INDs was that they suddenly legalized the very behavior of which Burzynski was due to be tried, actions he had long avoided taking. The investigator on any IND is always permitted to ship the drug he is testing to patients anywhere. So after almost 20 years of studiously avoiding the shipment of anti-neoplastons over state lines, and after almost 20 years of requiring that patients travel to Texas when they needed new supplies, Burzynski could now send as much of the drug as he wished to as many patients as he wished— legally.

His pre-existing patients all were placed on the same FDA-controlled IND while he was out on bail. Known as the CAN-1 trial, it was only one of 71 clinical trial protocols Burzynski would be awarded while awaiting trial. For all his clinical trials, Burzynski was compelled to file monthly progress reports on every patient. As a further condition of bail, he was not permitted to take on any new patients who did qualify under one of his INDs. Because the FDA would allow patients into the clinical trials only if no further conventional treatment was available to them, Burzynski now could usually take new patients only when they had failed two courses of both chemotherapy and radiation, as well as exhausted every conventional therapy.

This was always galling to Burzynski, who could see that almost all new patients coming to him were nearly at death's doorstep. "This is harmful, both to us and to our patients. Our patients have a much better chance if they have not been weakened by previous chemotherapy and radiation," he said. But he was never forced to give up treating even a single existing patient. This concession was won primarily because a flood of patient letters made a strong impression on Judge Lake. Another factor was a series of hearings that saw then FDA Commissioner David Kessler summoned before an oversight subcommittee of the House Commerce Committee. Members of that subcommittee also heard dozens of Burzynski patients explain that they desperately needed him to continue ministering to their needs.

The record keeping required for the CAN-1 trial soon provided the first statistical evidence Burzynski and his supporters believed was strong enough to merit an NDA, whose approval by the FDA would instantly remove antineoplastons from the realm of the experimental or alternative and immediately make them mainstream medicine. Burzynski believed from the beginning of his legal troubles that this would eventually happen, that antineoplastons would replace most cancer therapies of the 20th Century. "The alternative medicine of 100 years ago is the conventional medicine of today," he said, noting that doctors who insisted on bleeding their patients and subjecting them to leeches dominated the field in the 19th Century, but are viewed today as quaint and sometimes sadistic primitives.

From the moment he began gathering solid statistics in

order to report them to the FDA, Burzynski's case became easier to prove, even if the FDA consistently continued to downplay his studies. "We have had spectacular results in our clinical trials so far," read a September 1996 report from Dean Mouscher, then Burzynski's clinical trials director. "Approximately 35-40 percent of our patients have had dramatic reductions in the size of their tumors, with as many more showing stabilization of their disease. Keep in mind that most of these patients had failed conventional therapy and been told that there was no treatment available that could stop their tumors."

Over the next several years, the CAN-1 patients continued to do well. By the spring of 2000, Burzynski was able to report that of 35 brain tumor patients in the CAN-1 trial, nine had complete remissions, eight had partial remissions in which their tumors had decreased by more than 50 percent and 11 had stable disease—their tumors either had not grown or had been reduced, but by less than 50 percent. This 48 percent rate of complete and partial responses, combined with 32 percent showing stable disease, meant that antineoplastons had halted progress toward paralysis and then death in 80 percent of the brain tumor patients he was treating at the time of his indictment. All those patients had gained at least four years of life, when other doctors had given them no more than a few months to live.

Equally impressive numbers began to accumulate in some other Burzynski clinical trials. By the spring of 2000, Burzynski was able to report that of 36 patients in his trials with brain stem gliomas like the one that caused doctors to predict a quick death for Tori Moreno (see The Tori Moreno Story), 15 achieved either complete remissions or partial responses within less than three years (most far sooner) and 10 had stable disease. In another trial involving 10 children with astrocytomas, none had progressive disease; all the others were either in full or partial remission, or the growth of their tumors had been stopped. By contrast, the usual survival rate beyond five years for similar patients taking conventional chemotherapy and radiation is less than one in 1,000. Other Burzynski trials, especially those involving brain tumors, provided similarly dramatic results. But still there had been no approval from the FDA by the summer of 2000.

Never mind that the figures from his newer trials appeared to satisfy at least one of the objections voiced in 1997 by Dr. Robert J. DeLap, director of the FDA's Division of Oncology Drug Products. DeLap wrote that "Observations made in your clinical practice or in CAN-1 protocol patients cannot be used as the basis for a new drug application since they do not represent adequate and well-controlled investigations as defined in FDA applications." Patient acceptance protocols for the newer trials, of course, were far more rigorous than for the CAN-1 trial, which included all pre-indictment patients, no matter what treatments they had tried before coming to Burzynski.

But DeLap also declared that "The agency has never accepted data from a single investigator or clinic as the sole basis for approval of a new drug for cancer treatment. It is obviously important to know that the safety and effectiveness findings for a new drug can be replicated by more than one principal investigator." He added that "the cancer initiatives announced in March 1996 by President Bill Clinton and Vice President Albert Gore did not set aside any laws or regulations related to approval of new drugs for cancer treatment."

The latter part of DeLap's statement ran counter to the spirit of the Clinton/Gore announcement, which aimed to reassure Americans that cancer drugs would be put on a fast track toward approval. His comment also contradicted the 1989 statement of then FDA Commissioner Frank Young, who said it would henceforth be FDA policy to approve promising cancer drugs that had produced positive results in as few as 10 cases. Young's statement was never rescinded and remained nominal policy throughout Burzynski's indictment, his criminal trial and the years that followed.

But the firmly negative stance of the FDA toward Burzynski was never fully explained. In many attempts to elicit from the FDA and its top officials their reasons for their relentless campaign against antineoplastons, no official ever offered a clue. Some of the FDA's most severe critics among Burzynski's patients contended from the start that the agency was more concerned with protecting the financial interests of pharmaceutical companies than with finding successful cancer treatments. Drug companies regularly report profits in the billions of dollars from conventional chemotherapies, and hospitals, doctors and equipment makers earn more billions each year from radiation therapy. DeLap and others consistently refused to comment on this allegation, often saying the question was too insulting to merit an answer.

But in an exceptionally candid statement to veteran *USA Today* reporter Dennis Cauchon, which appeared in that paper's April 12, 2000, examination of the FDA's reluctance to permit switching of popular drugs from prescription status to over-the-counter, DeLap said that "You don't want to deep-six the drug companies." As Cauchon explained it, DeLap indicated this "could damage research into new drugs." So the FDA's top certifier of new drugs— the man who earlier ordered Zac McConnell off antineoplastons and then allowed him back on after the political wind shifted—admitted the financial well-being of pharmaceutical companies is a factor in FDA decision-making.

DeLap also indicated in 1997 he would never honor the commitment of his former boss, Young, to approve drugs that had drawn FDA-defined responses in at least 10 patients. Instead, DeLap put Burzynski on notice that it did not and would not matter what results he obtained in treating patients, even if those patients fit into FDA-approved IND protocols and had previously failed all conventional forms of treatment. By that time, of course, Burzynski had proven positive results in several times that many patients treated in FDA-approved clinical trials. (See Appendix: All Clinical Trial Patients chart) Nevertheless, he would need to find other researchers not merely to corroborate and vouch for the results he achieved in his own clinical practice, but also to duplicate those results in their own patients.

Burzynski had tried for years to accomplish both tasks, striving to take his medication through normal scientific channels while he was treating patients. This was why he approved the initial protocols and supplied the antineoplastons for the NCI-approved clinical trials begun in 1994 at the Mayo Clinic and Memorial Sloan-Kettering Cancer Center. It was why he supplied antineoplastons at no charge for years to the Japanese research group headed by Dr. Hideaki Tsuda—who used antineoplastons to cure the chancellor of his university, among others, of colon cancer that had metastacized to the liver. (See Appendix: Preliminary Results of Two Japanese Trials charts.) But the FDA was now saying this was not enough. If Burzynski didn't follow the same new drug approval procedures used by giant pharmaceutical houses whose research and development cost before bringing a new drug to market usually exceeds $400 million, he could forget about approval for his drug. DeLap was acting consistently with a 1982 statement from Richard Crout, then a top FDA official, who declared that "I never have and never will approve a drug to an individual, but only to a large pharmaceutical firm with unlimited resources." In short, the FDA was delivering an ultimatum to scientific entrepreneurs like Burzynski: Sign over the rights and profits from their inventions and discoveries into the hands of large drug companies, or never see them come to market; never see them save large numbers of lives.

Almost alone among scientists, Burzynski never knuckled under to this dictate. His refusal to give up his patents and his rights may have been the cause of nearly all his legal troubles. Burzynski's critics frequently accuse him of failing to save hundreds or thousands of lives because he operated outside established scientific procedures. They ignore both the FDA's negative attitude toward small, entrepreneurial scientific operations and the 13 years between the time Burzynski first applied for an IND and the time patients and politicians at last pressured the FDA into granting him dozens of them.

His status as a maverick often reviled in the mainstream medical press also made it difficult for Burzynski to find distinguished collaborators. One FDA rule requires that whenever a patient on an experimental drug protocol returns home and continues to take the medication, a local doctor must monitor that patient's progress and general health. Such doctors are referred to in the protocols as collaborators. While all Burzynski patients have such care, hundreds of physicians in all parts of the United States have refused to continue helping patients they previously saw at least in part because they wanted to avoid the professional stigma of being a Burzynski "collaborator." But Burzynski always persisted in seeking scientists to use antineoplastons experimentally in their own clinics and laboratories in order to prove that their effectiveness does not depend on some sort of placebo effect produced by his personality and eternal optimism.

One such associate reported great success at the 1998 International Congress of Chemotherapy in Stockholm, Sweden. Dr. P.J. Van der Schaar of the International Biomedical Center in Leende, The Netherlands, reported administering AS2-1 and A-10 to 27 patients, including five with astrocytoma brain tumors, three with glioma brain tumors, three with unknown types of brain tumors, one with a medulloblastoma brain tumor, two with prostate cancer and others with lung, kidney, liver, breast, pancreatic and stomach cancers, as well as several with malignant melanomas, malignant myelomas and osteosarcomas. "As with so many new treatments, for not completely under-stood reasons, results are improving with time," Van der Schaar said. He reported objective responses from patients with astrocytomas, prostate cancer, breast cancer, osteosar-coma and pancreatic cancer. He added that his patients were virtually free from side effects. "This study demon-strates that antineoplaston therapy is not restricted to hos-pitals," he reported. "It is a patient-friendly therapy with remarkably few side effects, which in most instances can be administered in an out-patient environment."

But the FDA often shows little respect for foreign research like that conducted by Van der Schaar and Tsuda, no matter how solid it may be. For this reason, Burzynski had high hopes for a relationship he was to begin in the spring of 2000 with the laboratory of Dr. Fred Epstein, director of the Institute for Neurology and Neurosurgery at Beth Israel Medical Center in New York City and a professor and department chairman at the Albert Einstein School of Medicine. Epstein, widely regarded as one of the world's leading pediatric brain surgeons, read Tori Moreno's MRI scans before her parents brought her to Burzynski in the fall of 1998 and again after two months of antineoplaston treatment. He found her tumor 23 percent reduced in that time. "What Burzynski has causes involution of cancers," he said. "In the case of Tori Moreno, there was clear-cut involution of the tumor due to the treatment. I didn't expect it, but I didn't fall over, either."

Epstein's lack of complete surprise was due to his prior familiarity with Burzynski's work. But he said the Moreno results convinced him to attempt to establish a scientific relationship with Burzynski. "This has to be taken seriously," he said of antineoplastons. Following up on that belief, Epstein sent several of his staffers to Houston in the spring of 2000 to receive training from Burzynski and his staff in the administration of the treatment. "It is very, very difficult to assess antineoplastons as yet, but I really, really hope we see something when we begin testing them here at Beth Israel," Epstein said.

Burzynski reported that Epstein had sent several patients with inoperable brain tumors to him over the last decade. "In most, we got good results. We have one of his patients on our treatment now and the patient is responding," he said in early 2000. Burzynski is convinced there will be positive results at Epstein's clinic, too. But he said a prerequisite for this was a positive attitude among Epstein's staff. "A positive approach provides the patient with much more motivation to comply with our rather complicated regimen," he said. "It is very, very important to take the medication systematically. If the patient doesn't believe antineoplastons will help him or her, they will not do it right." But Burzynski emphasized a positive approach like his cannot by itself dissolve brain tumors. "It is impossible for any placebo to have any effect on this type of tumor," he said. Epstein agreed. "Placebos do not involute brain tumors," he said.

Neither Burzynski nor Epstein expected serious problems in gaining FDA permission for Epstein to treat his patients with antineoplastons. Some Epstein patients were expected to qualify for treatment under Burzynski's clinical trial protocols. And beginning late in the year 1998, patients with low Karnovsky test results were almost automatically granted compassionate use exemptions allowing Burzynski to treat them even if they did not qualify for the clinical trials. Karnovsky tests measure physical capabilities; patients receiving routine compassionate use exemptions normally had scores of 50 or lower on the test, a level that ordinarily means they are almost terminal.

But as it did while Burzynski was free on bail in 1996, the FDA was continuing to set up obstacles for him and his patients long afterward. It wasn't merely the blizzard of paperwork forced on Burzynski in making monthly reports to the FDA on all his clinical trials, a load that forced him to hire two new secretaries and work late every night for years detailing the responses of each of his patients. Patients, too, were forced to jump through hoops. Whereas Burzynski might ask them to get blood tests once a month or every two weeks once their standard dose had been established, the FDA required blood tests at least twice a week—this for a drug that had already been ruled beyond the Phase 1 clinical trial tests for safety. For evidence that the federal agencies have long known antineoplastons are safe, there is this passage repeated in five patent applications for "phenylacetate derivative drugs" filed by the

National Cancer Institute: "Clinical experience indicates that acute or long-term treatment with sodium phenylacetate doses is well tolerated, essentially free of adverse effects." This government statement means Burzynski and his patients were on solid ground in claiming the requirement for twice-weekly blood tests for anyone undergoing antineoplaston treatment amounted to simple harassment.

But the most frustrating requirement was that almost all Burzynski's clinical trials include only patients who had not previously failed two courses of conventional treatment. The rule effectively meant that he was not allowed to treat anyone who didn't come to him a physical wreck. Even if patients desperately wanted to avoid conventional treatments and immediately begin antineoplaston therapy, they were usually thwarted.

The most prominent such case was that of four-year-old Thomas Navarro, an Arizona resident. He was brought to Burzynski's clinic in late 1999, because his parents did not want him subjected either to toxic chemotherapy or radiation to eliminate a localized medulloblastoma brain tumor.

Those therapies would almost surely debilitate him mentally for life, even if he should be cured of the cancer. The Arizona radiation oncologists who sought to use radiation on the similar brain tumor of Zac McConnell (see The Zachary McConnell Story) estimated their treatment might reduce his intelligence quotient by about 30 points. Dr. Larry Kun, chairman of the Department of Radiation Oncology at St. Jude Children's Research Hospital in Memphis, Tennessee, and chairman of the national Pediatric Oncology Group brain tumor committee, estimated Thomas Navarro might lose 20 to 30 intelligence quotient points if he underwent the standard treatment, which produced a 51 percent five-year survival rate in a St. Jude study involving 29 children treated between 1984 and 1999. "He would be below normal, but still at a level where he could learn and function," Kun said in an interview. Kun also said if Thomas' father Jim insisted on antineoplaston treatment rather than the standard procedures, "He is essentially saying he wants to let his child die and he's been ill-guided."

Kun added that "Burzynski's therapy has no documented success." But at that point Burzynski had treated 13 children with active medulloblastoma tumors, reporting two complete remissions, two partial remissions, five with stable disease and only four with progressive disease. This didn't satisfy Kun. "Burzynski had an opportunity to demonstrate the efficacy of his drug and did not cooperate," he said, referring to the abortive clinical trials orchestrated by NCI in the mid-1990s. But Kun admitted he had seen only snippets of the correspondence between Burzynski and the NCI (detailed in Chapter 6, The War Moves to the Laboratory), which demonstrates how NCI officials unilaterally changed the protocols of those trials in a way that would have guaranteed failure for antineoplastons if Burzynski had continued to participate.

Because his parents wanted to spare him the trauma of radiation and the almost certain accompanying permanent mental damage, they refused conventional therapy. Oncologists in his home state then obtained a court order removing Thomas from the custody of his parents and allowing the doctors to administer conventional treatment to him. To avoid this decree, the family was compelled to stay in Houston hotels for months while awaiting and lobbying for FDA approval of a compassionate use exemption. Even after six United States senators and four major presidential candidates signed petitions asking a compassionate use exemption for Thomas, the FDA did not relent. Officials insisted that Burzynski has achieved "no convincing results" against medulloblastomas like Thomas', while this tumor is one of the very few brain cancers where standard therapy has any significant effect at all. But the five-year-cure rate for standard therapies recorded at St. Jude's was not as good as the result reported by Burzynski in his clinical trial involving 13 patients who could be evaluated. (See chart, Appendix) So there was little give in the FDA's approach to Thomas Navarro and his parents, Jim and Donna. The agency was obdurate in refusing to allow Jim and Donna to choose Burzynski's treatment for their son, no matter how many leading government officials urged to bend and allow the parents to choose the treatment they thought best.

It was the case of David Smith that firmly established the courts would let the FDA exert this kind of control over choices made by patients or their families. In January 1993, while he was a 19-year-old living in Lexington, North Carolina, Smith was diagnosed with Stage 4 Hodgkin's disease, including metastases to the skeletal system. Between March and June of that year, he underwent 50 sessions of radiation therapy directed at his neck and chest. The radiation produced side effects that lasted from June 1993 until June 1994, including skin discoloration, physical exhaustion, continuous and severe sore throats, a dramatic drop in white blood cell count, severe hair loss, precipitous drops in his sperm count and an irregular heartbeat. By November 1993, however, this treatment had cleared Smith of his cancer. But not permanently.

In February 1996, Smith began experiencing severe bone pain in his left hip and leg, as well as night sweats and chills. These were diagnosed as recurrent Hodgkin's disease, which had spread to his bones. Smith's doctor advised him to undergo chemotherapy, recommending a treatment known as MOPP-ABVD (mechlorethamine + vincristine + procarbazine + prednisone—doxorubicin + bleomycin + vinblastine + procarbazine), and told him he might also require a bone marrow transplant. Among the likely side effects of all this, as conceded by the FDA: heart and lung damage, damage to the muscle connective tissue, destruction of the immune system, sterility, loss of appetite, nausea and vomiting, weight loss, fatigue and possible death. Smith learned, too, that chemotherapy might greatly reduce his life expectancy and that while such chemotherapy is often said to be effective against Hodgkin's disease, 35 percent of all patients who undergo the chemotherapy regimen proposed for him are nevertheless not cured.

By April 1, 1996, Smith had found his way to Burzynski's clinic, where he started onto antineoplastons. Less than six weeks later, a bone scan of his body showed "significant improvement" in his tumors. The previously visible metastases to his spinal column and his ribs were no longer identifiable. But Burzynski was forced by his conditions of bail to report his treatment of Smith to the FDA, applying in May 1996 for a compassionate use exemption that would have allowed Smith to continue taking antineoplastons. On May 23, the FDA ordered Burzynski to discontinue treating Smith, in spite of his obvious success. With financial help from other Burzynski patients, Smith immediately hired a Washington lawyer to ask the FDA to reconsider, submitting an affidavit in which he emphatically stated that he would rather die than undergo chemotherapy. Yet on May 27, 1996, the same day Smith's supply of antineoplastons was due to run out, the FDA denied his request. Smith then argued in federal court that the FDA's decision to deny him the chance to receive a potentially life-saving new cancer therapy violated his constitutional rights to due process and his right to privacy—the right to do whatever he wanted with his own body.

The FDA responded that "We cannot in good conscience allow Dr. Burzynski to proceed with administration of his investigational products to Mr. Smith. There is no justification for substituting an unproved, untested therapy for a proven treatment with a high rate of curing the disease." Almost four years later, Dr. Richard Pazdur, director of the FDA's Division of Oncology Drug Products, would echo that statement in denying antineoplastons to Thomas Navarro. "Ethically, giving a child an experimental product in such circumstances flies in the face of all the guidelines and regulations designed to protect children as research subjects," he said in an interview with *The Cancer Letter*. Pazdur declined to be interviewed for this book.

In Smith's case, the FDA added that "courts have refused to find an individual, constitutional right to receive unapproved new drugs as medical treatment." FDA lawyers also noted that Smith was "free to reject [conventional] therapy," but that if he did, he was not entitled to seek out whatever alternative he wanted.

In short, no matter what Smith wanted to do, the FDA demanded that he undergo chemotherapy, suffer whatever side effects it brought and have it fail him before the FDA would permit continuation of Burzynski's treatment. A drug that would lead to great suffering and debilitation was preferable to one that was already helping the patient. The FDA even argued that the bone scan Smith underwent to demonstrate the reduction in his disease did not matter, despite its clear showing that he had improved markedly while on antineoplastons. The agency cited a 1973 case in which the Supreme Court held that "the impressions or beliefs of physicians, no matter how fervently held, are treacherous." In short, the FDA said, it did not matter how many doctors, how many radiologists might read the bone scans and conclude that antineoplastons were working, Big Brother in the headquarters building at Rockville, Maryland, knew better. It's a clear-cut attitude of "don't bother me with the facts, I'm going to make you do whatever I want." It was the same approach the FDA later took with Thomas Navarro. The essence of the FDA's actions in each case was that it made absolutely no difference how well the patient was doing or whether Burzynski offered a good chance for remission; Burzynski could not treat these patients with antineoplastons. And a federal judge in Washington firmly upheld the FDA's position in the Smith case, setting a precedent later followed in denying Thomas Navarro's fervent pleas for a compassionate use exemption.

No one in Congress took any formal action after learning of the Smith case. But the Navarros gained so much national publicity, with appearances on CBS-TV, NBC-TV, the Fox News Channel, CNN and many local stations, that in February 2000 the chairman of the House Government Oversight Committee on Government Reform, Republican Dan Burton of Indiana, introduced the Thomas Navarro FDA Patient Rights Act. This bill would allow patients to choose experimental treatments over the standard ones so long as they are fully informed of all options and the risks involved with each.

Smith's ordeal, and Thomas Navarro's, represent clear-cut cases of legalistic sophistry triumphing over the individual will of the patients whose lives were threatened. In the end, Smith would survive and even continue taking antineoplastons despite the FDA's dictates and its court decisions. While Burzynski could not treat him or send him supplies, sympathetic patients who heard about his plight repeatedly sent Smith boxes filled with bottles and plastic bags of their own antineoplastons. Thomas Navarro and his parents would seek alternative treatment in Tijuana, Mexico.

Burton was not the only congressman to take an interest in Burzynski and his patients. One major change wrought by the Republican takeover after the 1994 congressional elections had been that California Congressman Henry Waxman, a Democrat and the FDA's single most enthusiastic supporter on Capitol Hill, no longer chaired any oversight committee with authority over the FDA. Instead, that role went for five years to Republican Joe Barton of Dallas, Texas. During the first two years Barton ran the House Commerce Committee's Subcommittee on Oversight and Investigations, he called then, FDA Commissioner Kessler on the carpet four times, with the FDA's handling of Burzynski and his antineoplastons a chief item for questioning each time. The congressional hearings featured some of the same patients who would later testify at Burzynski's criminal trials. "Without his treatment, my son will die!" testified a tearful Mary Michaels of Troy, Michigan; her son Paul's brain tumor had been shrunk and then held in check by antineoplastons.

Strikingly, during each hearing Kessler, Robert Spiller, DeLap and other FDA officials who had spent years pursuing Burzynski left the room before patients could begin their often heart-wrenching testimony. As in their court filings in the Smith case, it seemed that the fate of real-life individuals did not matter to them, especially in comparison with their concern for the power of their agency. It also seemed the FDA brass couldn't bear listening to patients who bore the brunt of their decisions. The FDA never acknowledged it publicly, but no one at Burzynski's clinic doubted that without the interest and questions from Congress, the agency would have insisted on its initial post-indictment proposal for conditions of bail: a complete shut-down of the clinic.

But after his criminal trial ended, a working relationship gradually emerged between Burzynski and the non-enforcement wings of the FDA. Where almost no patients were granted compassionate use exemptions during the indictment period, now those with very low Karnovsky scores were routinely permitted treatment. Where the FDA had once delayed granting requested INDs to Burzynski for more than a decade, now it did not often interfere as he conducted his clinical trials. But the agency persisted in sending out negative literature to all persons who inquired about Burzynski, never including in their mailings any of Burzynski's replies to the slurs against him. There was never a sign that antineoplastons had even a slight chance of enjoying the fast-track approval process that both President Clinton and the FDA itself had promised for anti-cancer drugs.

So Burzynski systematically for several years sought other legal ways to administer antineoplastons to patients, methods that would not place him afoul of the law. And in the summer of 1999, he discovered one. In the mid-1990s, Ucyclyd Pharma, a small New Jersey pharmaceutical company, had won "orphan drug" approval of a sodium phenyl-buterate compound for treatment of hyperammonenia, a rare childhood disease in which high levels of ammonia can cause liver failure. The orphan designation goes to drugs aimed at ailments which occur very infrequently. In the laboratories of the Burzynski Research Institute, several miles from the Burzynski Clinic, scientists working for Burzynski discovered that when taken orally, sodium phenylbuterate is metabolized in the liver into a combination of phenylacetylglutamine and phenylacetate, which then enter the bloodstream. Those two chemicals are the prime ingredients of antineoplaston AS2-1.

Since sodium phenylbuterate already had FDA approval, Burzynski could prescribe it for his patients without any danger of legal sanctions. The common practice in which doctors prescribe drugs for ailments other than those for which they have been approved is called "off-label" prescribing. Suddenly Burzynski could now treat as many patients as he liked, without need for compassionate use exemptions. Just not the patients in most urgent need. For taking this drug orally does not provide doses high enough to fight off aggressive tumors. But it can be useful in tumor suppression, Burzynski learned, both alone and in combination with some conventional chemotherapy treatments. It can also serve as a substitute for antineoplaston capsules for patients who have had tumors removed surgically and seek to prevent recurrences. By the middle of 2000, Burzynski was treating more than 100 patients with sodium phenylbuterate, which is marketed under the trade name Buterate. His patients needed so much of this drug that the Burzynski Clinic obtained a pharmacy license and began buying it in large quantities.

"Using sodium phenylbuterate, we are able to give our patients a higher-quantity of active ingredients than we can with our own capsule form of AS2-1," Burzynski said. "Oral AS2-1 also is partially metabolized into the same chemicals. But sodium phenylbuterate is easier for our patients to take because is has less odor than AS2-1. Most people didn't take more than 15 grams of AS2-1 daily. With sodium phenylbuterate, we can get as much as 30 grams a day into them. This is still nothing like infusing the drug directly into the bloodstream, but it helps us with some patient compliance problems where people were not taking the capsules as we instructed because of the odor. This formulation can also be useful if someone does not want intravenous treatment for other reasons. "

Burzynski would rather treat most of these patients with antineoplaston A-10, which he concluded in the late 1990s is more effective than AS2-1. "A-10 is the best treatment we can offer now, but the FDA severely limits our use of A-10. During 1999, we got about 1,000 requests a month for treatment and only about 25 of these people each month can be admitted to our clinical trials for A-10 and AS2-1. If I had a choice, I might use only A-10, which is a combination of phenylacetylglutamine and phenylacetylisoglutamine. It looks in our clinical trials like A-10 is the best, but we only learned this through the clinical trials."

The new oral regimen of sodium phenylbuterate also has made life more pleasant for many Burzynski patients. Burzynski has recorded several responses in treating children with astrocytomas by giving them a combination of Buterate and AS2-1 capsules rather than infusing antineoplastons via a chest catheter. "But this does not give us a high enough dose to treat gliomas—the glioblastomas, PNETs and brain stem tumors," he said. "For these we need a higher dose than we can achieve orally. But some patients can be treated intravenously for awhile and then switched over to oral medication. This tells us that sometimes the dosage must be high, but in other cases a high dose is not always necessary."

The FDA, of course, was not the only agency Burzynski had to contend with after his criminal trials were over.

There was also the state of Texas, whose board of medical examiners staged hearings in the early 1990s with the clear aim of suspending or lifting Burzynski's medical license. After long days of testimony during the summer of 1994, the Texas board found that several witnesses, including Dr. Nicholas Patronas, then chief of radiology for the National Institutes of Health, had testified that "antineoplaston therapy is necessary for the survival of many of [Burzynski's] patients." What's more, the board reported, "No evidence was received that was contrary to [that] testimony." Nevertheless the board in a decision that evoked comparisons with Alice in Wonderland ordered Burzynski's license suspended, then stayed the suspension and placed Burzynski on probation for 10 years. One condition of probation: that Burzynski dispense no antineoplastons without some kind of permit from the FDA. In short, like the FDA in the Smith case, the Texas board said patients' needs and wishes count for nothing. Because the FDA hasn't approved antineoplastons, it said, Burzynski should not use them and could be punished if he did. Therefore his patients were not to use the medication even though their very lives usually are at stake. Burzynski immediately appealed the Texas order and the state's case remained in limbo—and Burzynski's practice unchanged—as long as federal criminal charges were pending.

But the Texas authorities reemerged soon after the criminal trials in federal court ended. They scheduled civil proceedings in Austin and San Antonio, intending to threaten Burzynski's license to practice medicine. But since their case against Burzynski would have depended on many of the same witnesses who so frustrated federal officials in the criminal trials, the state eventually sought a settlement. At first, state lawyers wanted Burzynski to admit some form of wrongdoing. He refused, daring them to take him to a new trial. State officials backed off again. This time they reached a settlement in which Burzynski agreed to post a disclaimer in his clinic and in the informed consent forms all patients must sign before treatment. It says, "Antineoplastons are currently undergoing testing on human subjects in clinical trials being conducted to test their safety and effectiveness. Safety and effectiveness of antineoplaston medications have not been established."

Burzynski agreed to post this because it is virtually the same disclaimer given to all patients in any FDA-approved clinical trial. He paid $50,000 to the state for "reasonable attorneys fees and investigative expenses." He considered it a small price to pay for the freedom to practice without state interference. It was also a far cry from the $12 million the state initially sought when it scheduled civil trials.

Free at last from legal interference, Burzynski could attack a central question he had wondered about for decades: while he had no doubts that antineoplastons shrink or eliminate many cancers, he was not sure how they do it. Meanwhile, other researchers in a wide variety of studies published during the 1980s and 1990s established beyond much doubt that between 50 percent and 65 percent of cancers were associated with defective performance or non-performance by the p-53 tumor suppressor gene present in the DNA of each cell of every human body. This gene gets its name from the fact it produces proteins and its molecular weight is 53,000, meaning that one such gene weighs 53,000 times as much as a plain hydrogen atom. Burzynski observed that the varieties of cancer associated with p-53 gene problems also tended to be those that responded best to antineoplastons. But he did not fully understand why until Dr. Stephen Baylin of Johns Hopkins University in

Baltimore published a paper in the September 1997 issue of Science magazine. In that paper, Baylin reported that "almost half of the [tumor] suppressor genes known to underlie genetic forms of neoplasia...exhibit...hypermethylation in noninherited cancers." Translated from the biochemical jargon, this means almost half the genes that normally prevent the growth of cancers are covered with a coating of methyl groups.

This made instant sense to Burzynski, who had discovered in his laboratory at Baylor more than 20 years earlier that antineoplastons bind with methyl. Now he theorized that his medication works on many cancers by removing a coating of methyl groups from their surface, which permits them to resume operating. He saw this revelation as one with enormous potential future consequences and potential.

Burzynski's sense of the importance of hypermethylation, as the coating of genes with methyl groups is known, was based on the fact that at any given time, only a small fraction of the genes in any human body are active. There is little understanding of what makes genes turn on or off. Why, for instance, does the gene that causes kidneys to grow in a fetus cease to operate? Why does the gene which causes male baldness start to function long after fetal genes become inactive? Since his days in the anesthesia laboratory of Georges Ungar at Baylor, Burzynski had believed the peptides he calls antineoplastons are messengers carrying information and instructions to cells and their components. This information, he thought, had something to do with activating some genes and deactivating others. Now came Baylin, reporting in Science that "methylation patterns closely correlate with patterns of gene expression."

The new information at last allowed Burzynski to understand and explain how antineoplastons probably work. "The p-53 tumor suppressor gene causes abnormal cells to die. If the cell develops in an abnormal way, this gene kills it via programmed cell death," Burzynski explained. "When the p-53 gene sends out a protein, also called p-53, the abnormal, or malignant, cells form rigid patterns inside their cell walls. They do this by binding with isoglutamine, which is a component of our A-10 and is normally present in the bloodstream. Once possessing such a rigid framework, a cell will die by first shrinking and then disintegrating. It makes small tentacle-projections and they are gradually taken into the bloodstream by macrophages as the process repeats itself.

"This process of cell death is very gradual, so there is no disturbance inside the body. If all the malignant cells in a significant tumor were to die at once, the patient would have extreme fevers, inflammations, swelling, pain and toxic poisoning from pieces of dead tumor. So this process needs to be gradual for the body to handle it without damage. We have seen this process going on for a long time when antineoplastons are applied in cell culture to the DNA in many types of malignant cells, going back to the 1970s in the lab at Baylor."

Burzynski long suspected the inactivity of tumor suppressor genes which helped allow many cancers to grow may have been due to blockage of those tumor suppressor genes. He felt vindicated by Baylin's report.

"We long suspected that in the 50 percent or so of cancers associated with mutation or blockage of the p-53 gene, the blockage could be caused by a chemical attaching itself to the DNA," he said. "If the gene is covered, it is inactive. We now know that if we remove the coating by taking away most methyl groups, we allow the gene to operate." The process is called demethylation. Added Burzynski, "Our study done in the 1970s proved that antineoplastons remove methyl from DNA. But at the time, no one knew about tumor-suppressor genes. It was later proven that neurofibromatosis [better known as elephant man's disease] can be blocked by demethylating DNA." In fact, Burzynski patented a method of treating that disease with antineoplastons, and has succeeded in several cases.

Burzynski believes not all inactive genes are turned off by methyl group coatings. Other chemicals may be involved with other genes. "But we now know that hypermethylation can be caused by either inheritance or by environmental carcinogens like tobacco and certain chemicals. We postulated in the early 1990s in several papers that blockage of tumor suppressors through methylation is one of the mechanisms causing cancer and I believe this is now confirmed."

Other tumor-suppressor genes besides the p-53 can also become coated with methyl. One example is the VHL gene named for its discovers, the German scientists Von Hippel and Lindau, whose inactivity is often associated with kidney cancers. The fact that much of this phenomenon is hereditary, Burzynski says, may explain why the anti-cancer activity of antineoplastons sometimes varies by ethnic group. "We have had good success in treating colon cancer in Asians, especially Japanese," he reported. "But we have had less success with Europeans. This may also explain why Dr. Tsuda in Japan has had better results than we have had with colon cancer."

Several studies published after Baylin's provide even more detail on how tumor suppression works once it is reactivated by removal of gene coatings. They reveal that the p-53 gene does not directly activate the cell-death process. It activates another gene, the WAF-1, which is responsible directly for cell death.

Burzynski sees enormous potential in this new knowledge. "We believe the other 117 antineoplastons which we have isolated but not developed could have similar effects on other genes that may be methylated," he said. "We also know other genes can be unblocked by antineoplastons. We have had some success using them to treat auto-immune diseases."

One example: The cure of Dr. Stephanie Sadik, a Florida pediatrician who almost died from an extremely rare genetic disease known as Takayasu's arteritis, in which the victim's arteries become inflamed and gradually choked off. Dr. Sadik had been plagued by this condition since her early youth. In its initial stages, the disease caused her general pain and fatigue. Gradually, as the arteries leading to her arms closed off, she lost all blood pressure in those limbs. It became impossible for her to lift her arms, even to brush her hair. After scores of doctors had been unable to tell Stephanie what was wrong, the disease was finally diagnosed while she was a medical student at Tel Aviv University in Israel. Once the disease was diagnosed, she was put on a regimen of steroids, immune suppressants and chemotherapy agents including the drugs Imuran, Methotrexate and Cyclophosphamide. But her condition did not improve. The pain grew ever worse; her ability to use her arms deteriorated. She gained more than 200 pounds from years of the chemical regimen.

She found her way to Burzynski while still a medical student in 1993, after her mother heard the host of a radio show describe antineoplastons as a genetic therapy. "Dr. Burzynski had no idea whether his stuff would work for me or not," she said. "He had never treated anyone with Takayasu's arteritis before. But he gave me capsules of

AS2-1. After six months of taking the capsules, I started to feel better and eventually I felt normal again. I'm now in remission; I have no pain; I had no side effects from the drug. I believe my recovery was due to the AS2-1. If the symptoms ever recur, or if I am ever diagnosed with cancer, I will immediately go back to Dr. Burzynski. I believe he is a great man and a great scientist."

Burzynski believes Dr. Sadik's cure was due to demethylation of a gene—he doesn't know which one—which blocks development of this disease. "Other auto-immune diseases can also be cured by antineoplastons," he said in the spring of 2000. Anemia—both sickle cell and talasemia—can be affected. We can do this by unblocking the gene that produces hemoglobin F during life as a fetus. The gene is blocked after birth by hypermethylation. This is why some ethnic groups get inferior hemoglobin because of mutation of the genes that produce the hemoglobin. This prevents their blood from transferring oxygen throughout the body efficiently. These diseases can be treated by causing the body to create fetal hemoglobin in the patient's own blood. But even when you treat them that way, the problem can return, since the gene is blocked. We have treated this with capsules of AS2-1, by unblocking the gene for hemoglobin F. In research led by Dr. S.W. Brusilow at Johns Hopkins, they also did it with phenylactetate. The mechanism is similar to what is happening with our antineoplastons."

Burzynski concludes that methylation may be one of the main methods the human body uses to regulate genes, determining which ones will function at any given time. "We need different genes at different times of life," he said. "So we function like a clock that blocks some genes and not others."

Burzynski sees development of mechanisms to block some genes and restart others as offering not only the key to curing virtually all cancers, but also for many other purposes. "If we can unlock some genes, we could unlock the key to regenerating organs and limbs. We might not need nearly as many transplants, for instance, if people in kidney failure could regenerate their own kidneys. If they did this, the organs would really be their own, and there would be no need for the immune-suppressing drugs we now use to fight off rejection of transplanted organs. This could also lead to rejuvenating human beings and greatly extending our lives. With antineoplastons, we are making only the very first baby steps in this direction by unblocking some genes. There will be much more."

Burzynski knows he cannot possibly do all this by himself. At the time of his criminal trials, chief prosecutor Michael Clark complained that if he were convicted, Burzynski was offering no alternative for the care of his patients. "He was really playing hardball with the jury, hiding behind his patients," Clark complained. Replied Burzynski in 1997, "Who else could I get to work 18 hours every day, doing the paperwork, supervising the chemical plant, checking on the research into more concentrated and efficient versions of the drug, as well as seeing the patients? There is no one else crazy enough to do all this. Anyone else with a practice like mine would just keep the profits, not invest most of them in research and manufacturing."

But three years later, at age 57 in the spring of 2000, Burzynski realized that for the good of his patients, he had to train potential successors. "I would like to have at least three more doctors working with the patients," he said, noting that at that moment he had plans to hire four M.D.s to join three he then employed who were licensed to practice medicine in the United States. His staff also included 11 foreign-trained M.D.s not licensed in America. "I don't know if any one person can be a successor. We will have to see how good they are. But I am planning to train one of our new people in the overview of the whole enterprise."

His success and the clinical trial statistics Burzynski generated in the years after his courtroom ordeal have made recruiting quality physicians easier. "It was difficult to find good people because of our problems with the FDA," he said in the spring of 2000. "But things are a little better with the FDA, even if they are far from good, and now I have good people actively interested. Three of the people who want to come here this spring are currently on faculty at medical schools."

Burzynski also remained confident that antineoplastons would soon be approved by both the FDA and its European equivalent. "If we move ahead without interference from the FDA, our medicines will become a conventional treatment within a year or two," he said early in 2000. "They will no longer be seen as alternative. There is always resistance when a scientific paradigm is shattered. And when we establish that there is a biochemical defense system in addition to the immune system, we are doing just that, destroying ideas that have been held as gospel for many years. This is why I am being accused of being a quack and a fraud. Even the judge said there is no merit to those accusations. So I am immune to such accusations. I am comfortable with everything I've done."

But the old scientific paradigm may be about to fall. Cell differentiation drugs (chemicals that act only on malignant cells and do not affect healthy ones) became a fashionable subject for establishment cancer researchers during the late 1990s. One such drug is Herceptin, developed at

UCLA and marketed by the biotechnology firm Genentech and its parent pharmaceutical company Hoffman-LaRoche. It was in use against one form of breast cancer by the fall of 1999. At the 1998 and 2000 Science Writers Seminars sponsored by the American Cancer Society, full sessions were devoted to advances in cell differentiation.

No one now knows what will be the eventual outcome of this ongoing story. But it was certain by the summer of 2000 that worldwide scientific thinking was slowly coming around to Burzynski's point of view—even though many establishment scientists were unaware of who got there first. The well-publicized Herceptin had been approved. Like antineoplastons, it acts in a non-toxic way by affecting only cancer cells and ignoring healthy ones. But it acts on only one form of the disease, one that affects about 30 percent of breast cancer victims. Further indications of a change in attitude came at the 1998 American Cancer Society Science Writers Seminar in Newport Beach, Calif. The society's then-president, Dr. David Rosenthal of Harvard Medical School, remarked in an interview there that "Burzynski was clearly ahead of his time." The program for that seminar featured a full session on cell differentiation agents—chemicals that act on diseased cells but not on healthy ones. Yet no panelist there or in a similar session of the same seminar two years later even mentioned that a successful cell differentiation treatment had already been in use for decades, one that's been proven in more than 3,000 patients. It's called antineoplastons.

The Michele Curtis Story

Could Antineoplastons Have Saved Her Father Too?

Rarely has a daughter been as frustrated as Michele Curtis was during 1995 and 1996, watching her father wither and die from the ravaging effects of breast cancer. For Michele Curtis herself is a cancer survivor...and she had every reason to believe that the same treatment she sought in the early 1980s could also help her dad. But he would have no part of it.

Part One of the Curtis family cancer story began in a small elementary school just north of Detroit. At the time, Michele didn't think of herself as part of a cancer cluster, but she may have been. No government agency ever investigated what happened during the early 1980s at Avery Elementary School in the Berkley School District. During that time, four of the school's female teachers, as well as counselors and other employees—all working in the same building—were afflicted with soft-tissue tumors. Because there was no investigation, Michele was left with little but suspicion. She has no way of knowing whether any cancer-causing conditions existed in the building. She never taught in that school again after her cancer finally disappeared.

A Michigan native and the daughter of a man who spent most of his working life in the Buick assembly plant in Flint, Michele attended Eastern Michigan University in Ypsilanti and segued easily into a teaching career. By the age of 27, she was in her fourth year of teaching in the Berkley district, handling a special-education class of physically and otherwise handicapped children. She had two children of her own, twin sons named Aaron and Ryan, and her life in 1982 was so active that she tended to disregard the early clues that might have ensured her cancer was diagnosed before it caused much trouble.

Those early signs included severe periodic migraine headaches and sharp abdominal cramps, usually accompanied by diarrhea. Late in 1981, during a routine annual checkup, she told her gynecologist about the headaches, and he recommended seeing a neurologist. "Like a fool, I didn't go," Michele says regretfully years later. "I had had some colitis while I was in college, so I dismissed some of the early signs as just remnants of that. And I thought the headaches were somehow related to the stress of my job."

She was unable to ignore her symptoms any longer when they became more severe during Memorial Day weekend, 1982. "I had taken a sick day that Friday because a girl I taught was competing in the Special Olympics in Ypsilanti," she remembers. "While I was there, I felt very ill, so I went home and took some Tylenol. Because it was a Friday, I thought I could sleep it off over the weekend and be fine by the next Tuesday. Boy, was I wrong! The pains persisted in my stomach, and this time they were localized to my left side."

Her husband, Harry, drove her to a branch of the Pontiac Osteopathic Clinic near their home in Oxford, Michigan, about 40 miles north of Detroit. After she was examined, doctors recommended that she proceed to the hospital's main facility. But the Curtises went instead to Crittenton Hospital in the nearby town of Rochester, where her gynecologist was on staff.

By the time Michele arrived at Crittenton, it was early Saturday morning, and few doctors were available. In the hospital emergency room, blood tests were taken, and her abdomen was X-rayed. From the blood workup, the doctors knew something was amiss, but they were unsure what it was. The abdominal X-ray revealed no problems. So Michele stayed in the hospital for observation, with the admitting doctors telling her she ought to stay through the weekend.

"It was clear to me they knew something was wrong; that was why they kept doing more and more tests. They drew blood every few hours," she recalls. By Saturday night, Michele was in extreme pain and asked her nurses for a stronger painkiller than the intravenous Tylenol she had been given.

But this was a holiday weekend, so a different gynecologist from her doctor's group was on call each day. "Through the weekend, a different doctor would examine me each day, and each one had a different idea of what to do, which tests to run. Finally, my husband got angry and told the nurses to find someone who could figure out what was wrong with me," Michele remembers. Only after his demand, she says, did one gynecologist order a CT scan of her abdomen. It was taken on Monday, Memorial Day. And it showed that the source of her pain was a tumor on her left kidney, one that had already ruptured and was bleeding profusely into her abdomen.

Seeing this scan, Dr. Alan Morgan decided to operate. But Michele's internal bleeding had cost her so much blood that surgery was impossible until after she had several transfusions. Finally, she was operated on in the early morning hours of Tuesday. "I guess one lesson is that you should be careful not to have a crisis during a holiday weekend," Michele jokes later.

Morgan removed the tumor, taking the entire kidney out, too. "He told me he had to do that just to be cautious," Michele says. "And when the lab report came back, it was obvious that he was right." The tumor was a malignant leiomyosarcoma, a tumor of the soft tissue that occurs in about 1,080 Americans each year, according to American Cancer Society statistics. "That's when they called in an oncologist," Michele adds.

The oncologist, Dr. Ronald Izbicki, possessed a warm bedside manner, but he presented a cold message to the Curtises. "He said I had about a 40 percent chance of complete recovery if I underwent chemotherapy," Michele recalls. "Because the tumor had ruptured and I had a lot of internal bleeding, he believed that some cancer cells had landed elsewhere in my abdomen. That meant it was almost certain the cancer would metastasize."

Michele was frightened. "I was a basket case. To have cancer at 27 with two little boys at home was really scary. I thought about dying and leaving Harry to take care of the twins. But then Harry remembered a man he worked with whose high school-age son was sick with a brain tumor and leukemia. Radiation and chemotherapy had not helped him at all, and his doctors had told him there was nothing more they could do for him. The previous year they had given him three months to live. We had been following his progress all through his case."

The youth, Steve Hepp, traveled to Houston and sought treatment from Dr. Stanislaw Burzynski, who had told the teen's parents that he could treat their son's brain tumor, but that he had been having no luck using his antineoplaston medication against leukemia.

While recuperating from surgery, Michele asked Steve Hepp to come to her hospital room. "He told us all about the treatment, how he had to go to Texas and how he injected the antineoplastons. He talked about how he prevented his catheter from getting infected and he told us about the doctor and his clinic." The young man's brain tumor would soon clear up, and he went on to attend college, but years later he would die from his leukemia. "We all know that he would have died much earlier without the antineoplastons," Michele says.

The Curtises were still considering the chemotherapy option Izbicki presented. "I thought about losing my hair and getting sick and not being able to take care of my kids, and I didn't want anyone coming into my house to clean and take care of the boys, doing the things I was supposed to do," Michele remembers. "My family also didn't want any of that."

After Hepp's visit, the Curtises immediately telephoned Burzynski's clinic from Michele's hospital bed, requesting information and literature. They asked Morgan and Izbicki to evaluate the material they received. "Morgan said it sounded promising," Michele recounts. "Izbicki was neutral about it. But we were unsure. We worried because we needed these doctors to take care of me at home, even if I was on the antineoplaston treatment. So I asked Izbicki if he would still be my doctor even if I went to Texas. He said yes, so we decided to go. We figured if it didn't work on me, I could still come home and do the chemotherapy."

Within days of her release from Crittenton, Michele and Harry flew to Houston and made their first visit to Burzynski's clinic, then located in a small shopping center on the city's west side. "His staff was very kind and accommodating," she remembers. "They tried to help us through all the problems with insurance forms and hotels and arrangements. They even made some suggestions about who to contact at Michigan Blue Cross to get them to pay for the therapy. But we never got them to pay for any of it. They paid for the blood tests I had while on the treatment, but they even protested against paying for the CT scan I had in Houston before I started the treatment."

The scan revealed that all visible cancer had been removed during Michele's surgery just two weeks earlier. There was "no evidence of enlarged lymph nodes or any other mass lesion" in her abdomen, the CT scan report said. But Izbicki and Morgan had warned that new growths would certainly begin to sprout if Michele did nothing. So she decided to give antineoplastons a try, paying a $5,000 deposit at the start of treatment. "Later, Burzynski's office would try to bill the insurance company, but because it wouldn't pay, the clinic sent us a monthly statement," Michele explains. "They asked us to pay what we could, but they never hounded us for money at any time. Still, I worried a lot about the money it was costing. We'd been married only a little more than three years, and we didn't have much in savings. But when I visited Burzynski's lab facility where he was synthesizing the antineoplastons, I felt a lot better about the money because I could see how much he had invested in the equipment and staff he needed there. I could see it wasn't just a rip-off."

Michele had a subclavial catheter installed in her chest and immediately began injecting large amounts of antineoplastons four times a day. Her 25-cc dosage was so large that ordinary syringes could not accommodate it, so the bemused Curtises began buying their syringe supply from a veterinarian who normally used the large hypodermics in treating horses. Michele continued the treatment for three months until the tissue around her catheter became infected, and she wound up back in Crittenton after becoming dizzy and collapsing one day as she walked into her bathroom.

The hospital staff quickly removed her catheter and gave her antibiotics intravenously for her infection. She also underwent a spinal tap because she suffered a severe headache during her infection, and Izbicki feared that her cancer might have developed into a brain tumor. It had not. Her spinal fluid was completely clear, containing no cancer cells; her doctors concluded that her collapse was due entirely to her infection.

"I immediately called the clinic in Houston, and Burzynski suggested I start on the antineoplaston capsules he had just begun to make in his synthesizing plant," Michele reports. She stayed on the oral medication until November 1982 and has been clear of cancer ever since. She went back on the medication only once, in 1983, when Izbicki noticed a sudden drop in her white blood cell count. "Burzynski felt I should go back on a small dose, and I did," says Michele. "Then I had a CT scan in November 1983, which was clear. I've been clear ever since."

Years later, it was her father, Donald Noble, who was stricken in a new cancer crisis. He was reluctant even to admit he had a tumor but eventually was diagnosed with breast cancer, a relative rarity in a male, since men account for only about 1 percent of breast cancer cases. Michele urged him to travel to Houston to see Burzynski. "He wouldn't do it," she sobs. He died in September 1996. "He was 82, and he was the kind of person who hated going to doctors. He didn't ever want to put anybody out."

Michele learned of her dad's cancer in the fall of 1994, while she and her then eight-year-old daughter, Kristi, were visiting her parents at their winter retreat in Florida. "I talked to him then about going to Burzynski, and he said he didn't want to travel that far. He said he didn't want to spend so much money at his age. He knew about the trouble we'd had getting Blue Cross to cover me." Michele believes Burzynski's treatment had spared her from both the predicted spread of her cancer and the ravages of chemotherapy. She knew antineoplastons had worked well in many cases of breast cancer and believed they would be her dad's best option, as they had been for her.

But Michele backed off because she knew her father would resent her trying to involve herself in his decisions. She was forced to observe at close range as his health gradually deteriorated. His cancer was formally diagnosed after it metastasized to his arm in March 1995, taking the form of an open sore that oozed fluid onto his skin. "He'd cover it up," Michele recalls. "But it meant he could no longer go in the swimming pool, which he loved to do."

At the urging of other family members, Michele's dad eventually agreed to see a doctor. "The sore had him so scared that he finally went," she recalls. The physician immediately recommended radiation, and Don Noble underwent the treatment. But when he arrived home in Michigan later that spring, his abdomen was covered with a rash. Another physician convinced him that he was undergoing a second manifestation of his breast cancer, pressing him to try chemotherapy. The rash was gone within a month of beginning chemotherapy, and the family spent an uneasy summer.

The following winter, back in Florida, Michele noticed another open sore on her dad's arm. It was soon diagnosed as still another cancer episode, and he again underwent radiation. But this time he refused any follow-up chemotherapy, saying he feared that if he took any strong medication, he might never make it back to Michigan. By the time he arrived home in March 1996, he was having difficulty walking. Soon small lumps began appearing on his chest and back, one of which opened and continued to ooze until his death.

"All through this, I kept suggesting Burzynski because I knew Burzynski had had a lot of success against breast cancers," Michele says. "My dad would answer me, 'Look, I'm 83, and if it's my time to go, I'm gonna go.'" Still, he was willing to try one more therapy; he visited a homeopath in Pontiac, Michigan, who put him on an herbal diet. But Michele's father stuck with it less than a week. Meanwhile, a chest X-ray performed for the homeopath revealed that Noble had large tumors in both lungs and his liver. Eventually, he died from the cancer.

"It was incredibly upsetting for me to watch this when I felt there was something out there that could have helped him," Michele said tearfully just days after her father died."It's true that for a long time, I wasn't completely sure whether Burzynski's treatment of me was actually curative or whether I was just lucky and my cancer would not have metastasized anyway. But my doctors were so certain that my cancer would spread after my tumor burst open that when I think about it, I have very little doubt the antineo-plastons cured me. For sure, I know the medicine never hurt me. That made it very heartbreaking when my father refused to go to Burzynski."

Postscript

OXFORD, Mich., midyear 2000—Michele Curtis doesn't say much about her health these days. She doesn't think much about it, either, and she's glad of that. "There isn't much to say. I've been in great health and our kids keep my husband and me busy all the time."

Michele and Harry spend most vacations at their cabin near Alpena in northern Michigan, but she also travels sometimes with friends to exotic spots like Puerto Vallarta, Mexico, which she visited in the spring of 2000.

"Not much has changed for me," Michele says. "I'm still teaching first grade, I'm still feeling great. And if any cancer ever appeared again, I'd go see Dr. Burzynski again, for sure."

EPILOGUE

Patients

Antineoplastons are an activist therapy. Their success depends on the active participation of patients and families. It takes an effort to prime and load the infusion pump every day. It takes an effort to clean and sterilize the catheters most patients must use. It takes an effort for patients to carry the infusion pump with them everywhere, day and night, week after week, month after month.

The success of the therapy often depends on patients' willingness and ability to perform these tasks. "We have the best success with patients in two age groups: small children and adults in the 40- to 60-year-old age bracket," observes Dr. Stanislaw Burzynski. "The children do well because their parents force them to carry the pump and do most of the chores for them. But adults in their 20s and 30s and even some in their early 40s are often too impatient with the process. They expect instant results, and this process can often take months. At the same time, many patients older than 60 have given up on themselves. So among adults, we have the best success with patients in their middle-age years. They have patience with the therapy, and they are willing to put in the necessary effort."

This analysis has been borne out among the patients who sat in Burzynski's waiting room that sunny day in May 1996. Almost one year later, all are still alive. One of the four is an unqualified success, one at least a partial success, a third might have succeeded if she could have stayed on the therapy, and one dropped out after just three weeks.

William Boyd unquestionably benefited the most. After more than a year on antineoplastons, Bill was still infusing them regularly, and his brain tumor was at least 97 percent gone. "You have to remember, in early '96 we had been urged by the doctors and nurses in North Carolina to get radiation and chemotherapy just to buy a little time," said his wife, Shirley, in early April 1997. "Compared to just buying time, there's no doubt that antineoplastons have been the answer. Our neurologist here in Greensboro says he now has no doubt that the Food and Drug Administration should approve antineoplastons. He knows of at least two other patients besides Bill who have survived brain tumors just because of them.

"There is some confusion about whether Bill's tumor is completely gone. One report from our local hospital says the latest MRI scan shows the tumor has disappeared. But Dr. Burzynski said on our last visit to Houston that it is only 97 percent gone. And we know there is room for some different interpretations of these scans." In fact, simple swelling or edema can sometimes take on the appearance of an active tumor. So can scar tissue and masses of dead, or necrosed, cancer calls.

For William Boyd, the upshot was that he planned to continue infusing antineoplastons until he had spent 18 months on the treatment. If there was no doubt by then that his tumor was gone, he intended to switch to capsules for a while.

"Going to Dr. Burzynski was absolutely the best thing we could have done," Bill says. "I just continue to get better and better. How can there be any doubt about whether this stuff works?"

Meanwhile, one year after Mitzi Jo Goodfellow started antineoplaston treatment, there was some uncertainty about the degree of help she received from the drug. Like Bill Boyd, Mitzi Jo experienced dramatic reduction in the size of her tumor. By June 10, 1996, just 10 weeks after she began infusing antineoplastons, her tumor had shrunk by 67 percent. But she suffered recurrent infections, weight loss and occasional seizures, and she believed the treatment was making her exhausted. So she stopped taking the drug on Aug. 9, 1996. As of early March 1997, her once-aggressive glioblastoma tumor had not increased in size. A CT scan taken then, in fact, indicated that it might have shrunk slightly in the interim, a time span in which she underwent no treatment of any kind.

"So we don't know yet just how much she benefited," Burzynski said later that month. "The fact that the tumor did not grow in many months indicates that it may be gone. The remaining lesion we see may be scar tissue or necrosed cells. We can't be sure until we see more scans down the line and whether the tumor in fact begins to grow again."

If that happened, Mitzi Jo says, she would immediately return to Burzynski for renewed therapy. "I think I benefited a lot from the treatment, even though I lost about 20 pounds while I was on it. I only went off because I ended up having a few seizures and some weight loss." In the seven months after stopping treatment, she regained 15 pounds and resumed a normal life. "I would never go back to the radiation and chemo route," she says.

The course was not so definite for Sydney Seaward or Krystyna Pataluch. Seaward never felt she fit in among Burzynski's patients and stayed on the treatment just three weeks.

"I never believed I should be lumped together into a group of desperate patients," she says. "I was also in a minority of patients who had side effects." Seaward reports that she suffered debilitating fatigue while on antineoplastons and experienced two shattering nightmares worse than any she'd had before. "I was paranoid and aggressive," she remembers. "I kept thinking people were out to get me. I had shortness of breath. It was the first time during my whole bout with cancer that I really felt sick."

"We never had a chance to adjust her dose to her complaints," Burzynski said later. "Fatigue is common in the first few weeks on the treatment. It is part of the adjustment process and usually doesn't persist. And we never got her up to a full dose of the medicine." Seaward says her tumors nevertheless almost dissipated in the months after she stopped infusing. "I credit prayer," she says. "Yes, I eventually ran back to conventional chemotherapy, and they welcomed me with open arms." But she reports that her tumors were almost gone before she sought another round of establishment treatment.

"I think my biggest beef with antineoplastons was that everyone else I met had a spouse or a loved one or a parent to help them, and I had to do everything all by myself," Seaward says. "I was constantly dealing with needles and tubes, and I had no help. I had originally thought my roommate could help, but it turned out she was terrified by the sight of a needle." Though she went frequently to Burzynski's clinic for assistance, those visits, she said, often lasted a full day because doctors and nurses were occupied with other patients. "The three weeks I was on the therapy seemed like an eternity to me. It was the maximum time I could take physically and mentally."

Burzynski believes that Seaward never dedicated herself wholeheartedly to the treatment. "She insisted on having the catheter in her arm and not her chest, for one thing," he says. "Therefore, we could not adjust her doses precisely as we might have otherwise. And three weeks is simply too short a time to evaluate anyone's response."

Seaward offers no criticism of Burzynski. "I think he is a very kind and driven man," she concludes. "He earnestly wants to save people, and I think he is on to a way to do it for a lot of people. He is on the right track, even if it didn't work out for me."

For Krystyna Pataluch, there were no problems with side effects, only with doctors outside the Burzynski clinic. "Everything went OK for two months after she started the treatment and came home from Houston," reports her husband, Stan. "Her tumor was reduced, but in between, she needed blood transfusions because of internal bleeding. This had nothing to do with the antineoplastons, but it was when we began to have trouble.

"No one in Chicago wanted to work with us when they learned she was on Dr. Burzynski's therapy. When she needed blood—and eventually she needed transfusions about twice a week—we were forced to go to emergency rooms of the local hospitals. So after about seven or eight weeks, we stopped the treatment."

Krystyna eventually traveled back to her native Poland for two months of experimental treatment, but soon her tumor began growing again. After she returned to Chicago, it grew enough to block her colon completely and required her to use a colostomy bag. And because it was the only way to get local physicians to furnish other care she needed, Krystyna eventually consented to chemotherapy. Ten months after her first visit to Burzynski, the results of that conventional treatment were inconclusive.

"Basically, we know that none of what has happened is Burzynski's fault," says Stan. "We are 100 percent supportive of him. We stopped only because we could not manage the bleeding problem ourselves, and the doctors would not cooperate while she was taking antineoplastons. But she will go back to him for sure if the chemotherapy doesn't work, because we know we were getting results from Burzynski's medicine before we stopped." In May 1997, Krystyna Pataluch planned to return to Houston and restart antineoplaston treatment.

Postscript, Spring 2000

Sydney Seaward is dead. In the spring of 1997, she credited prayer with the reduction of her breast cancer tumors. But neither prayer nor conventional chemotherapy and radiation treatments could prevent them from recurring with a vengeance and spreading widely a few months later. She died in September 1998.

"We can't be sure if she would have responded to antineoplastons," says Burzynski. "But we can be sure she never took the full treatment, never gave it much of a chance. I wish she would have given us the chance to try to save her."

The stories of two other patients encountered in the Burzynski Clinic waiting room on that random day in May 1996 are far more cheerful. Mitzi Jo Goodfellow is alive and healthy, tumor free almost four years after going off antineoplaston treatment. William Boyd is also tumor free and politically active again, running for the North Carolina state Senate.

"I'm doing just fine," reports Mitzi Jo, taking time out from her part-time job. "I only spent three months on Dr. Burzynski's treatment, but it must have been long enough. My tumor was down to almost nothing when I went off, and I've been completely tumor-free for more than a year." Mitzi Jo still takes the anti-seizure drug Dilantin and she reports she has problems with short-term memory. "I've been told they touched part of my brain during the surgery before I went to Dr. Burzynski," she says. "But I'm alive and my doctor, Dr. Decker, says he's surprised, that it's a miracle."

It is no miracle, says Burzynski. "She didn't stay on the treatment as long as many patients, but it was obviously sufficient," he says.

The ultimate outcome was more tragic for Krystyna Pataluch, who died in late 1997. "She never went back to Dr. Burzynski because she was just too weak," said her husband, Stan. "Her hemoglobin was so low that she had to receive blood transfusions every week, or even more often, during the last months of her life. I wish she could have been strong enough to travel. If she could have returned to Houston, I think she might have lived much longer."

Bill Boyd did live, and quite vigorously. He thinks his survival is a miracle. But he knows the cause. "It's the anti-neoplastons, and I'm doing what I can to try to get them approved by the FDA so other people can get the same benefit. I also want to get insurance companies to cover this kind of alternative treatment, so it can be available to everyone," he says. "That's one reason I'm running for office again."

Bill reports no health problems since his tumor completely disappeared on a scan taken in early 1998. "I go to work every day and I love it. I have no health problems."

But his wife Shirley has encountered trouble. She's undergone surgery for endometrial, breast and colon tumors and another surgery for a pelvic mass was likely in the spring of 2000. "I had three chemotherapy treatments a year and a half ago and they did no good. I may go down to Dr. B pretty soon. I know how well Bill is doing, and I'm sure I'll do well, too."

Burzynski feels these patients, plus the nine others

whose stories are covered in even greater detail in this book "make up a small sample, but an important one." He notes many of the patients arrived at his clinic after undergoing massive chemotherapy and radiation, while a few had no prior treatment of any kind.

"To have the best chance, they should come to us first," Burzynski says. "They have a much better chance before they are affected by chemotherapy and radiation. I think, for example, if Thomas Wellborn had come to us first, he might have lived significantly longer."

But until antineoplastons receive FDA approval, most patients cannot come to Burzynski until they've already undergone one or two courses of this era's standard cancer therapies. If there is one principle that appears to have governed the fate of the 13 persons whose case histories are detailed in this book, it is that there was a tragic outcome for those who altered the prescribed dosage of antineoplastons and those who either abandoned the treatment on their own volition or under FDA coercion.

"We have no doubt that compliance, staying on the treatment just as we prescribe it, is a major factor in our patient outcomes," says Burzynski. "Lack of previous treatment with chemotherapy and radiation, which can affect patients' immune systems, their respiratory abilities and their blood vessels, is also an advantage. It is certain that if a particular case is not managed well, this can lead to a negative outcome."

ALL CLINICAL TRIAL PATIENTS

Includes all evaluable patients treated with antineoplaston A10 and AS2-1 injections in clinical trials supervised by FDA since 1988

(All results preliminary, reported as of May 15, 2000; Patients listed with stable disease on that date may improve and become partial or complete remissions)

Cancer Type—	Patients (numbers of)	Complete Remission	Partial Remission*	No Recurrence**	Objective Response Total	Stable Disease***	Progressive Disease
All Brain Tumors	211	25	34		59	73	79
(Various types of brain tumor included in above total)							
Anaplastic Astrocytoma	29	5	3		8	10	11
Anaplastic Glioma	2		1		1		1
Anaplastic Oligodendroglioma	3		1		1		2
Astrocytoma	10		4		4	6	
Brain Stem Glioma	36	5	10		15	10	11
Ependymoma	5					4	1
Glioblastoma	78	4	7		11	26	41
Glioma	2		1			1	1
Gliosarcoma	1						
Meningioma	3	1			1	2	
Mixed Glioma	13	4	1		5	3	5
Oligodendroglioma	7	2	2		4	2	1
Pilocytic astrocytoma	2		1		1	1	
PNET (medulloblastoma)	13	2	2		4	5	4
Rhabdoid Tumor	3	1			1	1	1
Schwannoma	1					1	
Visual Pathway Astrocytoma	3	1	1		1	1	
Other Cancers							
Adrenal Gland Cancer	1					1	
Breast Cancer	21			5	5	8	8
Carcinoma (of unknown primary)	3					1	2
Colon Cancer	10					2	8

340

Cancer Type–	Patients (numbers of)	Complete Remission	Partial Remission*	No Recurrence **	Objective Response Total	Stable Disease ***	Progressive Disease
Esophageal Cancer	8	2			2	1	5
Head and Neck Cancer	6					4	2
Leukemia	3					3	
Liver Cancer	2						2
Lung Cancer	21					6	15
Malignant Melanoma	6						6
Mantle Zone Lymphoma	4					4	
Mesothelioma	3					1	2
Multiple Myeloma	3			3	3		
	(all 3 cases are improved; other categories do not apply to this cancer)						
Neuroblastoma	2		1		1	1	
Neuroendocrine Tumor	1						1
Non-Hodgkin's Lymphoma	48	6	5		11	29	8
Ovarian Cancer	2						2
Pancreatic Cancer	7		1		1	1	5
Prostate Cancer	21	1	1	4	6	6	9
Renal Cell Carcinoma	8					5	3
Small Intestine Cancer	1						1
Soft Tissue Sarcoma	7						7
Stomach Cancer	2			1	1		1
Urinary Bladder Cancer	1						1
Uterine Cervix Cancer	7					5	2
Total:	409	35	41	13	86	151	169

* FDA definition: 50 percent or more reduction in tumor size which persists longer than 4 weeks

** Patients arrived with no tumor after surgery or other treatment and cancer did not recur

*** Less than 50 percent reduction of tumor, but no progression, which persists for a minimum of 12 weeks.

341

SPECIAL (COMPASSIONATE USE) EXCEPTION PATIENTS*

Includes all patients treated on special exceptions granted by FDA since 1996

(All results preliminary, reported as of May 15, 2000; Patients listed with stable disease on that date may improve and become partial or complete remissions)

Cancer Type—	Patients (numbers of)	Complete Remission	Partial Remission*	No Recurrence**	Objective Response Total	Stable Disease***	Progressive Disease
All Brain Tumors	97	1	14		15	40	42
(Various types of brain tumor included in above total)							
Anaplastic Astrocytoma	15		3		3	7	5
Anaplastic Ependymoma	2						2
Astrocytoma	3		1		1	2	
Brain Stem Glioma	14		3		3	8	3
Ependymoma	1					1	
Ganglioneurocytoma	1						1
Glioblastoma	45	1	4		5	17	23
Gemistocytic Astrocytoma	1		1		1		1
Glioma	2					1	
Gliosarcoma	2		1		1	1	
Meningioma	1					1	
Mixed Glioma	3						3
Oligodendroglioma	1					1	
Pilocytic Astrocytoma	2		1		1	1	
PNET	2						2
Rhabdoid Tumor	2						2
Other Cancers							
Adrenal Gland Cancer	1						1
Breast Cancer	15					3	12
Carcinoma of unknown primary	7		1		1	3	3
Colon Cancer	24					7	17
Esophageal Cancer	4						4

Cancer Type—	Patients (numbers of)	Complete Remission	Partial Remission*	No Recurrence **	Objective Response Total	Stable Disease ***	Progressive Disease
Head and Neck Cancer	9					4	5
Leukemia	1					1	1
Liver Cancer	1						1
Lung Cancer	18					6	12
Lymphoma of the Central Nervous System	1					1	
Malignant Melanoma	4			1	1		3
Mesothelioma	6					2	4
Multiple Myeloma	1					1	
Neuroblastoma	1						1
Neuroendocrine Tumor	1						1
Non-Hodgkin's Lymphoma	7		1		1	5	1
Ovarian Cancer	4		1			2	2
Pancreatic Cancer	4	1			2		2
Prostate Cancer	6					2	4
Renal Cell Carcinoma	9					3	6
Small Intestine Cancer	1						1
Soft Tissue Sarcoma	7					2	5
Stomach Cancer	2					1	1
Urinary Bladder Cancer	4					1	3
Uterine Cervix Cancer	1					1	
Waldenstrom's Macroglobulinemia	1					1	
Total	237	2	17	1	20	86	131

* Almost all patients treated under special exceptions have failed all other available treatments and are very ill when accepted for treatment. Most have life expectancies of two months or less when they arrive.

** FDA Definition: 50 percent or more reduction in tumor size within a six month period.

*** Less than 50 percent reduction of tumor size within a six-month period, but no progression

COMPLETED CLINICAL TRIALS

Results of Phase II clinical trials in which antineoplastons produced at least four complete or partial responses in groups of 40 or fewer patients

Results as of May 2000, in patients whose treatment began in 1996 or later

Nature of trial	patients (number of)	Complete Remissions	Partial Remissions *	Stable Disease **	Progressive Disease
Children with low-grade astrocy-toma brain tumors	8	2	3	2	1
	25 percent complete remission, 37.5 percent partial remission, for total of 62.5 percent FDA-defined objective response to antineoplastons.				
Adults with mixed glioma brain tumors	11	3	1	2	5
	27.3 percent complete remission, 9.1 percent partial remission, for total of 36.4 percent FDA-defined objective response to antineoplastons.				
Patients with brain-stem glioma brain tumors	21	3	4	5	9
	14.3 percent complete remission, 19 percent partial remission, for total of 33.3 percent FDA-defined objective response to antineoplastons.				
Patients with primary brain tumors	11	1	5	4	1
	9.1 percent complete remission, 45.5 percent partial remission, for total of 54.5 percent FDA-defined objective response to antineoplastons				

*   FDA definition: 50 percent or more reduction in tumor size which persists longer than 4 weeks

**   Less than 50 percent reduction of tumor, but no progression, which persists for a minimum of 12 weeks.

PRELIMINARY RESULTS OF TWO JAPANESE TRIALS
Reported in Spring 2000 by Hideaki Tsuda M.D., Kurume
University School of Medicine, Kurume, Japan

Cancer Type	# patients	# with increased time with no tumor recurrence	# with increased time to recurrence	# with shorter time to recurrence
Heptocellular Carcinoma (liver cancer)	8	2	5	1

All patients treated with AS2-1 after initial treatment removed tumor.
Tsuda report stated: "Hepatocellular cancer almost always recurs after
successful initial treatment." Initial standard treatment in Japan usually
consists of ethanol injections, microwave coagulation necrosis, trans
arterial embolization and chemotherapy administered to the hepatic
artery.

Tsuda further reported: "The survival curve of these 8 patients treated
by antineoplaston AS2-1 looks better than any other treatment for hepatocellular cancer at this moment (we have to increase the number of
patients, but we are feeling very good about the response)."

Colon Cancer	8	Recurrent site	
		Liver	Lung
		1	0

Study compares the recurrence rate after surgical removal of colon and
metastatic liver cancer. All patients treated with combination of oral
AS2-1 and injections of A10 for periods of one to two weeks (after surgical removal of tumors from colon, liver and/or lung). Only one recurrence of tumor found after 19 months. Tsuda reports normal recurrence
rate of tumor in liver is 63 percent and in lungs 48 percent within the
same time period. "Antineoplaston A10 and AS2-1 reduced recurrence
rate," Tsuda reported. He added: "Our former president of Kurume
University underwent (colon surgery) and microwave coagulation in
1995 on some metastatic cancers, but not all that he had. He has taken
antineoplaston AS2-1 since then and has been free from cancer. He has
lived five years and a half without limiting his usual activity. No (other)
patient of colon cancer with multiple liver metastases has lived longer
than 28 months regardless of what kinds of treatment he took in
Kurume University Hospital."

Index

212, 263, 326
development of, 25-36, 99-106,
122-132, 147-159
insurance payments for, 21, 36, 49, 55,
66-71, 140-141, 156, 183-184, 238,
247, 263-264, 325-326
interference of conventional treatments
with, 25-30, 114, 142-144, 300, 338
interference of lung impairment with,
16-18
JAMA literature, 253-266
monitoring, 209-210
NCI grants for developing, 124-125
NCI investigation, 220-221, 227
NCI studies, 32-33
patents, 35-36, 154-155
patient age as a factor, 23, 331
and patient energy level, 113-114
patient involvement, 331-338
pharmacodynamics, 311-317
and recurrences of cancer, 249, 345
sodium loads experienced by patients,
267-269
sodium phenylbuterate as, 307-309
species-specific qualities, 129,
157-158, 219-220, 259
See also antineoplastons; antineoplaston
treatment side effects; case histories;
dosage for antineoplaston treatments;
FDA; legal issues; pharmaceutical
companies; response rates for antineo
plaston treatments; studies of
antineoplaston treatments
antineoplaston treatment side effects
catheter complications, 28, 326-327
cramps, 202, 205
fatigue, 282, 333-334
flu-like symptoms, 171-172, 202, 205
hypernatremia, 267-269, 271-272
increased energy, 113-114
lack of negative side effects, 29,
113-114, 232
mental changes, 333-334
arteritis, 315-316
astrocytoma
antineoplaston treatment response rate,
340, 342, 344
case histories, 74-75, 83-94, 275-287
chemotherapy, 279-280
radiation treatment, 86-87, 279-280

surgical treatment, 84-85, 278-279
survival rates, 86
Avadassian, Emma, 25-28

B

babies. *See* infants
Bachorik, Larry, on the FDA Burzynski
trials, 81
Baylin, Stephen, on cancer biochemistry,
311-312
Baylor College of Medicine
Burzynski's research at, 105-106,
121-132
internal politics of, 130-131
Beth Israel Medical Center antineoplaston
study, 297-299
biochemical defense system, 127
biochemistry of cancer, 103, 122-123,
311-315
biographical information on Burzynski,
95-106
bladder cancer
antineoplaston treatment response rate,
341, 343
case histories, 30
blood in urine as a renal-cell cancer sign,
162-163
Blue Cross
antineoplaston treatment policies, 49,
55, 68-69, 325-326
knowledge of antineoplaston treatments,
69
Blue Shield antineoplaston treatment
policies, 247
bone cancer
case histories, 25, 26, 28-29
Ewing's sarcoma, 25, 26, 28-29
bone marrow tests, 243-244
bone marrow transplants, 245-246
side effects, 246
survival rates, 246
Boyd, William, 18-21, 331-332, 336
brain peptides, 121, 125-126
brain stem glioma, 37-56
antineoplaston treatment response rate,
340, 342, 344
brain tumors
antineoplaston treatment response rate,
17-18, 76, 263, 292-293, 297-299, 301,
302, 340, 342, 344
astrocytoma, 74-75, 83-94, 275-287

FDA, 48-49, 50-51
Karnovsky test, 50-51
Navarro case, 300-302, 304
compliance in antineoplaston treatments,
331-338
congestion of lungs, preventing, 16-17
congressional hearings on FDA
antineoplaston treatment policies,
306-307
Consolidated Administrator's Group,
antineoplaston treatment payments, 21
conventional cancer treatments
bone marrow transplants, 245-246
cell differentiation drugs, 318-319
compulsion by law, 300-306, 338
cost, 139, 264
interference with antineoplaston
treatments, 25-30, 114, 142-144, 300,
338
lymphoma, 245
side effects, 238, 245, 303
See also chemotherapy; radiation
treatments; surgical treatment
corticosteroids, side effects, 88, 89
cost of antineoplaston treatments, 89-90,
114, 139, 140-141, 150, 212, 263, 326
conventional treatment costs compared to,
139, 264
cramps as an antineoplaston treatment side
effect, 202, 205
Curtis, Michele, 321-330

D

death, as a radiation treatment side effect,
142-143
DeLap, Robert, 203-205, 293-295
delayed effects of radiation treatments,
264-265
demethylation, 311-316
demonstrations
1995 FDA trial of Burzynski, 34
1997 (January) FDA trial of Burzynski,
63, 74
diet as an alternative therapy, 112
diffuse large-cell lymphoma, case
histories, 72
dosage for antineoplaston treatments,
16-18, 23, 51, 113, 117, 171, 298-299
increases, 114-115, 207-208, 209-210,
224-226, 239
interruptions and changes, 204,

205-206, 207-208, 209-210, 298-299
large dosages, 326
and lung impairment, 16-18
maintenance dosage, 92
NCI trials, 224-226, 228
oral sodium phenylbuterate, 309
studies, 127, 224-226, 259-260
test dosages for individual patients, 51
double-blind studies of cancer patients,
264-265
drug approval process, 31-32, 186,
289-299

E

effectiveness
as an issue in the Burzynski trials,
33-36, 57-77
interleukin-2, 168
visualization, 111
See also chemotherapy response rates;
radiation treatment response rates;
response rates for antineoplaston
treatments; surgical treatment
effectiveness
Elan Corporation
antineoplaston arrangement with
Burzynski, 215-218
phenylacetate trial support, 232-233
ependymoma, antineoplaston treatment
response rate, 340, 342
Epstein, Fred
on antineoplaston brain tumor case
histories, 48, 54
antineoplaston study, 297-299
esophageal cancer, antineoplaston
treatment response rate, 341, 342
Ewing's sarcoma, case histories, 25, 26,
28-29

F

facial palsy as a sign of brain tumors,
40-42, 85, 93
fatigue
as an antineoplaston treatment side
effect, 282, 333-334
See also lethargy
FDA (Food and Drug Administration)
1977-1978 antineoplaston policies,
152-153
1983 lawsuit against Burzynski,
158-159, 175-181

1995 FDA trial of Burzynski, 30-36, 185-190
1997 (January) FDA trial of Burzynski, 57-77, 80-82, 289
1997 (May) FDA trial of Burzynski, 77-82
compulsion of conventional treatments, 300-306, 338
congressional hearings on FDA antineoplaston treatment policies, 306-307
FDA antineoplaston treatment intervention, 202-205, 208-209
FDA antineoplaston treatment restrictions, 17, 21-22, 284-285, 289-291, 299-309
fraud, 66-71, 188-190
IND permits, 32-33, 35, 139, 157, 177-178, 290
interstate drug shipment, 59-60, 62-63, 66-71, 79-80, 180, 182
malpractice suits for radiation treatments, 144-145
patent infringements, 233-235
patient rights, 36, 300-306, 338
Texas board of medical examiners investigation of Burzynski, 185-188, 309-311
See also 1983 FDA lawsuit against Burzynski; 1985 federal grand jury testimony by Burzynski; 1986 federal grand jury testimony by Burzynski; 1991 federal grand jury testimony by Burzynski; insurance companies
leiomyosarcoma
case histories, 321-330
chemotherapy, 324
surgical treatment, 323-324
lethargy
as a radiation treatment side effect, 200-201
See also fatigue
leukemia
antineoplaston treatments, 324-325, 341, 343
as a radiation treatment side effect, 246
Levit, Clay, testimony by, 59-60
liver cancer, 258
antineoplaston treatment response rate, 341, 343, 345

Lubens, Perry, on antineoplaston brain tumor case histories, 41-42, 53-54
lumps as renal-cell cancer signs, 165-167
lung cancer, antineoplaston treatment response rate, 341, 343
lymphoma
antineoplaston treatment response rate, 341, 343
case histories, 59-60, 72, 74, 107-119, 237-251
central nervous system, 343
chemotherapy, 110
diffuse large-cell, 72
metastasis, 243
non-Hodgkin's, 59-60, 74, 237-251, 341, 343
remissions, 248
surgical treatment, 109-110
visualization, 111

M

McConnell, Desiree, 191-210
McConnell, Shawn, 191-210
McConnell, Zachary, 191-210
FDA intervention with antineoplaston treatments, 202-205, 208-209
McDonald, Gabrielle, 179-181
McNally, Mary Ann, 73
macroglobulinemia, antineoplaston treatment response rate, 343
maintenance dosage for antineoplaston treatments, 92
malignant melanoma, antineoplaston treatment response rate, 341, 343
Malkin/Buckner paper on antineoplaston treatments, 227-228, 271-272
malpractice suits for radiation treatments, 144-145
mantle zone lymphoma, antineoplaston treatment response rate, 341
manufacture of antineoplastons, 58-59, 149-150, 153
Mask, William
on antineoplaston response rates, 29-30
and early antineoplaston trials, 27-30
Mayo Clinic report on antineoplaston treatments, 227
Mazur, Marian, 104-105, 147-148
M.D. Anderson, antineoplaston research grants, 124-125
medications

22-23
side effects
  bone marrow transplants, 246
  conventional cancer treatments, 238
  surgical treatment, 93
  See also antineoplaston treatment side
    effects; chemotherapy side effects;
    medication side effects; radiation
    treatment side effects
Siegel, Mary Jo, 237-251
Sigma Tau antineoplaston trials, 258-259
signs
  brain tumor signs, 40-42, 85, 93,
    193-194
  renal-cell cancer signs, 162-163, 165
small intestine cancer, antineoplaston
  treatment response rate, 341, 343
Smith, David, 302-306
Smith, Michael, testimony of, 73
sodium loads experienced by patients on
  antineoplaston treatments, 267-269
sodium phenylbuterate
  as an antineoplaston treatment,
    307-309
  approval as an orphan drug, 307
soft tissue sarcoma, antineoplaston
  treatment response rate, 341, 343
Spiller, Robert, on FDA trials of
  Burzynski, 80-81
spontaneous remissions, 116, 172, 248
stable disease, definition, 269-270
Steed, Robert, 30
stomach cancer, antineoplaston treatment
  response rate, 341, 343
studies of antineoplaston treatments,
  122-132, 295-299
  animal tests, 129, 157-158, 219-220,
    259
  antineoplaston A, 150-151
  Beth Israel Medical Center, 297-299
  brain tumor studies, 297-299
  breast cancer studies, 126-128
  CAN-1 trial, 290-293
  dosages used, 224-226, 228, 259-260,
    298-299
  double-blind studies, 264-265
  FDA clinical trials (tables), 340-343
  Green article, 253-262
  ND permits, 32-33, 35, 139, 157,
    177-178, 290

International Biomedical Center
  (Netherlands), 297
Kurume University (Japan), 186,
  257-258, 345
laboratory studies, 26-27, 256-257
Mayo Clinic/Memorial Sloan-Kettering
  report, 227, 271-272
National Cancer Institute trials, 32-33,
  157-158, 219-235, 259-260, 267
NIH trials, 212-214
phenylacetate studies, 216-219, 222-
  223, 227-235
protocols, 266-267, 272, 293
Sigma Tau antineoplaston trials,
  258-259
in vitro studies, 256-257
See also research; response rates for
  antineoplaston treatments
surgical treatment
  astrocytoma, 84-85, 278-279
  brain tumors, 19, 43-45, 47-48, 75-76,
    85-86, 135, 195-197, 206, 209, 211,
    212, 278-279
  glioblastoma, 211, 212
  infants, 43-45, 47-48
  kidney cancer, 323-324
  leiomyosarcoma, 323-324
  lymphoma, 109-110
  medulloblastoma, 195-197, 206, 209
  PNET (primitive neuroectodermal
    tumors), 195-197, 206, 209
  renal-cell cancer, 163-164
  side effects, 93
  See also surgical treatment effectiveness
surgical treatment effectiveness
  brain tumors, 43-45, 47-48, 75-76,
    85-86, 211
  lymphoma, 109-110
survival rates
  astrocytoma, 86
  bone marrow transplants, 246
  medulloblastoma, 195
  PNET (primitive neuroectodermal
    tumors), 195
  renal-cell cancer, 161-162
synthesis of antineoplastons, 153-155
Szymkowski, Barbara, testimony by, 61

T

Takayasu's arteritis, case histories,
  315-316

Index   357